Andrés McKinley has penned a beautiful, moving love story – a stunning tribute to his family and country of birth and to his family and country of re-birth. Read it also as a tribute to a generation whose best and brightest members seized the opportunity to be a part of the social justice movements that were unfolding around the world. Theirs was not a journey for fame or for fortune. Baby-boomers, read this book to remember; others, read this to understand not only the sacrifices made but, more importantly, the fulfillment gained. May others follow Andres's path to love, wherever it may take take them.

> — **Robin Broad** (Guggenheim Fellow) and **John Cavanagh** (director, Institute for Policy Studies), coauthors of *The Water Defenders: How Ordinary People Saved a Country from Corporate Greed* (Beacon Press, 2021).

The voice is simple, authentic, articulate, and consistent and coherent throughout. Given the unique and dramatic personal story that Andrés tells, it is actually under-stated and quiet—restrained intensity is how I might describe it. What really sets it apart, though, is the intimacy, care and respect with which he describes and tells the stories of the Salvadorans with whom he shared life and struggle throughout these years (and for that matter the villagers in Liberia in his early Peace Corps years). ... It is a work of great humility, even as it tells a heroic tale without flinching, and in great detail. Nor is he romantic about the course that the struggle has taken; he is unflinch-ing in that as well, and so leaves history open-ended but blessed with the grace of those who struggle.

> — **Brian K. Murphy**, writer and organizer, former policy analyst at Inter Pares, who writes at **MurphysLog.ca**

This is a very impressive book which tells a truly remarkable personal story, without the story becoming purely personal. In fact, there is a great deal of political history in the book, which I can confirm as I also studied as well as lived through some of the Salvadorean civil war. The truly incredible Salvadorean peasants who stayed in the war zones despite army incursions and US backed aerial bombing, are just as he describes them. They led me also to a lasting respect and love for them, even with-out the long term depth of experience of the author. The way the author brings us so many personal stories is very powerful. We get to know the friends he makes and then to feel as he did, when they lost their loved ones in this horrendous violence un-leashed on the Salvadorean poor and their allies by the Salvadorean wealthy elites, their military and US backers.

> **Jenny Pearce**, Research Professor, Latin America and Caribbean Centre, London School of Economics

Andrés McKinley's book *For the Love of the Struggle* is a moving and personal account of his involvement in the fight for justice in El Salvador during the civil war of the 1980s. But more than the events he describes, with great detail and political insight, it is his love for the people of El Salvador that sets this book apart. From working with church related organizations, to joining the guerrillas in the liberated zones, to his work along the communities opposing metallic mining, it is his relationship with the people, particularly the humbler ones, which stands out.

Most books that deal with the civil war in El Salvador end with the signing of the Peace Accords, which put an end to the armed conflict and laid the foundation for a more democratic and just El Salvador. As important as the Peace Agreements were, they did not solve all the problems and conflicts of the country. When several rural communities were threatened in the early 2000s by the efforts of transnational gold mining interests, they rose in defense of their rights through social organization and peaceful opposition. In spite of the repression they suffered, after 17 years of struggle they finally prevailed, showing how people united, can bring about change.

This belief is particularly important now, at a moment in which our democratic institutions are being threatened precisely by those who should be the first to protect them. It is the role of organized civil society to defend what we have conquered and McKinley's book is an excellent and timely reminder that this is something possible and necessary to achieve.

— **Francisco Altschul** is a former Salvadoran
Ambassador to the United States

For the Love of the Struggle

Memoirs from El Salvador

For the Love of the Struggle
Memoirs from El Salvador

Andrés (Drew) McKinley

Daraja Press

Published by Daraja Press
https://darajapress.com

© 2020 Andrés McKinley

Book and cover design by Kate McDonnell
Landscape photo by Maren Barbee, Creative Commons

Library and Archives Canada Cataloguing in Publication

Title: For the love of the struggle : a memoir of El Salvador / Andrés
McKinley. Names: McKinley, Andrés, author.
Description: Includes bibliographical references.
Identifiers: Canadiana (print) 20200316001 | Canadiana (ebook) 20200316079 |
ISBN 9781988832814 (softcover) | ISBN 9781988832821 (EPUB)
Subjects: LCSH: McKinley, Andrés. | LCSH: Political activists—El Salvador—
Biography. | LCSH:
Community development personnel—El Salvador—Biography. | LCSH:
Americans—El Salvador—Biography.
| LCSH: El Salvador—Biography. | LCSH: El Salvador—History—Civil War,
1979-1992. | LCSH: El Salvador—History—1992| LCGFT: Autobiographies.
Classification: LCC F1488.42.M35 A3 2020 | DDC 972.8405/3092—dc23

In Loving Memory of
Maria Teresa Polanco de Rivas

Those who profess to favor freedom and yet
depreciate agitation are men who want crops
without plowing up the ground.

They want rain without thunder and lightning.
They want the ocean without the awful roar of its waters.

This struggle may be a moral one, or it may be a physical one,
or it may be both moral and physical, but it must be a struggle.

Power concedes nothing without a demand.
It never did, and it never will.

– Frederick Douglass, August 4, 1857

Contents

Foreword

Charlie Clements

Andrés McKinley and I were born in the United States within a few weeks of each other in 1945, just after the end of World War II. This meant we grew up in the shadow of the Cold War and were high school students when President Kennedy challenged our generation to 'ask not what your country can do for you, but what you can do for your country.'

We responded in very different ways – McKinley became one of the early Peace Corps volunteers and I attended the USAF Academy. Years later in the early 1980s we would both end up in El Salvador living and working with peasants in a mountainous 'free fire' zone that was bombed, rocketed, or strafed daily by U.S.-supplied aircraft, some of which I had once piloted. We had found our separate way to El Salvador out of anger about what our own government was doing there, me to use my skill as a physician, and Andrés to doggedly accompany Salvadorans as a humanitarian worker – two gringos trying to send a very different message than our government was sending daily.

Andrés McKinley and I never met. I only stayed a year; McKinley stayed more than forty years and lives there today. This book is his story, and the story of the people of El Salvador in struggle.

Before serving as a pilot in Vietnam, I had to attend jungle survival training in the Philippines where I learned to eat insects. Andrés relates that as a Peace Corps Volunteer in Liberia he grew accustomed to a local diet of bats with three-foot wingspans as well as other items that were new to him as well, 'like snake meat, smoked elephant and monkey meat, toasted rhinoceros beetles, fat juicy bamboo worms and termites.' He says it 'broadened his perception of available options for human consumption on our planet.'

While he would not enjoy that kind of variety again, McKinley learned to accept and get by with whatever was of-

.n—good practice for what lay ahead for him in Central
.ca. Learning to clear land, plant, tend crops, and harvest
.ie rhythms of subsistence farming, much the same in many
ρarts of the world – would also serve him well amongst the peasants in El Salvador. It was in Liberia that he first experienced
communal life of a village and how activities done individually in
the west such as agriculture, hunting, fishing, gathering firewood
were accomplished collectively.

As for me, I learned the rhythms of peasants' lives during a
year's leave-of-absence from medical school spent in rural India.
The story of how I got from Vietnam to El Salvador is described
in my memoir *Witness to War* (Bantam, 1984). Now, Andrés
McKinley's remarkable memoir, *For the Love of the Struggle*,
tells about his pathway there, and about the life he has shared
in struggle with the Salvadoran people for the better part of four
decades.

Both Andrés McKinley's life and my life were impacted by
a document written when we were only three years old, a 'Top
Secret' document that wouldn't see the light of day until more
than four decades after it was written. Authored by George Ken-
nan, the 'father' of the U.S. containment strategy that under-
girded the Cold War, in part it stated:

> We have about 50 percent of the world's wealth, but only
> 6.3 percent of its population.... In this situation, we cannot
> fail to be the object of envy and resentment. Our real task in
> the coming period is to devise a pattern of relationships which
> will permit us to maintain this position of disparity.... *We need
> not deceive ourselves that we can afford today the luxury of al-
> truism and world-benefaction.... We should cease to talk about
> vague and... unreal objectives such as human rights, the raising
> of the living standards, and democratization.* The day is not far
> off when we are going to have to deal in straight power con-
> cepts. The less we are then hampered by idealistic slogans, the
> better." (emphasis added)

Slowly I began to see for myself in Vietnam that the U.S.
government was neither interested in human rights, nor democ-
ratization – and certainly not about raising living standards in
the midst of war. I had intentionally requested a role, as a C-130

pilot, in which I wouldn't have to take someone's life. The C-130 was a four-engine turbo-prop transport aircraft that was designed to land and take-off from unprepared runways and capable of carrying anything from huge bladders full of gasoline to a pallet with an anesthetized elephant. However, after more than fifty combat missions I began to realize I was fooling myself. I may not have been killing anyone personally, but I was making it possible for everyone else to do that by carrying soldiers to remote firebases, dropping paratroopers into battles, carrying wounded soldiers from field hospitals to medevac centers where they could be whisked to Japan or the U.S., or re-supplying arms to outposts under siege.

In early 1970 I flew a top-secret mission for what we were told was a diplomatic mission to Phnom Penh, and I saw large parts of Cambodia that looked like the moon. The only weapons capable of that kind of destruction were American B-52 bombers, but the U.S. was not at war with Cambodia – that would only come when it invaded Cambodia on May 1 of that year. On April 30, 1970, having carried planeload-after-planeload of combat-ready American soldiers to a jumping-off point called the Parrot's Beak, it was clear what was coming. I refused to fly further missions. I had concluded that what I was being asked to do was immoral.

I was placed in a locked psychiatric ward and eventually discharged with a 10% disability (mental). Had I been an enlisted man, I'm sure I would have ended up in a penitentiary. Later when I realized that being only 10% disabled implied that I was 90% abled. I took the 90% and went to medical school, choosing a small hospital in Salinas, California, for my family practice residency.

While a family medicine intern at Natividad Medical Center, I began to meet undocumented Salvadorans who fled death squads to find employment as farmworkers. Then, as the U.S. began to send military advisors and fleets of helicopters to El Salvador, it seemed like a *déjà vu* of Vietnam. Upon leaving the military, I had become a Quaker in part because I was attracted by their commitment to non-violence. Like Andrés, I was angry at what my own government was doing and decided to volunteer to provide medical care to civilians being targeted in El Salvador. Later, I would be asked to testify in Congress and eventually led several Congressional fact-finding missions to El Salvador and some of its neighbours in the region. After the FMLN (*Frente Farabundo Martí para la Liberación Nacional* – Farabundo Marti Front for National Liberation) ultimately fought the Salvadoran government and its U.S. sponsor to a stalemate, I was a special guest at the formal signing of the Peace Accords in Mexico City in January 1992, ending the brutal twelve-year civil war.

I can attest to all of Andrés' stark descriptions of life in the combat zones. His remarkable story tells about his pathway to El Salvador and about the life he shared in struggle with the Salvadoran people. This memoir gives a unique, often disturbingly honest, on-the-ground description of the conditions that led hundreds of thousands of Guatemalans and Salvadorans to flee the region during the 1980s. And it tells a personal story of McKinley's accompaniment of a people joined together in struggle within the insurrectional movement of the FMLN.

The Greek playwright Aeschylus once wrote, 'Even in our sleep, pain which cannot forget falls drop-by-drop upon the heart, until in our own despair, against our will, comes wisdom through the awful grace of God.' Andrés McKinley's book is built around the story of his relationship with Antonio and Teresa Rivas, hard-working, generous, and open-hearted Salvadoran peasants who embraced him into their struggle, and their family. Over the decades that he has lived in El Salvador, their courage and their pain, and that of their compatriots, which he has been determined not to forget, fell "drop by drop upon his heart," eventually emerging as this poignant memoir. And through his experience and the telling of his story, McKinley discovers and shares a humane and transcendent wisdom about life and pain, friendship and struggle.

The book relates how McKinley came to understand how his own government was aiding and abetting the repression and genocide that he was seeing in Guatemala, where he first worked when he arrived in Central America as a development worker in 1977. Forced to leave Guatemala as his sympathies with the popular movement became apparent, he moved to El Salvador and began to form the relationships that would alter and define his life. During Andrés McKinley's first decade in the country, the U.S. would spend billions in military and economic assistance trying to defeat the guerrillas of the Salvadoran liberation movement, the FMLN. A major part of this book tells the story of the Salvadoran struggle led by the FMLN over this period, and McKinley's personal engagement with it – a story of courage and high adventure, of terrible tragedy and deep compassion, of transcendent friendship and solidarity.

After the signing of the Peace Accords in January 1992, McKinley continued living in El Salvador with his Salvadoran wife and two sons and working with local communities through various international NGOs. Peace allowed life to gradually return to normal, sadly including the profound poverty that had been one of the historic causes of the civil war. But community organizing also flourished, and McKinley remained at the heart of such activities supporting his Salvadoran companions-in-struggle trying to build a just basis for a permanent peace.

An important part of this story is McKinley's role in supporting impoverished communities fight to protect the precious water resources of their tiny country against the destructive effects of foreign mining companies, a movement that achieved a remarkable victory when, in 2017, El Salvador became the first country in the world to ban all activities of metal mining within its borders. The ban has helped other communities in the region to develop their own local anti-mining strategies.

One of the most destructive legacies of the decades of U.S. intervention in Latin America is that the 'war on drugs' it sponsored in Colombia and in the wider Andean region forced the drug cartels to use Central America both for transit and as a market. Salvadoran narco-gangs, who learned the ropes of the drug trade in Los Angeles, brought that experience home with them when they were deported. They have, as a result, made El Salvador and Honduras two of most violent countries in the hemisphere.

For the Love of the Struggle includes a description of the current situation, the failure of governments (ours and theirs) to cope with the consequences, and the challenges that the Salvadoran people face going forward. The book is essential reading to better understand the realities behind the deadly quagmire of regional migration, the travesty of current U.S. immigration policy, and why parents would let their young children attempt to cross alone the dangerous border to the U.S.

The American Friends Service Committee is a Quaker organization. A traditional part of Quaker faith is their belief in 'bearing witness' or standing with people who are experiencing injustice to share their burden. This is done both by their very presence and as well by oral or written testimonies, sometimes referred to as Peace Testimonies. Andrés McKinley is not a Quaker, but he has provided an extraordinary gift to the poor and oppressed of Central America by bearing witness to their struggles, by walking beside them in perilous conditions for more forty years, and by writing this Peace Testimony – *For the Love of the Struggle.*

I salute him and the Salvadoran people we both grew to love.

Charlie Clements, M.D., M.P.H.
Author of *Witness to War*
Former Executive Director of the
Carr Center for Human Rights Policy
at the Harvard Kennedy School

Florida, March 1986

Dearest Drew,

Your letter was a treasure, thank you. It took me a week to get through the enclosures [on Central America] with a sense of terrible helplessness – feel wasted and defeated – all so lost and unknown. Miracles are needed.

My life saving theory of "God knows all things" is severely challenged – and yet I remain convinced that He does indeed know....

I am imploring you not to lose yourself, to somehow take good care of you and remember always how much I love you and to somehow leave there one day.... There are so many needs right here, so many places you could enhance, but not in your present sense of anger and resentment. I understand, but it's unfair and presumptuous of you to assume that we are all gross and uncaring and that your insults will enlighten – they only hurt and sadden...

I am as always so proud of you, your strength and the goodness of your heart....time moves so slowly there, but it will move and in the interim you must not lose yourself or a prospectus for us – and appear harsh and cold and judgmental because our sufferings are not familiar to you at the moment....

Love,

Mom

Note to the reader

By the time I finally got around to finishing this book, a project I have been working on for almost 20 years, I had lived most of my life in Central America, that small explosive chain of poverty-ridden nations connecting continents, separating oceans and blending the very best with the very worst humanity has to offer.

When I arrived in this region in 1977, the isthmus was on fire as poor and traditionally marginalized sectors of society struggled against five decades of military dictatorship and centuries of poverty and injustice, and I was quickly engulfed by the flames of political violence. I had been exposed to poverty during four years as a Peace Corps volunteer teaching school in impoverished communities of northern Liberia. I knew little of social struggle, however, and even less about revolution. I was quick to perceive, nevertheless, the historical importance of the moment, marking the pinnacle of a prolonged era of liberation struggles of poor people throughout Latin America and the Caribbean. I was also forced to recognize that the United States government – my government – was on the wrong side of these struggles, allied with murderers and thugs in a desperate effort to defend over a century of hegemony in its "own back yard."

El Salvador, the smallest country in Central America with an area of slightly more than eight thousand square miles and a population of six million people, quickly became the site of America's most prolonged and expensive military endeavor since Vietnam. To win the continuing support of the American people during 12 years of bloody war by proxy, successive U.S. regimes promoted a devious distortion of Central American reality, characterizing a legitimate struggle by the region's poor as "communist subversion" and arguing that military intervention was necessary to halt Soviet expansion in the western hemisphere. Farmers impoverished by generations of landlessness, overexploited factory workers battling for a minimum wage and the social activists who supported them were described as "terrorists" and "delinquents."

Between 1981 and 1992, billions of dollars of U.S. military aid were spent in the systematic slaughter of over 250,000 innocent

Central Americans. As a U.S. citizen who witnessed the horror of these policies on the ground, I became overwhelmed with anguish at the levels of human suffering that my own government was willing to inflict on innocent human beings in the name of "national security," and with the ignorance and complacency of the American people in the face of such blatant disregard for human life. My allegiances became firmly realigned in favor of the victims of U.S. aggression. My heart became hardened in self defense against the insanity of everyday life, and my country of origin, along with friends and immediate family, were often the target of my growing rage.

It was many years after the war in El Salvador had ended that I was finally able to reconcile my anger with the nation of my birth. Politics in Central America evolved into something less urgent and less dramatic than the life and death struggle it had once been, and U.S. intervention became more subliminal and benign. I am still moved to anger by America's continued commitment to the use of political intrigue, economic pressure and military force to shape the world in accordance with its own interests, and I have been appalled in recent years by the U.S.'s continued propensity to intervene in harmful ways in the internal affairs of the nations in the region, shoring up anti-democratic and often corrupt regimes and pushing for neoliberal economic policies that prioritize the interests of local elites over poor majorities. At the same time, however, I am constantly reminded by Central Americans themselves that the U.S. role in this region and in other parts of the world cannot be explained by the hearts and minds of the American people.

In the spring of 2002, ten years after the signing of Peace Accords in El Salvador, I came across a series of letters that my now-deceased mother had written in March 1986 emphasizing the goodness in the human heart and demanding tolerance from a son she was finding increasingly difficult to reach at the time. I was deeply moved by the levels of pain and frustration I had failed to see and I was forced to recognize my own inability to help the people that I most loved understand my anger towards the country of my birth. I had not shared adequately the human experience of a war that had bled my adopted country white and changed me forever. I had been unable to bring to life the personal histories of its heroes and martyrs and I had been unable to record more faithfully the hopes and aspirations that had pulled me into their struggle.

This book was born from the desire to meet this challenge, for those of my family who remain alive and for others of good will intent on building a more just and peaceful world. As you read it, you will find several stories woven together as threads. The first, and perhaps most important, is the story of Antonio Rivas and his wife Teresa, born into poverty in the rural countryside of El Salvador and caught up in the violent struggles of their time. The second thread focuses on the history of a prolonged people's struggle to overturn centuries of poverty, exploitation, repression and foreign domination, and the third is my own story of awakening, of transition, of what could rightly be called "salvation," in a country appropriately named The Savior (El Salvador).

The book is not an autobiography. I have chosen carefully the memoirs included herein, measured by their ability to inform and to enhance the book's general theme. I have excluded, for example, a number of wonderful relationships that I have had with amazing men and women who accompanied me during different periods of life's journey, and make references only to Ana Eugenia, my eternal light, soul mate, guru, and mother of my children who influenced my path in so many key ways during my years in Central America.

In many ways, the book is an act of catharsis, an effort to "clean out the attic" and bring closure. It is a harsh critique of U.S. policy, programs and practices in the region, but it is intended to foster understanding and truth, not to stir hatred towards nations or peoples. Most importantly, this book is about remembering at a time when today's generations are forgetting one of the most important and inspiring periods in El Salvador's history with its heroes and martyrs and authors of change whose enduring hope and unconquerable will defined the immense struggles of their day.

– Andrés (Drew) McKinley
San Salvador, 2020

Prologue

San Salvador October 1996

We stood in a circle around the plain gray casket in a parched, windswept corner of the public cemetery in San Salvador. The midday sun beat down without mercy, and the tears of Antonio and his six surviving children merged with droplets of sweat and rolled off their anguished faces onto the dusty ground.

The murderous incursions of government troops that had destroyed the home of this humble peasant family, and thousands of others like them, had been halted. The endless marches through the night and the terrifying days of hiding in dark, damp tunnels without food or water were just a haunting memory. The U.S. bombs and rockets that had driven a third of El Salvador's rural population from their villages of origin were now silent. A war that had taken over 75,000 innocent civilian lives – and almost ended my own life on more than one occasion – was over, and life had returned to "normal."

Antonio's wife, Teresa, had passed away in the early morning hours three days earlier after a prolonged and painful bout with breast cancer that had spread to her liver, an illness which takes the life of hundreds of peasant women with no access to adequate health care each year. Her death had been imminent for weeks, but the radiance and delight of her presence prior to her illness left us all stunned and bewildered in the face of such an overwhelming loss.

I held my three-year-old son, Andresito, in my arms for emotional comfort (mine more than his) while Ana Eugenia, my Salvadoran wife, and our oldest son, David Miguel, tried to shield Antonio and his children from the harsh scene evolving at a gravesite nearby, where two callused workers heaved and sweated as they removed bones and a human skull from the tomb of a family too poor to pay the annual cemetery fee. It was like a post mortem eviction and a grotesque reminder that the poor of El Salvador remain as vulnerable in death as they are in life.

Such irony would not have been lost on Teresa, born into poverty and wizened early by the cruel reality of life and death in the Salvadoran countryside. She had been conceived through the rape of her mother, who died from gangrene within 24 hours of giving birth. She had been victimized by a life of exploitation and repression in a country where being born poor meant dying poor and where those who protested this great injustice were hunted down and brutally killed.

Government security forces had tortured to death two brothers-in-law in 1979 and 1980. She had suffered the loss of her oldest daughter, a brother and a niece in the bloody civil war that wracked El Salvador during the 1980s. Yet, in all the years that I had known this woman, I had never seen the slightest sign of resentment or hatred, nor did I ever have a sense that she coveted the material comforts denied to her in the humble world to which she belonged. All I ever saw was the enormous joy that she derived from her simple life and the love she felt for her beautiful family who now mourned her.

Teresa had shared with me some of the pieces of her life's dramatic puzzle during long and sometimes painful conversations in the final months of her battle with cancer. She told me of her birth in the smoky darkness of a oneroom mud shack on June 17, 1952 in the small rural village of Peñones, near the town of San Pablo Tacachico in La Libertad province. At the time of her birth, 20 years had passed in El Salvador since the slaughter of almost 30,000 indigenous peasants by the military dictatorship of Maximiliano Hernandez Martinez, but little had changed to inspire hope for the rural poor.

Teresa's mother, Julia Duarte, was 18 years old on the day of her daughter's birth. Like most peasant women of the period, she had received no pre-natal care during her pregnancy, nor did she have the services of a trained health professional at the moment of birth. The rudimentary skills and frantic efforts of the local midwife were insufficient to resolve the complications that arose during the birth process, and Julia Duarte died of gangrene 24 hours later.

It was not startling news in this peasant village less than 40 miles north of the capital city. The tragedy that surrounded the birth of Teresa was rooted in the centuries of injustice and repression that defined the history of El Salvador's rural poor. But it was unable to quell the hope that arises with new life, bringing light to the darkness and joy to life's endless struggle.

Teresa's grandmother was Patrocinia Polanco, born in 1920, like Teresa, in the village of Peñones. In the conversations that I had with her over the years, she revealed that she had no recollection of her exact date of birth, nor had she ever celebrated a birthday. She was approximately four years old when her own mother died of pneumonia. And her father died a year later from the unattended bite of a poisonous lizard.

Like most peasant women of her time, Patrocinia entered into a commonlaw marriage at an early age. Her young "husband," Cleto Duarte, was a heavy drinker who had won local fame as a slightly crazed *pistolero* (gunfighter). He was involved in frequent encounters with machetes and firearms and, during Patrocinia's seventh month of pregnancy with their first child, he was ambushed and chopped to pieces by an enraged neighbor who had had enough of his drunken insults and abuse.

With the death of her husband, Patrocinia was left with nothing. The small adobe house where they had lived belonged to the owner of the *hacienda*, and she was forced to abandon it in the final month of her pregnancy. She gave birth to Teresa's mother, Julia Duarte, at the age of 16 in the mud shack of a neighbor, and, within days, set off with her infant daughter to look for work.

Patrocinia's search led eventually to the *hacienda* where her father had labored as a field hand many years prior, and it was there that she met Pedro Avalos, with whom she quickly entered into a second common-law marriage. Pedro welcomed Patrocinia's newborn child, Julia, and family life began anew. Together, they had three additional children in rapid succession: Santos, Graciela and José Victor.

In the constant search for work and for a small piece of arable land to cultivate, the family eventually migrated to the village of Las Araditas, situated on an extensive *hacienda*, El Matazano, near the town of El Paisnal. Like other peasant villages of the period, Las Araditas was a sparse settlement of small huts made of mud and sticks with roofs of clay tile or grass. The houses were

dispersed over the most arid portions of the *hacienda* and workers were allowed to occupy them as long as they were providing
labor to the *hacienda*'s owner. Additional lands were sometimes
allotted to the workers for the production of corn and beans, the
basic staple of peasant families since the times of the Pipil, El
Salvador's original inhabitants.

The *hacienda* of El Matazano stretched over thousands of
acres of rolling hills and shallow ravines, producing basic grains
and maintaining dairy cattle. The terrain was harsh and sparsely
forested with dry vegetation during six months of the year. But
with the first rains of June, the area turned to a lush green, renew-
ing hope among its inhabitants that life would somehow go on.

China Mountain, on the edge of the *hacienda*, was the highest point in the municipality. It rose like a bell curve out of the
midst of the impoverished villages scattered along its lower
slopes. It received its name from its rounded and treeless summit
which bore a resemblance to the stereotypical bald Chinaman of
local people's imagination, and it served as a key point of reference for travelers from near and afar.

Pedro Avalos found work as a farm hand on the *hacienda* for
a wage of 10 cents a day. His work day began before sunrise and
rarely ended before nightfall, but there was never enough money
to meet even the most minimal needs of his small family. During the months of December, January and February, Pedro hired
himself out as a seasonal worker on the nearby sugar cane plantation, La Cabaña. Sugar was new to El Salvador, and its production and processing were rudimentary, so there was always a
need for additional men with the back for manual labor during
peak periods.

Patrocinia established a small store in their home and traveled frequently to the surrounding villages to peddle her goods.
It was during one of her absences that Pedro became involved
sexually with Patrocinia's daughter, Julia, 17 years old at the
time. It is not known how many times or under what conditions
Pedro abused his stepdaughter, but it was soon apparent to all
that young Julia Duarte was pregnant.

The shame of Pedro's act impelled the family to send a bewildered Julia away to the village of Peñones, the birthplace of her mother. There she lived out her pregnancy in the home of an uncle, washing clothes, cleaning house and cooking. Patrocinia received no news of her daughter during this period, until the dry dusty mid-morning of June 18, 1952, when a telegram arrived from Peñones. Nobody in the family could read or write, so the reluctant mailman delivered aloud the simple message on the crumpled white sheet of paper he had been holding in his sweaty hands: "Come quickly! Your daughter Julia is dead."

That same day, an exhausted and half-crazed Patrocinia, along with her six-year-old son, José Victor, traveled by train to Peñones, buried Julia in the municipal cemetery of Tacachico, wrapped her newly-born and unnamed grandchild in a small towel and returned to Las Araditas. She later named the infant Ana Teresa, endowed her with her own surname of Polanco, and raised her as a daughter.

Patrocinia never forgave Pedro for the sin he had committed. While they never separated, they lived the remainder of their lives in tension. Nor did Patrocinia ever overcome her resentment towards Teresa, a constant reminder of Pedro's infidelity and perceived by her as the cause of her real daughter's death.

The first year of Teresa's life was filled with anxious uncertainty about her survival. In the absence of a warm breast to provide her with a mother's natural nourishment, she was hand fed a daily ration of corn broth mixed with the milk of Ranchera, the family cow. This provoked frequent teasing from villagers who insisted that the docile old animal was Teresa's true mother, since it was her milk that kept this frail baby alive.

Other features of Teresa's early childhood have been more difficult to ascertain, even after many conversations with family members following the war. After many frustrating attempts, I finally acknowledged that the drudgery and routine of life for rural peasants is too frequently lacking in distinguishing landmarks required to help one recall the details of their lives. One day flows into another, like the water molecules of steadily moving river.

What is certain is that Teresa's days, from the time she could walk, included an overdose of harsh physical labor: cleaning an adobe house with floors and walls of packed earth, washing clothes in a nearby stream, sewing patches over worn patches to mend the family's clothing, tending to the livestock, gathering firewood for cooking, hand-grinding corn for *tortillas* and helping tend to the family store. There were few friends to play with, as the small adobe homes of El Salvador's peasant villages were widely scattered, and young children, especially the girls, were kept busy with household chores.

Both the rainy and dry seasons brought their own difficulties for a small peasant girl burdened with responsibilities beyond her age. In dry season, the small rivers that served as a source of water for drinking, bathing and washing clothes often dried up. In rainy season, water was abundant, but so were water-borne illnesses like malaria, dengue and intestinal parasites.

Patrocinia showed little gratitude for her granddaughter's labor, but Teresa's father, Pedro, more than compensated for the lack of a mother's affection with abundant love for his youngest and favorite daughter. He was a quiet and patient man, haunted by the errors of his past, and silent in the face of Patrocinia's constant reminders. These qualities were assimilated by Teresa and became deeply embedded in her character. She developed a stoic yet indomitable spirit that would not submit to the harsh and sometimes hostile surroundings of her youth and learned to find joy and delight in all that she did, turning tedium into pleasure and work into games.

According to her brother, José Victor, she had only one toy, a small rubber doll given to her by her father and cared for well into adulthood. She loved jumping rope and playing house, or watching José Victor play soccer with a ball made from rags rolled tightly together and knotted with string. Her greatest love, however, was school.

Her older brothers and her sister had been unable to study because there was no school on the *hacienda* when they came of age. The first schoolhouse was built when Teresa was 7 years old, and she walked barefoot in her best tattered dress two miles each day to attend classes.

She was inquisitive and exceptionally bright – the "teacher's favorite," as José Victor remembered in later years – "good at memorizing things and writing poetry." Few peasant girls of her day enjoyed the "luxury" of formal study, but sheer determination took Teresa all the way to fourth grade, a significant accomplishment in a village where only a handful of people knew how to read and write. Further study, however, would have required daily travel to the distant town of El Paisnal at a cost far beyond the means of this humble family; so, at the age of 11, Maria Teresa Polanco's formal education came to a halt.

She never lost her love for schooling, and remained an ardent advocate for education throughout her life. Education, for her, was a treasure, never to be squandered, but to be widely shared. In her later life, when the war was at its peak in El Salvador, Teresa would share her knowledge daily with the children of her village in Amayo, with no official recognition and with no pay, just a firm conviction and a desire to help others find their way to dignity.

Sunday was market day in the city of Aguilares, several hours walk from Las Araditas, and brought a brief respite from the drudgery of life in the countryside. Young Teresa and her family rose before dawn to ready themselves for the arduous journey, gathering beans, corn, maize and other items for sale in the market. With the money it earned, the family purchased basic necessities like salt, limestone for cooking corn, kerosene for their lamps, matches, soap and *dulce de panela* (brown cane sugar). The latter was used for sweetening the morning cup of ground toasted corn kernels which the peasants drank instead of real but unaffordable coffee, a distinct irony in a country where coffee was king.

The market was followed by church services and, if any money remained, an inexpensive meal of *pupusas* (a popular Salvadoran food made from *tortillas* stuffed with beans or pork) or perhaps some honey-filled candies. The family would then gather together under the steaming afternoon sun and prepare for the long walk home.

Sunday afternoons on the *haciendas* were dedicated to local soccer matches, and Teresa loved to accompany Patrocinia to sell refreshments when the teams from the surrounding villages gathered to play. It was during one of these Sunday matches that 12-year-old Teresa caught the eye of a player from the village of Amayo named Antonio Rivas Ruiz.

Antonio was 25 years old at the time, thin and muscular with curly black hair and a face already weathered and heavily sunburned from long hours of labor beneath an unforgiving sun. He had the high cheekbones of his indigenous ancestors and the customary well-trimmed mustache worn by all peasant males in celebration of their manhood. He was the youngest son of Macario Rivas and Celestina Ruiz, and he was famous throughout the villages of El Paisnal for his athletic skills. His mother had died of "fever" when he was 13 years old. Like his five brothers and one sister, he had never been to school and was unable to read or write. His family was well known for its honesty and diligence, however, and he possessed a vast knowledge of agriculture for which he remained grateful to his father throughout his life. His only "vice," he would say today, was soccer.

His younger sister, Fidelia, had married Teresa's older brother, Santos, several years earlier, and Antonio finally summoned the nerve to speak one day to Teresa following a Sunday soccer match. This conversation led to a flurry of visits to Patrocinia's store where Teresa could always be found. Once Antonio had convinced himself that the attraction was mutual, a formal letter was sent from Antonio's father to Pedro seeking permission for his son to court Teresa, in accordance with the tradition of the time. Upon receiving an affirmative response, Antonio was allowed to become Teresa's *novio* (steady boyfriend), although, due to her young age, courtship was to be highly supervised and limited to the family home.

Antonio lived an hour's walk from Las Araditas, but his visits were frequent and soon led to a formal engagement. Teresa insisted at first that they wait until her eighteenth birthday to wed, but Antonio was impatient and, with the blessing of both fathers, the couple married just days after Teresa's fifteenth birthday in 1967. Family members who recall the ceremony paint a picture of a fairytale princess in wedding gown mounted on horseback at Antonio's side as the young couple returned from the simple church in El Paisnal to their village of Amayo. Teresa was too young for marriage in the minds of most, but in many ways wiser and more mature than Antonio. And when asked by her daughters years later how she could have left her youth behind and married so early, she responded unequivocally that the youth she had left behind was the youth she never had.

Antonio and Teresa on their wedding day, with brothers Santos and José Victor.

I pondered all of these things as the burial proceeded, comforted by the certainty that we were not burying Maria Teresa Polanco de Rivas on that hot dusty day, but were simply returning to the earth the privileged temple that had housed this extraordinary spirit for 46 years.

CHAPTER ONE

Introduction to an Impoverished World

I was born at 7 a.m. on Christmas Eve in 1945 in New Haven, Connecticut. As my mother recalled in later years, the event occurred under the studious gaze of a dozen young students from the Yale Medical School, explaining perhaps the joy I still derive from performing before a live audience.

I lived in several different towns during my youth, but my most fervent childhood memories are of Hingham, Massachusetts, a small prosperous New England town on Boston's south shore whose history goes back to the time of the early Pilgrims. It had been settled by members of the Massachusetts Bay Colony who, seeking religious freedom, had fled from their village of Hingham, England, in the early 1630s. In my day, it was inhabited primarily by second generation families of Irish and Italian decent, with a small cluster of African Americans gathered tightly together in an area which some referred to as "Little Africa."

Hingham was known for its natural beauty, with abundant forest lands still intact, orderly tree-lined streets, clean rivers, ponds and a picturesque harbor where fishermen brought in an abundance of lobster and from where large ferries transported commuters to their jobs in Boston. I grew up on Main Street, said to have been described by Eleanor Roosevelt during a visit in 1942 as the "the most beautiful Main Street in America."

It was a magical place, caressed by perennial fresh sea air, laced with the fragrance of blossoms and fresh cut grass in springtime and burning leaves in autumn, hinting of eternal well-being and insulating its inhabitants from the more turbulent world beyond. The most serious issues of the day were generally local, and were resolved in monthly town meetings, a proud holdover from the early Pilgrims.

We marched down Main Street, content and secure, singing at all hours of the night, built snowmen and sledded or skated in winter, sang Christmas carols throughout the neighborhood on Christmas Eve, hunted for painted eggs on Easter Sunday and went out trick-or-treating on Halloween. During boring summer evenings in our early teen years, my friends and I stooped to more delinquent activities in search of adventure, stealing cattle trucks from the local dairy farm and driving them down Main Street, or "borrowing" a boat and driving it across Hingham harbor to the Paragon Amusement Park. Irresponsible, but innocent.

I was the second of six children and was influenced early on by the love of a mother somehow capable of convincing each one of us that he or she was her favorite and only treasure. She was, in her own words, "an old soul," wise and loving, inured to the silence of the late night, when she would escape from the drudgery of housekeeping to indulge herself alone in poetry and novels.

She had been born and raised in the rough and tumble Irish working class neighborhoods in New York City, referred to at the time as "Hell's Kitchen." And, while she clearly loved Hingham, I always felt that she somehow missed the wild urban streets of her youth. The subtle lessons she passed down to her children based on the colorful histories of the hard-living figures of Hell's Kitchen permeated our young minds and souls and have much to do with the adults we all became in later years.

My maternal grandmother was born in New York City of Irish immigrants and spoke with a brogue until the day she died. Her name was Maisey McCormick, and she had worked cleaning the homes of New York's wealthy neighborhoods while trying to keep a tight leash on her adventuresome daughter. My maternal grandfather was a New York City policemen, the most the son of Irish immigrants could aspire to in that day. His name was Mickey Davis, referred to by friends and family as "the Mick," but the local press honored him with the title "Terror of the Tenderloin" for his high-profiled exploits on the tough streets of New York's Tenderloin district.

He once captured five hold-up men after being shot in the jaw, and my mom always cherished the picture of her as a little girl receiving his medal from the mayor of New York. He won the annual boxing championship of the New York Police Department several years in a row, and one of New York's most famous nightclubs played the hit song of the day, "East Side, West Side," every time he walked in. We never knew him, since he died of a gunshot wound before our time, but he was a hero to us all and continues to inspire awe to this day.

My paternal grandfather, Joseph Andrew McKinley, after whom I am named, was a bellowing Irishman from Donegal. He was the last of nine children born in a single-room cottage with a thatched roof in a social system that awarded all family assets, especially land, to the oldest son; so, with little hope for a future in the Ireland of his day, he had jumped on a ship in his twentieth year and migrated to Nova Scotia. There he met and married young Jenny Black, a woman of Irish descent who he had found in a boarding house hiding from an abusive father and caring for her invalid brother. They moved eventually to New Jersey where my grandfather entered the meat business with his older brother, William, until William stole the business from him, as the story goes.

Visiting "Pop" and "Grandma Jane", as we called them in their retirement years, was one of my fondest memories of growing up. They had settled by that time next door to a small dairy farm in rural Kent, Connecticut. The famous Connecticut River flowed nearby and both grandparents would take us frequently to swim in its shallow waters, search for arrowheads, collect shiny obsidian rocks and capture spotted salamanders along its rocky shore. To keep us from wandering off during these excursions, they assured us that the wooded hillsides that rose up on the other side of the river were filled with "wild Indians" and rattlesnakes.

My grandfather had a goat which he called Bessie and kept in a small wooden shack with walls lined with newspapers. He claimed that he was teaching Bessie to read, and derived great pleasure from releasing this aggressive animal in the open cow fields by his house and watching her chase after us as we fled in panic.

At nights, Grandma Jane would gather us all together on the living room floor while she read from the Old Testament. It was before TV, so we remained entertained for hours with the stories of Daniel and the lions, David and Goliath, Samuel and Delilah and Joseph's coat of many colors.

On many days, my grandfather would fill the hours with tales of his youth in the "old country." He told of his exploits fishing in the rough and icy waters of Donegal Bay and of his days as a champion wrestler of Ireland, Scotland and Wales. We were young, innocent and easily beguiled in those days, and confident that I carried his genes, I excelled as a wrestler myself in later years. It was only in adulthood that I learned that he had actually worked with a traveling circus, pitting his strength against local farmers in the towns and rural villages of these three countries.

My grandfather despised people who feared dirtying their "lily-white hands" in an honest day's labor, referring to them as "cake eaters," and often including myself and my five brothers and sisters among the accused. He instilled in me a profound respect for the working class, however, and pleasing him was probably the key incentive for my incessant attraction to hard physical labor during most of my youth.

His second son, my father, shared these values closely and enforced them throughout his life. He also suffered from many of the peculiar idiosyncrasies of the Irish and told me once when I was quite young that his greatest ambition as a child was to work on a garbage truck. He studied civil engineering at Penn State University instead and became a high level executive in one of Boston's largest construction firms, building some of the city's tallest and most important buildings. He later went on to become Head of Real Estate for IBM, travelling the world. His older years, long after his divorce from my mother, were spent in much humbler career options that I always attributed to a late-life-search for simplicity. He ended up, I am told, delivering mail in rural North Carolina where he lived with his second wife.

He was frequently absent from home when I was growing up, given his work as a civil engineer and weekend golf tournaments. He had been a football player and a champion university boxer in his younger years, so he must have had some amazing qualities, but he hid most of them from us, and I am saddened to say that I have few memories of moments together. He always loved horses, however, and this love was somehow engendered in me, inspiring me to learn to ride at an early age, and for that I have always been grateful.

Our home life as young children was not a happy one. With a father descended from stern and sober Presbyterians from Northern Ireland, and a mother descended from fun-loving, raucous and heavy-drinking Catholics from county Cork in southern Ireland, our family reproduced its own version of the home country's vicious civil war between Catholics and Protestants. My grandma Maisey from my mother's side

Suburban cowboy

used to say about the McKinley family from Donegal that "a good laugh would kill them."

When I think back on those days, I understand that divorce was built into my parents' marriage from the very beginning. My father had been humiliated prior to marrying my mother by having to sign a document promising to raise his children as Catholics, a requirement of the Church at the time for all mixed marriages. He was also sworn to avoid birth control, which he increasingly resented as the birth rate in our family accelerated out of control, leaving him finally with three boys and three girls.

Life's expectations were gradually dashed for both of my parents and conflicts became uglier and more frequent as time moved on, leaving the six of us looking on and wondering who was at fault. It was a complex dynamic beyond the scope of this book. But when my brothers and sisters gather today, our conversations inevitably turn to those painful years in an unsuccessful attempt to remember, process and resolve repressed sentiments and shed some light on the causal factors of our dysfunctional family.

In October 1997, almost a decade after my mother's death and several years after the end of the war in El Salvador, I wrote my father to tell him that I loved him, to thank him for the support he had provided for my upbringing and education and assure him that I forgave his absence and neglect during our youth. I told him that all was OK with us and that I would love to see him during my next trip to the U.S. or if ever he had the opportunity to travel to Central America. I received the following letter back:

Oct. 17, 1997

Dear Drew,

Thank you so much for your letter. I will che it for as long as I live.

You have so much to be proud of with the sacrifices you have made for others. When you really think about it, there is no real explanation for the times we all have suffered with a split up, broken down family. It is only the memories that we want to have that are left.

It would be a step into heaven to truly be with you and your family, but I'm afraid that is impossible. There is so much that could be said, but can't and won't.

I am very very proud of you and I only wish our relationship had been closer and better. I pray to God to bless you and your loved ones. Take care and live with God.

Your loving father

A few months later, a second letter arrived from his lawyer informing me that he had died, and I was thankful that I had been inspired to take this initiative of forgiveness and reconciliation prior to his death. Several of my brothers and sisters attended his burial in North Carolina and informed me later that many of his friends of that period had come up them during the funeral ceremonies and expressed their surprise that my father had children.

A rough emotional beginning in life left all of the McKinley brothers and sisters a bit wiser and tougher – and probably a bit harder to love. We were armed, however, with the understanding that life is a struggle; and I'm pleased and proud to see what amazing human beings all of my siblings became. My older brother Dave, an angry soul who was expelled for fighting from every school he attended, and with whom I fought almost daily during our youth, went on to become a highly successful and widely recognized recording engineer in the studios of Nashville, Tennessee and was recently inducted into the Country Music Hall of Fame. My younger brother Tim, who served time in the military and later in prison for drug dealing, became a commercial airline pilot, flying from Florida to the Bahamas, and found peace in his final years as a flight instructor until a snapped rudder cable on an ultralight aircraft sent him to his death just before Christmas in 1995. My younger sister Jemmy taught school for 40 years in Colorado and is now retired. Close to 70 years old, she can still run 10 miles a day and finish a 500-mile bike race through the Rocky Mountains. Kathleen has worked much of her life running her own import business, selling arts and crafts from Africa. She is the sweetest and wisest of us all, and the most severely damaged, I am afraid. She reminds us all of our mom and, at this writing, she works in a Buddhist monastery in northern New York. Finally, my youngest sister Amy is a studied and highly skilled natural healer and practicing Buddhist. She has worked most of her life in solidarity with women in prisons and with victims of paralysis, to several of whom she has restored the gift of mobility.

I was an average student and a mediocre but determined athlete in high school, playing ice hockey and football and wrestling. I had a friendly greeting for everyone in the hallways, and for that was elected to two terms as class president and voted "most popular boy," clearly the substance of "cake eaters," my grandfather would say. It was common at that time in traditional IrishCatholic families for second sons or daughters to join the religious life and I had strong leanings in this direction. I served

With my brothers and sisters in 1984:
From left to right, Amy, Tim, Kathleen, Jemmy, myself and David.

as an altar boy in my young years and felt certain about joining the priesthood throughout most of my four years of high school, but my calling was silently lost somewhere along the way in the face of my father's staunch opposition.

At Villanova University in Pennsylvania, I majored in psychology, played ice hockey, wrestled and captained the university's crew team. I quickly fell in love with rowing, since the only required attribute for success was a disposition to pull your heart out at the end of an oar and drive yourself beyond the pain barrier. I knew that any Irishman could do that, and with the genes of my ancestors alive and well, I excelled at this sport, winning a gold medal at the U.S. National Rowing Championships in Philadelphia in 1967 with a boat full of Irishmen with names like O'Malley, Monahan and McKinley.

If I had been born in a different time, I surely would have bought into the modus vivendi of American life following graduation from the university, but I was living in an era of profound social change and was gradually awakening to the realities of poverty, racism and injustice around the world. It was a time of hippies and flower power, of free love and protest. The civil rights movement was at its peak. The struggle against U.S. involvement in the Vietnam War was in its early stages. African nations were battling to escape a long and complex history of colonialism, and the humble classes of Central and South America were struggling to construct social, economic and political alternatives to decades of exploitation, military dictatorship and foreign intervention. I was the product of small-town New England with all of its comforts and privilege, but my searching soul and underlying sense of adventure were screaming to break free from this small and confining world.

The author, fourth from the left

My politics were evolving as well. When I first began my university studies, I had hoped that the Vietnam War would last so that I could participate in all of its patriotic glory. By graduation, however, the tragedy of the war, both for Vietnam and for the United States, was broadly recognized among my generation. Anger was rising at what we considered to be an evil and flawed foreign policy holding the U.S. hostage to its own arrogance.

Upon graduation, I left behind a long chain of jobs held during my youth as a construction laborer, roofer, house painter and plumber's assistant and embarked on a career in social work with the Pennhurst State School and Hospital for the mentally handicapped in rural Pennsylvania. I applied my studies in psychology to a job which I loved immensely, participating in an experimental program to get patients – many of them long-term residents – out of an institutional setting and back into the community. I was ultimately looking for something more audacious, however, so I applied to the Peace Corps, hoping for an assignment in Central America. I was offered a position in West Africa instead and, in spite of my poor mother's fears and protestations, I accepted it readily, with the enthusiasm, idealism and inspired hope of a youthful seeker committed to building a better world.

I spent the next four years, from 1969 to 1972, teaching school in a small jungle village of mud and thatch huts in northeastern Liberia, where elementary school teachers were being sent back to teacher training institutes for continued education, leaving a temporary shortage of teachers in the remote rural areas of the country. It was a perfect fit for me and I quickly fell deeply in love with this mysterious continent and its myriad of cultures and peoples.

The Peace Corps had once served as an alternative option for young American males wanting to avoid being drafted into the military and sent to Vietnam, but by my time it was no longer draft exempt, so the risk of being called up for military service hung over my head throughout the duration of my tour. The draft board to which I had been assigned was located in rural Virginia, however, where lots of poor rural and jobless youth were itching to join the army and go to Vietnam, so its annual quotas were easily filled without having to bother more privileged and idealistic dreamers like myself. This was a blessing to me, since by this time I had become a staunch opponent of the war, viewing it as an unjustified aggression against a nation which could in no way be perceived as a threat to the United States. Had I been drafted during those years, I surely would have ended up in jail, in Canada or on the run.

I knew of course that Africa was poor, but I was unprepared upon my arrival to Monrovia, Liberia's capital, for the dusty trash-strewn streets crowded with young barefooted children in tattered shorts and T-shirts with fly-infested open sores and bellies extended by parasites and chronic malnutrition. Hygiene was seriously lacking, and open sewage was the norm for disposing of waste. Housing consisted of small run-down shacks of adobe and sticks with roofs of thatch or rusting zinc, with no running water, no phone system and no electricity. The majority of urban males were jobless and had few educational opportunities for pulling themselves up by the bootstraps.

Liberia is a small country of 43,000 square miles on the western coast of Africa. Its current population numbers slightly less than five million people. It is the oldest republic in Africa and one of only two countries, along with Ethiopia, that was never colonized during the European scramble for the continent in the late 19th century. It was founded in 1822 by freed slaves organized by the American Colonization Society with the aim of returning black people to Africa. These original pioneers remained primarily on the coast and later became known as Americo-Liberians.

In spite of its natural resource wealth, including diamonds, gold and iron, and a variety of tradeable agricultural commodities such as rubber, coffee, cocoa, cassava, rice, palm oil, sugar cane, bananas, sheep, goats and timber, Liberia is considered to be among the poorest and least developed countries in the world. At the time of my arrival, it was controlled politically and economically by a powerful minority of Americo-Liberians, while 16 indigenous tribes scratched out a meager living in the jungles and highlands of the interior.

I was assigned to a small village up country in Nimba County called Nengben, inhabited by approximately 150 families of the Mano tribe, residing in traditional homes of mud, bamboo and thatch, built in close proximity. The thatched roofs of the houses had the advantages of keeping a home cool in the overbearing heat of midday and silencing the heavy rains of monsoon season. They were also easily cured by the constant smoke of interior cooking fires which drove away poisonous insects, snakes and pesky rodents. The village was divided into "quarters," where extended families lived and where intermarriage was strictly prohibited.

The Mano people had resided in this area for thousands of years and now made up slightly more than 7% of the country's population. The surroundings were harsh and life had few comforts, but hardships were generously interlaced with the joys of traditional village life. A lack of running water was compensated for by frequent trips to the village well, where the women would leave me spellbound by hours of playful dialogue. The absence of electricity brought long evenings around the cook fires under starlit skies, with drums and traditional dancing whenever the moon was full.

Formal schooling was a new phenomenon in this remote region of Liberia. It had started only seven years prior to my arrival and I found myself teaching grades two through six to students who frequently were several years older than myself. Many of them came from surrounding villages where there were no schools available yet. They were hungry for learning, anxious to absorb anything I could teach, and it was a joy and a privilege to work with them.

I adapted easily to life in the jungle, 8000 miles from the tragedy of Vietnam. I was constantly surrounded by a large contingent of children ready for merriment and song and full of curiosity about this young white foreigner in their midst. Their small hands were constantly upon me, rubbing my skin in an attempt to remove the whiteness and see what color lay underneath, and running their fingers through my hair, amazed at its softness. And I did the same with them, realizing how removed I had been in the early years of my life from people of color.

I taught school in the mornings and was respectfully referred to by my students as "teacher." On most afternoons, I accompanied my students into the jungle, where our roles were abruptly reversed: I became the student and they became my teachers, patiently revealing the secrets of the jungle and sharing their vast knowledge of hunting, fishing, planting and, best of all, making palm wine. During those moments, my students called me by my tribal name, "Nya Flumo," given to me by the elders of the village and meaning "Second Son" in the Mano language. At other times, when they wanted to tease, they called me "Yókemi," Mano for "Palm Wine Maker," in recognition of my abundant appetite for this delicious and highly alcoholic drink.

On weekends, they often took me to swim in the murky crocodile-infested waters of the St. John River separating Liberia from French-speaking Guinea. Guinea was run at the time by a socialist government, unfriendly to the U.S. The Mano tribe had been divided in the colonial period by a border that they now paid little attention to and crossed at will to visit friends and family, but it was an uncomfortable challenge for me, given the consequences of being caught by Guinean migration authorities or being eaten by a crocodile lurking unseen in the rust-colored waters. I trusted my students to keep me safe, nevertheless, and was always a willing participant in these adventures.

During school vacations, some of my students who were not from Nengben would carry me deep into the jungles to their villages, often several days walk from Nengben, where we were frequently met by terrified mobs of scurrying and screaming women, grabbing up children and fleeing into the jungle at the site of this white man, whom they took to be a spirit. Once my students were recognized and we were adequately bathed in the nearest river, however, the women would slowly and cautiously return to observe me with great curiosity and prepare a welcoming meal.

Since Liberia itself had never been colonized by European powers, the customs and traditions of the tribal peoples of the interior were still very much intact. The Mano tribe was ruled by a "paramount" chief. Under this regal figure were a number of clan chiefs and town chiefs. All were men, and they generally ruled until death, at which time their authority was passed down to their eldest son.

Polygamy was common and women were "purchased" in matrimony, generally through a payment of goats. The first wife was the "head wife" and ruled over all of the wives that followed. Jealousy and conflict were frequent, however, and men with more than one spouse lived a life of constant turmoil. Marriages were often pre-arranged, and it was not uncommon for girls as young as seven or eight to be promised in matrimony to elderly men, although they remained with their families until puberty. I protested with fervor, but with little results, when young female students of mine were promised to old (and ugly) men of privilege and power in the tribe, but the cultural practices at that time were firmly entrenched and a young Peace Corps volunteer could do little to change them.

I heard rumors on occasion of other frightful practices like covering newborn babies in chile pepper and leaving them under the sun to see if they could resist, assuring that scarce tribal resources would not be squandered on someone too weak to survive the tribulations of life in the jungle. On another occasion, I was told that twins were believed to have only one soul between them, so to be sure about who possessed the soul, one of them would be buried alive in a termite hill with the assurance that the soul would pass to the survivor.

There were also rumors of cannibalism in the Mano tribe's distant past, but, during my four years with these people I never saw signs of any of these practices. Instead, I found a warm and caring people who looked after each other with a sense of pride, belonging and personal identity derived from membership in the tribe.

To be sure, there were traditions that could chill the soul of any foreigner, including voodoo and witchcraft, which were practiced with a disturbing frequency. Village zos (witchdoctors) wielded great power and the secret Poro Society, with branches in every village, was assigned the task of preserving order. There were no government police in the villages of the Mano people. In fact, there was no government presence at all. Respect for law and tribal authority was maintained by the tribal chiefs, the village elders, the Poro Society and the zos.

To help them in this task, they had at their beck and call a blood-chilling array of jungle "spirits," men of the Poro Society dressed in large swirling grass skirts with headdresses and wooden masks, who came out of the bush at night, and, occasionally, during the day, to judge and to punish wrong-doers, sometimes with death. During such moments, only the initiated male members of the secret society could be present. The women, children and I had to flee into our houses, slamming shutters and doors at the first haunting sounds, from deep within the jungle, of flutes and shouts of "the devil is coming."

Annual ceremonies or "bush schools," as they are called, were held every few years for the initiation of young men into the Poro Society. This involved living for several months in the jungle (in the belly of a dragon, the old people would say) learning tribal secrets, medicines and traditions, and being circumcised. Physical scarring around the neck and shoulders was also carried out, symbolizing the dragon's teeth marks and serving as a sign of passage into manhood. The harshness of the customs and practices reflected the harshness of life itself. Survival depended on the strength and unity of the tribe. The jungle was untamed, and danger lurked in its shadows. Food was only come by through planting, fishing or hunting and for this the tribe still depended on bows and arrows, machetes, spears and other rudimentary instruments. While seasonal rains brought an abundance of food, dry season could bring starvation. During this time of year, animals became scarce and more difficult to hunt. Stores of rice, the basic staple, were depleted prior to the new harvest. Tempers grew short in a desperate search for eatable roots, leaves, and insects and people began to make reference to "hungry time." It was during this period each year that many families in the interior of Liberia succumbed to the humiliating practice of consuming their own domestic cats and dogs. And, on more than one occasion, I joined them.

We also consumed the smoked meat of the enormous fruit bats that migrated north each year darkening the skies over our village with their threefoot wingspan. We hunted them in the afternoons as they slept hanging upside down from the palm trees on the outskirts of the village. Our daily diet frequently included other items that were new to me as well, like snake meat, smoked elephant and monkey meat, toasted rhinoceros beetles, fat juicy bamboo worms and termites, broadening my perception of available options for human consumption on our planet.

On weekends during planting season, my students joined ranks with the other young men of the village to form a communal work force to go into the jungle to cut the bush and prepare the soil for "making farm." They formed small collectives, referred to as ku, and I often accompanied them on this adventure, honoring the memory of my working class Irish ancestors and challenging prejudices about the frailties of the white man. The night before each ku, a member of the community would pass through the village blowing a goat horn, and I would begin to prepare myself psychologically for the physical challenge of the coming day.

Slash and burn techniques, common throughout the developing world, were used by Mano farmers, but rice fields were allowed to rest for five years between plantings in order to prevent a deterioration of the delicate subtropical soil. We arose long before sunrise and departed from the village, machetes in hand, to begin the day's toil in the relative coolness of the early dawn. The work was arduous and dangerous, as the jungles were filled with poisonous snakes, large black scorpions, tarantulas and a variety of more aggressive animals higher up on the food chain. With the steady rising of the morning sun we would all be sweating profusely, and I would be trying to ignore the burning blisters and torn skin on a body unaccustomed to working in the jungle.

While the morning was still young, the women would arrive in their colorful lappas (cloth wrapped around the waist as a skirt) and bright head scarves, with large bowls of freshly-boiled rice, potato greens, monkey meat, or fish. We would all be exhausted and starving, but thoroughly immersed in the joy of camaraderie, and easily revived by the female presence and the accompanying aroma of food.

Eating was a leisurely affair, sitting in a circle around a single large bowl of rice and soup and hands serving as our only utensils. But once the last grain of rice had been scooped from the bowl, we would return immediately to the task at hand. For the rest of the morning, with lunch on the fire, the women would join us, singing and clapping to the rhythms of traditional Mano songs set to the steady sweep of our machetes, providing a magical source of renewed strength and stamina. We would eat again at midday, work until late afternoon and then drag our worn bodies back to the village, usually arriving in a silent group shortly after dark.

My exhaustion and painful blisters from the weekend's labor would last well into the school week and undoubtedly affected the quality of my teaching during that time of the year. But my students were patient and supportive, and they beamed with pride when word began to spread throughout the county of the young white foreigner – their teacher – who could withstand the toil of "cutting the bush."

My obvious love for tribal tradition began to allay the fears of village elders concerned with the dangers of western influence on tribal youth. On occasion, these wise and highly respected old men would come by my house in the early evening and sit for hours in silence. Their visit was a sign of respect and talk was not required to strengthen the bonds that had taken root.

On other evenings, they would invite me to accompany them into the jungle to help harvest their palm wine and we would sit in a circle for hours, drinking the sweet intoxicating liquid from a shared gourd, gazing at the moon and listening to the night. They spoke no English and my Mano was rudimentary, so conversation was inhibited until the palm wine took effect, loosening our tongues and rendering all languages understandable.

The old men talked of the tribal wars of previous generations against the Kran, the Kru and even their brothers, the nearby Guio. They described handto-hand battles in which their fathers had participated as young men, and told of warriors with magical powers that allowed them to fly and to resist injury by spear, arrow or gunshot.

They were filled with curiosity about the faraway land on the other side of the "great water" from which the Peace Corps was sending young people from America to serve as teachers, agronomists, doctors, nurses and other technical "experts." They called America *kwipa*, meaning "land of the civilized." I often wondered what notion of history – or propaganda – had produced such a cognomen, recalling the ongoing tragedy of my country's policies in Vietnam. I also remembered from history that African kings were drinking beer from golden goblets before western man had discovered the wheel.

By the 1970s, Liberia had become America's doorway to Africa. A system of government resembling that of the United States had been violently imposed on the tribal peoples of the interior. The national flag was designed after the American flag. English was established as the national language, although only those with a formal education spoke it. Large tracts of agricultural lands and mineral rights were ceded to U.S. and Swedish transnational interests, and national holidays celebrated the slaughter and rape of the country's original inhabitants.

At the time of my tour, Liberia hosted the largest Peace Corps delegation of any country in the world. Most of the volunteers that I knew were deeply in love with the country and were totally dedicated to improving the lives of its people. But after a number of years in country, we were humbled by the limitations of our contribution. We were also more politicized and shared concerns about the Peace Corps' true mission of convincing a hungry world of the American Dream and the virtues of capitalism. The Cuban revolution had toppled a resilient U.S.-supported military dictatorship, and was promoting revolutionary change, while the U.S., through John Kennedy's Alliance for Progress and programs like the Peace Corps, was fighting to hold off the winds of change in Latin America and around the world.

Nevertheless, the Peace Corps offered an amazing opportunity to young North Americans, like myself, to break free from the restrictive bounds of the United States, to experience the realities of the Third World's poor and to further the search for truth about the structural roots of injustice that were shaping our world.

In my small village in Liberia, I began to observe and understand alternative options for organizing society. African socialism expressed itself in all aspects of community and tribal life. There was no private ownership of lands among the peoples of the interior. All lands were collectively owned by the tribe. Agricultural production was a joint venture carried out communally, as was hunting, fishing, gathering fire wood, washing clothes, "making market," and other essential tasks of survival.

There was little sense of personal ownership of anything.

Even clothing, scarce in the jungle, was shared with no sense of loss or gain. There was no such thing as an illegitimate child or an orphan. Children belonged to the tribe, and babies born out of wedlock, or those whose parents had died, were quickly taken in by another family and raised with love and acceptance.

Social status was determined by a person's contribution to the welfare of his or her community, and one's sense of dignity derived from the simple act of belonging to the tribe. The tribal collective was the mechanism for individual survival. The concentration of personal wealth and the accumulation of capital were unknown concepts, and community development models that benefited elite minorities at the expense of the majority violated cultural values and norms.

This was the beauty of Liberia, and this was the mystique that would hold me in her embrace for the remainder of my life. By the end of my fourth year, I knew that I had changed and grown as a result of my experience. Liberia had become a part of my soul and I felt deeply grateful for having had the opportunity to experience the beauty and vibrancy of a culture so dramatically different from my own.

It was with a heavy heart that I finally said goodbye to my students, the young children, the old people and the amazing women of Nengben at the end of my second Peace Corps tour in 1972. Fearful of its volunteers becoming too immersed in the local culture and losing their sense of national identity, the Peace Corps did not allow a third term. And there were few options available to an American in Liberia with no institutional backing.

I knew that I would deeply miss Liberia and this troubled continent, so abundantly blessed with natural resources and cultural wealth, yet so afflicted by poverty and violence; and I fought back the tears knowing that I would probably never return to this land that had so captured my soul and to the thrill of life as Yókemi, the "Palm Wine Maker."

CHAPTER TWO

Coming Home

En route to the United States, after four years in the jungle, I traveled through Senegal, Mali, Morocco, then up to Spain where I remained three months studying Spanish. I backpacked through France, Italy, Switzerland, Germany and England. It wasn't until I crossed the Atlantic and returned home, however, that I suffered from my first attack of culture shock.

I was overwhelmed by the wealth and the glitter, and by the exaggerated displays of nationalism. Enormous American flags waved over used car dealerships and McDonalds restaurants. They decorated the front porches of private homes, gravestones in public cemeteries, banks and libraries. They hung from schools and other public buildings. In all of my travels through Africa and Europe, I had never seen such exaggerated patriotism.

Millions of American dollars that could have helped eradicate poverty in countries like Liberia, or in the United States itself, were still being consumed by a useless war in Southeast Asia that would eventually claim the lives of over two million Vietnamese and 58,000 American soldiers drawn from the ranks of the underprivileged classes. I could find little cause for such elevated levels of national pride.

Growing numbers of North Americans were protesting bravely against the war, but many remained convinced by their government that a country on the other side of the globe somehow threatened the security of the United States. The domino theory argued that if communism was not halted in Vietnam, it would spread like a plague to the rest of Southeast Asia, to Africa, Latin America and eventually threaten the United States itself. In response, a nation of immigrants, in growing fear of the world in which they lived, tried to reassure itself of its greatness and confirm its belief in the American dream.

It was complex and unsettling for one still vibrating from the warmth of community and the authenticity of life in a poorer and humbler world light years away. And I began to suffer the heartfelt longings for a full moon slowly rising over the jungle, decorating the profound silence of the African night.

By late 1972, I had settled in Philadelphia, where I had studied in the university during the 60s, worked as a roofer during the summers repairing the high steeples of the city's many gothic churches and spent many painful but rewarding hours rowing on the Schuylkill River. It had always been one of my favorite cities, with its strong ethnic neighborhoods, beautiful architecture and abundance of historical sites dating back to the American Revolution.

I found a small studio apartment in Center City and, with the help of friends, attained a job working with poor African-American and Hispanic families in the ghettos of North Philadelphia in one of the nation's first experiments in Health Maintenance Organizations, sponsored by Temple University and funded through President Lyndon Johnson's national program, "Great Society."

The gang-ridden streets of North Philadelphia were dangerous at that time and the job did not pay well, causing many of my co-workers – all AfricanAmericans or Hispanic inhabitants from the local communities – to ask why a college graduate was unable to find more lucrative and safer employment. I never responded adequately to these questions, but I knew in my heart that the job was part of my journey in search of "home," offering the opportunity to be with people again for whom life and struggle were synonymous.

My days on the streets provided more than a glimpse of the enormous social inequities afflicting U.S. society at the time and had a dramatic impact on the way I later perceived government responses to poverty in "the land of milk and honey." My job consisted of trying to convince community residents about the benefits of preventive healthcare and enroll them in Temple

University's Comprehensive Community Health Care Program. This meant spending days with old men in the shadows of abandoned and crumbling houses crouched in dark hallways or heating themselves by the flames of an old stove in the dead of winter. I met old women and school-aged youth imprisoned in their homes by neighborhood gangs. Small children with inadequate clothing and no place to play ran noisily through the garbage-strewn streets, and door stoops were littered with the semi-conscious bodies of junkies and alcoholics. I had seen the same faces in another jungle a world away, and was deeply saddened by the tragic transition of Africa's princes and kings.

This world, filled with gang violence and drugs, was frequently redeemed by its fascinating personalities. I met highly talented artists, self-made scholars with little formal education, unemployed musicians, athletes, and Hispanic migrants overcoming the limitations of speaking English as a second language. It was a major change from the villages of Liberia, but the memories of my mother's childhood in Hell's Kitchen, New York, had been embedded in my soul, and I quickly fell in love with the vibrancy of life on the bustling city streets.

Through this job, my interest in health administration as a career option quickly grew and, at the end of my first year, I bade farewell to the many friends and spiritual teachers I had met in the ghettos of North Philadelphia and travelled south to Florida where I spent the next two years in a masters degree program in Health and Hospital Administration at the University of Florida in Gainesville. I did my residency at University Teaching Hospital, a 400-bed facility serving low-income residents of Jacksonville, Florida. Upon receiving my degree in the spring of 1975, I was offered a position as administrative assistant overseeing several departments of this hospital.

Jacksonville is a beautiful city. The Saint John's River, one of the few city rivers in America at the time clean enough to support aquatic life – including porpoises – runs through its center. Fernandina beach, a picturesque town of shrimp fishermen, is less than an hour away with its annual shrimp boat races and country music festivals where I played my guitar and sang my songs each summer. I fell in love with northern Florida and thrived on the challenges of hospital administration, thrilled with the opportunity to render a complicated morass of health services to the overwhelmed, poorly educated and impoverished families that frequented our doorstep. My life was good and my future was promising, but my soul was missing my beloved Liberia.

After two and a half fruitful years at the hospital I could resist the tugging on my heart no longer and began searching for employment with international development and relief organizations. Most job opportunities in Africa at the time were in the French-speaking northern Sahel region, plagued by prolonged draught and a humanitarian disaster of startling proportions. I spoke only English and Spanish, so was not an appropriate candidate for the positions with humanitarian assistance organizations that were open at the time. I continued my search, however, and was finally offered a position as Program Assistant with Catholic Relief Services (CRS) in Guatemala; a position which I quickly accepted, buoyed by the confidence that I would transfer to Africa at the first opportunity.

I arrived in Guatemala City in December 1977 with the lessons of my four years with the Peace Corps, a year in the ghettos of North Philadelphia, almost three years as a hospital administrator in Florida, a large suitcase of clothes and a guitar. I had been exposed to poverty and injustice in Liberia and in my own country, but I was still inexperienced politically and was again unprepared for what I found in the city streets and rural villages of this explosive new world.

Guatemala is a country of exquisite beauty, inhabited by over 27 different sub-groups of Mayan people referring to themselves as Akchí, the people of corn. Its landscape is adorned with a chain of active volcanoes and crystalclear lakes with a back-

ground of towering mountains clothed in deep green forests of
pine, unrivaled by anything I had seen in my previous lifetime.
In an effort to attract tourism, the primary source of income for
the country, the Guatemalan government exploited the country's physical beauty and its exotic indigenous cultures through
travel magazines and posters portraying well-fed models in colorful indigenous dress among the volcanoes and lakes. I would
soon learn, however, that the reality of indigenous peoples in
Guatemala was characterized by a much crueler scenario built
upon levels of exclusion and oppression closely resembling South
Africa's apartheid of earlier years.

Indigenous peoples made up the poorest of the poor in
Guatemala, with high rates of landlessness, unemployment, illiteracy, rampant malnutrition, poor housing and inadequate
healthcare. A reformist government under Jacobo Arbenz had
attempted to overturn this situation in the early 1950s, but when
his land reform program impacted the enormous extensions of
agricultural lands controlled by the U.S. transnational United
Fruit Company, the U.S. government organized and financed a
coup that overthrew him in 1954, installing a military dictatorship that endured until the early 1980s.

At the time of my arrival, "popular organizations" of landless peasants, overexploited workers, urban slum dwellers and
students were demonstrating in the streets of the capital city,
demanding economic and political reforms and respect for basic
human rights. In response to the growing protests, these same
organizations were being systematically decimated by right-wing
death squads and government security forces.

On May 29, 1978, just seven months after my arrival, the
Guatemalan army, together with the National Police and hired
guns of local land barons, massacred 114 Kekchi people in the
town of Panzos in the eastern province of Baja Verapaz. Five
women with babies drowned as they tried to escape across the
Polochic River while others were hunted down or died several
days later for lack of medical attention. The Kekchi people had
come peacefully to demand support from the town's municipal
government in securing agricultural lands for planting corn and

beans, necessary to feed their families, but were seen as a threat to the interests of large local landholders producing crops for export. The massacre of Panzos marked a turning point in Guatemala's political life and warned of the violence to come. In its wake, 17 union leaders of the National Worker's Union (CNT) were kidnapped and "disappeared," student leaders were gunned down in public and even middle-class professionals eventually became victims to the growing violence of a U.S.-supported military dictatorship resisting change.

The situation took a dramatic turn for the worse in January 1980, when 19 Mayan people – among them the father of future Nobel Peace Prize laureate Rigoberta Menchú – staged a non-violent occupation of the Spanish embassy in Guatemala City. They had been sent by their communities to seek the formation of an international commission to investigate a widespread reign of terror being perpetrated by the Guatemalan army in the northern province of Quiché. Fearing violence, the Spanish ambassador had requested that government security forces not intervene, but the National Police stormed the embassy on January 31 and burned all 19 of the Mayans alive, along with 20 other civilians.

The event served as a warning to urban and rural poor that public protest would not be tolerated in Guatemala. In the face of decades of electoral fraud and military dictatorship, it also confirmed fears that non-violent options for change were rapidly disappearing. Civic organizations which had previously operated openly became clandestine and, as in the case of neighboring El Salvador, their frustrated but determined membership began to consider the option of armed struggle.

In my role as Program Assistant and later as Country Director of Catholic Relief Services, I worked primarily with Mayan communities in the western highlands, financing the construction of schools, housing, sanitary facilities and markets and promoting small-scale production in agriculture, weaving and animal husbandry. All of our projects were designed to alleviate the profound levels of poverty in the rural sector. To minimize paternalism in these efforts, projects were founded on the principles of self-help. Villagers were encouraged to organize themselves into local "development committees" to provide labor and logistical support, while CRS provided funds, materials, and technical advice.

The government soon became suspicious of the organizational component of our work, given the increasingly volatile political mood of the country. Many of our counterparts began to experience levels of repression that forced the closure of projects. One emblematic example of this growing trend happened in the town of Chupol in the province of Quiché where several leaders of a local development committee promoting the construction of a marketplace were assassinated by an army-sponsored death squad. A few days later a group of new leaders from that community visited our offices, insisting that the project continue. In a gesture of solidarity, CRS agreed, but within the month, several members of this committee had been assassinated as well.

I was inexperienced at the time in political violence and had little to guide me through this moment of decision-making. I was embarrassed as a North American, knowing the sad history of U.S. intervention in Guatemala and the role the U.S. had played in the training and equipping of Guatemalan security forces. I was also still struggling to understand indigenous culture and felt frustrated at my own inability to communicate effectively with indigenous leaders about all that was occurring in the rural areas of the country.

When a third coordinating committee from Chupol came knocking on our door in an effort to convince us that their market must be built, we relented and agreed again to continue providing the necessary materials. The death squads struck a third time, however, this time killing the president of the committee and threatening the other members with a similar fate. Refusing to risk more innocent lives, CRS terminated the project. A half-built market, designed in accordance with centuries-old Mayan architecture, was abandoned. And this bewildered CRS program assistant contemplated the horror that would soon be raging through Mayan villages where other CRS projects were struggling to survive.

In the mountains of Quiché province, Ixil people, with CRS assistance, had built a large honey-producing cooperative based in the town of Nebaj. Over the years, the project had consolidated a network of over 60 member communities, organized and trained in the latest techniques for constructing and maintaining beehives, for processing honey and for marketing their product internationally. As production grew, the cooperative had begun to export to buyers as far away as Switzerland.

It was perhaps the most successful venture I had seen in my years as an international development worker, with the promise of raising hundreds of Mayan families out of poverty. The Guatemalan army, however, again viewed the level of social organization generated by the project as a threat and took measures to destroy this hopeful initiative.

Local leaders and cooperative members whom I had come to know and love were killed or disappeared. Others, perceiving their lives to be in danger, drifted silently into the surrounding mountains to join the guerrillas. The director of the cooperative, a young Quiché with whom I had developed a close personal friendship, was severely beaten and threatened with death. He disappeared one day without a trace and I began to doubt that he remained alive until a year later, when a mutual acquaintance brought the following letter.

October 1979

My Esteemed Friend,

I have wanted to write to you for many months, but work did not permit. Now that I have this opportunity, I want to tell you a little about our organization. I am working in the area of Nebaj again, but am now clandestine, since working openly and legally is no longer possible....

Here in the mountains, the Guerrilla Army of the Poor (EGP) becomes stronger each day, with hundreds of people wanting to participate. The truth is we are still unable to provide adequate food supplies and other materials to support the growing numbers of combatants.

Our plans are centered on building local cells in the surrounding towns and villages in order to disorient the enemy. We are now holding four courses for new guerrilla cadres each year providing political orientation and military training. In this struggle there is no rest. Every three months, four or five platoons of new guerrilla combatants are trained and new recruits are then sent in. In the past months, between 300 and 400 new recruits have arrived from other towns. In this struggle we work 24 hours a day.

I am a political cadre focusing on organization. Others form the guerrilla army. All are Indians from Nebaj, Chajul and Cotzal, and we are beginning to open new fronts in order to force the [government] army to disperse its troops. At present, there is too much concentration of force in Nebaj.... Our plan is to eventually take power, although we know that the people must be better organized first.

Life in the mountains is very difficult. There is great suffering, mud, rain, cold and so much illness, but we are prepared to resist all of this to free our people. We have no personal interests here. We do not seek high-level positions or honor. I am simply a revolutionary orienting the people....

Well my friend, I send you a revolutionary greeting and many hugs, hoping that we can see each other again one day.

Until victory

The Guerrilla Army of the Poor
EGP Guevara

When the guerrilla organizations around Nebaj began occupying coffee farms and threatening local land barons, the town and the surrounding countryside were completely militarized by the government. An army base was built on the outskirts of the town. Civilians suspected of guerrilla sympathies were arrested or simply "disappeared." And nuns in a convent nearby began to share spine tingling testimony of nights filled with the agonizing screams of tortured Mayan farmers accused of subversion. Then the local parish priest, another close friend whom I had met during my first visit to Nebaj and with whom I had coordinated over the years, was forced to flee under threat of assassination.

During this period, the Catholic Church, with whom our agency coordinated many of its development activities, was being accused by the government and military of supporting the guerrilla movements and was fiercely attacked. Between 1975 and 1981, 12 priests were assassinated, and many others were forced into exile. Community leaders and church workers involved in our rural and urban development programs began "disappearing", to be found later crucified to tree trunks, often beheaded, or with other equally terrifying forms of physical mutilation.

By early 1981, four years after my arrival, I had stopped counting the treasured friends and acquaintances that I had lost to political violence in this country. During that year alone, 3,000 rural peasants were massacred by the Guatemalan army. That same army then went on to wipe from the face of the earth over 440 villages of indigenous people, assassinate over 100,000 of its own people and win for itself the distinction of being named the "worst offender of human rights in the western hemisphere." Even neighboring El Salvador could not rival the Guatemalan regime in its murderous rampage.

In the midst of such horror, it became clear that the kind of local community development work that we had hoped to carry out in Guatemala was neither feasible nor relevant. It also became clear that I was not immune, myself, to the threat of kidnapping and torture.

A Jesuit priest and friend, Luis Pellecer, was kidnapped by security agents in 1981. After six months of government denials, authorities, under strong pressure from the Vatican, finally released him. He continued to reside on a military base in the capital city "for his own protection," according to the military, and, during the months that followed, was brought frequently before the press to share his damning testimony against the Catholic

Church and its role in support of guerrilla organizations. He sometimes named individual church workers, and many of these later turned up dead, displaying signs of severe torture.

As I watched him on television from my small rental apartment in Guatemala City, I was amazed at how he had changed. His physique seemed bloated and his rhetoric coincided too much with the standard government line. It was in fact true that many activists within the Catholic as well as Protestant churches in Guatemala and El Salvador supported the growing insurgency out of a Christian commitment to relieve human suffering and to build a more just society. Father Pellecer's testimony, however, ignored the underlying causes of that struggle and the frustrated efforts of the country's leading social forces over the previous decades to construct a non-violent alternative for change.

Brainwashing experts hired by the Jesuits concluded that his personality had been modified through the probable use of sustained torture, mind-altering drugs and threats against his mother and brothers. Undaunted by questions of credibility, the U.S. State Department took him to Washington to testify before the Senate on the role of the Latin American Church in subverting public order. As a result of his testimony, church workers, including nuns and priests throughout Guatemala were forced into exile. Church-sponsored development or humanitarian assistance projects were suspended, and many lay activists were tortured and killed.

I was never able to talk directly to Luis after his reappearance. I was warned a short time later, however, that he had mentioned my name to military intelligence agents and that a plan had been designed to "deal" with me "in the same way that Pellecer had been dealt with." Several days later, armed men appeared at the CRS offices looking for me. On another occasion, our offices were surrounded by the army.

With CRS projects in shambles and most of my friends either dead, in exile or joining the rapidly growing ranks of guerrilla organizations, my life in Guatemala became a series of maneuvers to evade capture by the death squads. I purchased a pistol which I carried at all times and kept in a nearby drawer when I slept.

Fearing that the death squads could sneak into my apartment at night, I began sleeping with it under my pillow and was soon dozing off with it in my hand underneath the covers.

Life became a chain of psychotic episodes in which no one but the closest of friends could be trusted. A car following too closely, a person waiting too long on a street corner, a lone man on a motorcycle, someone asking too many questions on a park bench all became probable kidnappers, torturers and assassins.

By the end of 1981, the CRS program in Guatemala had been forced to close the majority of its projects. A large number of our counterparts had been assassinated or forced into exile; the Minister of the Interior was advising international aid workers not to wander beyond the limits of the capital city and I was requesting meetings with top CRS management in New York to assess together where to go from here. But I was getting no answer.

It was a complex moment for CRS as an institution and for CRS program directors working in an increasingly polarized region threatened by violence. We had been seeing signs for more than a year of a worrisome institutional trend of growing collaboration between CRS management in New York and the U.S. State Department, and there was suspicion that the CIA was pressuring management at the highest levels to modify programming in Central America and eliminate program staff in this region sympathetic to the Theology of Liberation and the spreading struggle for change.

The CRS country Program Director of Nicaragua, a capable and deeply committed woman, was fired for political motives at the insistence of the director of the US Agency for International Development (USAID) in Managua. The country director of Honduras was warned away from supporting peasant organizations and human rights workers close to the Catholic Church but perceived as subversive by the local embassy, and I was receiving no solidarity at a moment of growing disarray.

I finally got the OK to fly to New York, and was met in CRS headquarters by executives already armed with the State Department's version of current events in Central America, confirming our fears back in the region. They had little interest in debriefings and analysis on how to defend our social justice, human rights and sustainable development objectives in Guatemala.

On the day of my arrival, I was aggressively cornered, interrogated and informed that I would not be returning to my position of Program Director in Guatemala. There were no clear reasons given, and I wasn't being fired. I was offered, instead, a position as Program Director in Kenya or in the Dominican Republic, and as I heard these words, my soul took a leap. I had travelled to Kenya and spent a month camping in its glorious wilderness during my years in Liberia. I also loved the Caribbean, and, in a different context, would have jumped at the opportunity to transfer to either of these countries. But there was too much injustice and betrayal embodied in the option of leaving Central America in this difficult and crucial period of its history.

It was a lonely and confusing moment for me and I was feeling lost and without direction, not knowing if I should remain in the U.S., go back to my beloved Africa, as I had originally planned years earlier, or go, without a job, to some other country in Central America.

Relocating to El Salvador was an obvious option. I had visited the country frequently during my four years in Guatemala and had developed friendships among young revolutionaries already organized in clandestine cells and planning their struggles against their country's brutal military government. Several of them had even visited me in Guatemala and I had taken them to the mountains of Quiché and other remote areas of the country where indigenous peoples were organizing and guerrilla armies beginning to exert more influence.

I had also formed a deepening bond with a Salvadoran woman, working closely with the Catholic Church and committed to the struggle of her people. Her name was Ana Eugenia. She was intelligent and beautiful with a majestic presence that belied her humble background. She was mature, patient and centered, so I decided to call her and share with her my dilemma. With no surprise or hesitation, she said something to me that changed my life forever: "Just come home."

It was an abrupt awakening for me, and a first step on a path which would absorb my energies and emotions for the rest of my days. My homeless wanderings had ended. I had found a home and a person in it who would continue to offer direction in my moments of dispersion and eventually become a source of balance in the midst of the insanity of El Salvador's brutal civil war. She would offer tolerance and understanding of my ignorance of her culture and help me fall in love with her country and with her people, through her eyes and her heart. She would later become my wife and the mother of my children, my guide and my guru whom I would follow always, even in times of physical separation, like a small mountain stream tumbling towards the sea.

CHAPTER THREE

A Simple Matter of the Heart

The situation I found in El Salvador in 1981 was similar in many ways to that which I had left in Guatemala. Government repression was rampant as the army battled an increasingly organized and radicalized civilian population pushed to the limits by decades of electoral fraud, military rule, and massive poverty. The most startling difference, to my eye, was the extent of U.S. government involvement in the efforts to defend the established order.

With the inauguration of Ronald Reagan as President in January 1981 and the naming of Alexander Haig as Secretary of State, the Salvadoran conflict was suddenly framed within the context of the cold war. Landless farmers demanding agrarian reform were referred to as "terrorists." Social activists supporting them were described as "communist subversives." The demands of the Salvadoran people for democracy and social justice were explained as part of a Soviet plot to build a communist beachhead in the Americas, while U.S. policymakers proceeded to build, train, equip and advise a proxy army to wage a war in defense of elite economic interests and U.S. "manifest destiny."

The death squads were running wild, kidnapping, torturing, and assassinating anyone suspected of leftist sympathies. This included long-haired students, women in blue jeans and foreigners, like me. A network of luxury homes of El Salvador's traditional oligarchy served as safe houses for the illegal imprisonment and torture of suspected terrorists, applying prolonged beatings, electric shock, submersion, the *capucha* (a rubber hood filled with lye and placed over the head to provoke suffocation), sexual mutilation, and prolonged isolation in small cramped cages. Rumors began to leak out to the foreign press about the involvement of high Salvadoran intelligence officials in this "dirty war." And growing evidence confirmed the collaboration of foreign mercenaries from countries like Chile and Argentina, experienced in their own dirty war during the prior decade.

It was a messy endeavor for a U.S. regime intent on convincing its own citizens that American intervention was about preserving democracy and freedom. All objectivity was eventually lost in a blind and determined effort to justify a deepening involvement in the conflict. The historical causes of the struggle were ignored while insanity crept into an already faulty U.S. foreign policy in El Salvador that would go on to fuel 12 years of bloody civil war.

By the time of my arrival, Archbishop Oscar Arnulfo Romero, much loved for his incessant battle in favor of human rights and social justice and later elevated to sainthood, had been assassinated by a right-wing hitman while celebrating Mass. And the largest of the death squads, the Secret Anticommunist Army, had published an all inclusive list of additional human targets flagged for assassination. Among those named were:

> ...."all of the leadership of the Salvadoran Communist Party, international agents, all members of the government Junta connected to leftist groups, all leadership of the popular organizations and guerrillas, all common killers, thieves, robbers, rapists, homosexuals, prostitutes, drug addicts, phony priests, traitors in the military, lawyers, professors who indoctrinate, corrupt government functionaries, unscrupulous loan sharks, and all the other good-for-nothing rabble of El Salvador."

The spicy communiqué produced a mixture of humor and contempt at the national and international levels, but clearly signaled the initiation of a new and more pervasive wave of repression against an ever-broadening spectrum of Salvadoran society.

In May 1980, two months after the slaying of Bishop Romero, several hundred infantrymen and National Guardsmen had spread through the villages of Chalatenango province, killing civilians and destroying crops, livestock and housing. They then headed north towards the Sumpul River in an effort to entrap the fleeing villagers. In a "hammer and anvil" operation coordinated with the Honduran army, they overran the civilians in the village of Aradas; and, as bullets began to fly, the unarmed population threw itself into the river's raging current in a frantic effort to escape. They were met on the other side by Honduran soldiers who pushed them back across the river or killed them outright. In the chaos, many of the children and elderly drowned, and when the dust had finally settled, an estimated 500 unarmed civilians were dead.

In November 1980, four U.S. churchwomen – Dorothy Kazel, Ita Ford, Maura Clarke and Jean Donovan – were detained by national guardsmen on a dark and lonely highway leading from the international airport to the coastal town of La Libertad. They were then driven to a secluded area approximately half an hour's drive from the airport, raped, shot dead and buried. All four of the missionaries had worked with rural peasants displaced from their villages of origin by military operations in the northern countryside. Ita Ford and Maura Clark had worked in the province of Chalatenango where they had received repeated threats from the local military commander and once found a note posted on their door that read:

> "In this house are communists. Everyone who enters here will die."

It was widely understood that no soldier of lower rank would dare attack a U.S. churchwoman without a direct order from above, but the Salvadoran government refused to acknowledge any links between the killers and higher military authorities.

The following year, just before Christmas, government troops launched a major incursion into northern Morazan province, cynically named "Operation Rescue." The maneuvers were headed up by the newly-formed Atlacatl battalion, fresh from the tutelage of U.S. Special Forces advisors in Fort Bragg. On December 10, the soldiers entered the village of El Mozote and, on the following day, interrogated, tortured and then killed all of its inhabitants: men, women and children alike. In the days that followed, the troops marched on the surrounding villages of La Joya, La Ranchería, Los Toriles, Jocote Amarillo and Cerro Pando, killing every civilian they came upon. The exact numbers were difficult to verify, but it is believed that over 800 unarmed civilians were massacred in this single operation.

As word of the killings leaked out, human rights organizations and international media, including Ray Bonner of the *New York Times* and Alma Guillermoprieto of the *Washington Post*, traveled to the site and witnessed the horrific scene of decaying corpses and destroyed housing. Salvadoran authorities and their U.S. patrons, however, continued to deny that the massacre had occurred and refused to conduct an official investigation.

The issue of violence had always been a problem for Bishop Romero and for Christians in general in El Salvador, but a clear distinction was increasingly being made in the minds of most between the institutionalized violence of the government and the growing violence of civilian resistance. There were those who argued, both in Guatemala and in El Salvador, for Gandhian-style nonviolent resistance. But I knew that Gandhi would never have survived either country. A Martin Luther King would have been assassinated, as he was in the United States. A George McGovern, arguing for moderate reform, would have been forced into exile. A Jesse Jackson, with a Rainbow Coalition questioning the status quo, would have been tortured and killed.

While the debate over the use of violence to bring about necessary change was never resolved on a theoretical level, in practice many people in El Salvador came to view violence as the only remaining option. Five guerrilla organizations, the Popular Liberation Forces (FPL), the People's Revolutionary Army (ERP), the National Resistance (RN), the Revolutionary Party of Central American Workers (PRTC) and the Armed Liberation Forces (FAL), all with historical roots in El Salvador's Communist Party, had combined forces to form the Farabundo Martí National Liberation Front (FMLN) in 1980 and, in January of 1981 had launched a nationwide offensive, marking the formal onset of the civil war. The offensive was not highly successful in the capital city where a citizenry terrorized and decimated by years of repression failed to respond. In the rural sector, however, it left extensive areas under guerrilla control. In the face of the growing storm, the U.S. administration was providing riot control equipment, trucks, communications technology, helicopters, weapons, ammunition, uniforms, training and maintenance, along with economic support funds for military use.

As the armed conflict heated up in the rural areas, increasing numbers of peasant families began to flee their villages in the face of massive and indiscriminate bombing and murderous incursions by government troops. Little distinction was made between unarmed civilians and rebel combatants as government aircraft leveled peasant villages and infantry units slaughtered humans, domestic animals and all other forms of life. By the end of 1981, over 300,000 Salvadorans had fled to neighboring countries or north to the United States. And civilians continued to pour out of the countryside in waves, seeking the security of nearby towns and larger cities. By 1981, church-sponsored reception centers had been set up in and around the capital city. The centers were quickly flooded by hordes of bewildered and severely malnourished women, children and elderly, most barefoot, threadbare and highly traumatized. It was in this volatile and chaotic environment that I accepted a position with a French humanitarian agency called Doctors of the World (Médecins du Monde) to design and implement a humanitarian aid program for the victims of the war. With funding from the European Union, we purchased 17 acres of land in the municipality of Zaragoza in the southern province of La Libertad and began to build a center for displaced persons that would later be called Betania.

I coordinated my efforts early on with El Salvador's Green Cross, a local humanitarian organization modeled after the Red Cross and which, at the time, was transporting and caring for large populations of peasants fleeing from the chaotic province of Cuscatlan. A young and deeply committed Green Cross volunteer named Eliseo Franco took a special interest in our project and became my confidant and mentor in the months that followed.

Apart from his voluntary efforts with the Green Cross, Eliseo was a skilled mason. He had been contracted a year earlier by the government to renovate the main buildings of an old *hacienda* in the historic valley of La Bermuda, where El Salvador's capi-

tal city had been briefly
situated during the co-
lonial period. The peas-
ant village of San Rafael
was nearby, and several
of the men from this
community had hired
on with Eliseo as day
laborers.

San Rafael was a
small community of
poor dirt farmers pro-
ducing subsistence
crops of corn and beans
and hiring themselves
out as cane cutters to
supplement their mea-

Eliseo Franco of the Green Cross

ger annual incomes. Nevertheless, it had merited a red flag on
the large wall map of the local National Guard, signifying that it
was a beehive of subversive activity.

When the village came under heavy mortar fire from a government artillery position near Suchitoto in October 1980, the
population fled en masse to the only refuge they knew: the *hacienda*, La Bermuda, under the direction of Eliseo Franco. As
Eliseo told it later, he looked around one night after a hard day's
labor and found 30 terrified families camped on the grounds of
the *hacienda*. On the next evening, he looked around again, and
the number of families had grown to over 100.

A temporary Green Cross base was established to provide
emergency foods and medicines, and *champas* (rustic lean-tos)
soon dotted the countryside around the *hacienda*. The area
around San Rafael was quickly militarized, and army patrols frequently visited the Green Cross base in La Bermuda, stealing
food and harassing civilians. During one such visit, soldiers carried 18 men off into the night never to be seen again, and Eliseo,
himself, was severely beaten. In June 1981, almost eight months
after the first families of San Rafael had arrived in La Bermuda,

the army came again, this time with trucks to transfer the population to a newly constructed prison in nearby Suchitoto. As eyewitnesses later described it, the people were offered two options by the officer in charge: "either move to Suchitoto, or die in the La Bermuda." The population resisted in spite of the threats, so soldiers began grabbing small children and the defenseless elderly and throwing them "like sacks of potatoes" onto the waiting trucks. By the end of the day, when the army finally departed, the population in La Bermuda had been reduced by almost half.

The civilians who remained knew that the soldiers would return the next morning to take them by force to Suchitoto, so they began frantically planning their escape. Temporary housing, a clinic and community store, built with arduous labor over the previous months, were dismantled. Clay pots for storing water and grains were smashed in anger. Mothers sent their young children with Green Cross volunteers to the capital city of San Salvador, then later followed.

Through the efforts of Eliseo and the Green Cross, the population was finally reunited in a quickly erected refugee center in the city of Santa Tecla, in December 1981. The new location provided greater security, but being located in the center of a city meant that space was limited. It quickly took on the appearance of a fenced-in ghetto with rusted zinc and cardboard shelters, and hordes of children and elderly men scattered about the premises in inert boredom. It was a fishbowl existence in a sea of urban clutter far from the fresh breezes and rural fields and hillsides of San Rafael.

Within months, Eliseo and I began to transfer the families in Santa Tecla to the new site in Zaragoza. Eliseo named the center Betania, and news of our project began to spread. Displaced families from other provinces began arriving in search of refuge, and the population quickly grew to over a thousand.

We repaired an old adobe house on the grounds that had once served as a retreat for Catholic nuns but was now in a state of severe disrepair from years of abandonment and neglect. During

Everyone worked in Betania

the next six months, this old rambling building would serve as a collective dormitory and meeting hall. It was there that we held our nightly sessions to plan the following day's labor, to discuss community problems and to provide classes on basic hygiene and health.

We also built a collective kitchen, peasant style, where rotating teams of women prepared three simple meals a day for the growing community. We visited a local fishing cooperative in the nearby port city of La Libertad and convinced its membership to share its catch when the fishing was good. We talked local citrus growers into providing a steady supply of oranges and lemons for the children, and were granted approval from the Social Secretariat of the Archdiocese to receive emergency foodstuffs and medicines.

Everybody shared equally in the physical task of building a center that we hoped would serve as a model for future programs for the displaced. In the sweltering heat of dry season we cleared the thick brush from the fields with machetes, built housing units for hundreds of families, dug latrines and planted the fields with corn, beans and vegetables. A small school and clinic followed, along with a community store and a small hatchery for fish, all with the impossible hope of building a productive, healthy and relatively self-sustaining community in a country at war.

I worked alongside the elderly men of San Rafael with machete in hand, as I had done in the jungles of Liberia a lifetime ago, and I quickly became their ardent student of herbal medicine as they patiently explained the special properties of each stubborn bush I was mercilessly slashing. They would frequently gather the broken limbs and hold them out for me to smell or taste, then describe in detail how one served for curing infections while another served for healing farm animals bitten by bats, and still another helped prevent malaria or treat the parasites making their home in the extended bellies of most of the children.

The hillside that we had selected for the barrack-style housing was inaccessible by vehicle, so building supplies had to be transported on foot. Long lines of men, women and children wove over the broken countryside like ants, carrying sand, gravel, cement, steel, plywood, zinc roofing, nails and water. My enthusiasm for physical labor frequently surprised the population and challenged traditional stereotypes of the wealthy and privileged *gringo*. And, in spite of my government's role in the war against these humble but determined people, relationships of trust and sharing began to develop.

Few of the men had ever talked to a North American before, and they began to take advantage of any opportunity to engage me in conversation, especially about the war. They taught me much about peasant culture and custom and provided a wealth of insights into the harshness and vulnerability of life in the Salvadoran countryside. Most were thin and worn from a lifetime of hard labor and malnutrition, with heads that belonged on a larger body. Their hands were gnarled and callused from years of harsh physical labor, and their skin was a leathery brown from the unforgiving tropical sun.

As in Liberia, the young children became my constant companions, an unruly mob of sweating, undernourished ragamuffins, distrusting at first of the strange bearded foreigner in their midst, but quickly won over by my obvious affection. I teased them incessantly and gave them special nicknames, many of which stuck well into adulthood. A shy young boy named Pedro became *Pedro Poderoso* (Peter the Powerful), a pot-bellied and mischievous waif named Leonel became *El Alcalde*

(the mayor). They introduced me to their world of magic and superstition, filled with frightful goblins that haunted the night, handed down from Pipil mythology and kept alive by rural parents to terrorize their children into obedience. I learned of the *Cadejo*, that mysterious dog that appears along lonely trails in the late night hours. Its eyes gleam red like fiery coals, and those who come too close can lose their minds or, at best, fall seriously ill with fever. The *Siguanaba* is "the woman who cries." Like the *Cadejo*, she appears in the late night hours, usually at a river crossing. She has long black hair covering a large beak, and breasts that hang to her waist. She lures unsuspecting victims closer with her soft wail then sends them scampering in panic with hideous and mocking laughter. The *Cipitío* is a short male figure with a large *sombrero*, protruding belly and both feet in reverse who feeds on the ashes of the fires used to cook molasses.

I was introduced to the world of witchcraft, practiced by some in El Salvador but seldom spoken of with foreigners out of shame. I learned of the *brujos* (witches) from the Pipil town of Izalco in the province of Sonsonate where a myriad of illnesses

could be cured or where a curse could be placed upon one's enemy. And I learned of the *mal de ojo* (evil eye) that could afflict young infants if an adult looked upon them too intensely, and of the bracelet of red beads that mothers put on the wrists of their newborns to protect them from this curse.

The children taught me *caliche*, the popular version of Spanish spoken by rural peasants, heavily laced with Nahuatl, the language of El Salvador's original inhabitants, and an abundance of foul words used by men and women alike. They also teased me incessantly about my own mangled Spanish and frequent violation of cultural etiquette. They snuggled beside me on cold evenings and snuck up on me during afternoon naps, surrounding me like the Lilliputians of Gulliver's Travels, whispering and giggling as I pretended to sleep, and daring each other to pull on my beard.

It was the women, however, who provided most of my political education and helped me to understand the enormous suffering and terror that had driven these families to abandon their homes. Many had lost husbands, sons, daughters and the material possessions of a lifetime. All were highly traumatized, and too many were clearly on the edge of insanity in the face of personal loss beyond the limits of the human heart.

In the evenings, we would sit together in the darkness on the open hillsides in Betania, exhausted from the day's labor, and gaze into the heavens at the endless explosion of stars above us. As trust grew, these sessions became filled with horrifying tales of death squads, of "disappeared" relatives, of villages burned to the ground, of young children thrown in the air by crazed soldiers and caught at bayonet point, and of pregnant women slit open to kill their unborn babies before they could grow up to be "communists."

I heard about the endless marches through the night without food or water to avoid being captured or killed when government soldiers penetrated guerrilla-controlled areas. The people referred to this common practice as *guinda*. And I learned of the valor of young guerrilla fighters who often gave their lives to defend the civilian population in flight. The names of most

With the women and children of Betania

of these women have slipped from my memory, but their stories remain vivid, and a few personalities still come to mind in intimate detail:

Ana Menjivar was a strong and independent woman, and a natural leader from the village of San Rafael. A difficult relationship with her mother had driven her from her home at age 11 and, by age 13, she had moved to the capital city where she worked as a maid. By age 18 she had entered into a common-law marriage with a man from her village, several years her elder.

By the late 1970s, Ana had given birth to four children, and both, she and her husband, had become deeply involved in political activities to oust the military dictatorship of General Carlos Humberto Romero. During the height of the repression, with death squads wreaking havoc in the area of Suchitoto, she and her family continued to participate in popular organizations operating at the national level. Like other families from the village, they were forced to seek refuge each night in the hillsides around San Rafael, and Ana watched angrily early one morning from one of those hillsides as death squads burned her small home to the ground and stole all of her remaining possessions.

She gave birth to her last son soon after her arrival in the La

Ana Menjivar, with her mother and children

Bermuda and named him after Eliseo. Eight months later, she fled with her children to San Salvador to avoid capture by the army, then sat stoically in the Green Cross center in Santa Tecla as she received the news of her husband's death in an ambush just north of their village of San Rafael. Ana, now widowed, became a key leader in Betania. She was elected by the population to serve as president of the community, ran the local health clinic, helped set up the school and participated in the physical labor of building and planting.

Christina Menjivar, Ana's mother, was a thin woman who still showed signs of having possessed stunning beauty in her youth. But the birth of nine children and a life of privation had taken their toll. Our first meeting occurred in an uncomfortable silence one stifling afternoon in Betania as her tears fell into a dark pool of bean soup that sat untouched on the table before her. She was too injured to speak, and I withheld my questions, but eventually learned that she had just received word that government soldiers had killed her oldest son in battle on the outskirts of Suchitoto. She would lose two more sons, several brothers and other close family members before the war was over and would suffer from serious heart ailments caused by prolonged stress in her later years.

Talina

Talina was a small and frail woman, too tormented by her losses to recapture the joy of living. She spent her days in silent rage, and the central aim of my life became making her smile. Her only son, Antonio, had been killed by the National Guard in March 1980, just days before the assassination of Archbishop Romero. He was buried in the basement of the National Cathedral in San Salvador alongside the remains of Romero himself, but this enormous honor had done little to alleviate Talina's anguish and overwhelming sense of loss. Then her husband disappeared a year later in La Bermuda, carried away one frightening night by the army and never heard from again.

Ofelia had five young children when I met her in Betania. Like Talina, she had lost her husband in La Bermuda to army assassins. Ana Andrades had lost her oldest son in combat in 1982. Maria Santos lost her husband and two sons between 1980 and 1982. Nena lost her husband in 1980 – and the endless litany of tragedy goes on.

The army began to visit Betania soon after the first truckloads of displaced families had arrived. Sometimes they came peacefully, wanting only to demonstrate that they knew of our presence. On other occasions they were more menacing, surrounding the refugee camp before sunrise and greeting the awakening population with weapons readied. Eliseo and I were interrogated frequently, and it was only due to the backing of the European Union and my being a North American that no physical harm came to us or to the population during those years.

We were also visited frequently by international delegations from the United States and Europe. They came in search of the truth, and they left with anguish and a burning desire to share their troubling findings with the peoples of the world. With each visit, we organized discreet encounters between delegation members and selected women from the population of Betania. These were always heart-wrenching sessions, as the women could never hold back their tears at having to recount in vivid detail all that they had suffered and all that they had lost. I sometimes felt that the meetings were an abuse, but the women themselves viewed their testimonial as their own special contribution to the struggle.

In late 1982, Mary Travers of the famous musical trio Peter, Paul and Mary came to Betania. She had been interested in El Salvador since the war began, and Peter, Paul and Mary had recently released a song honoring the people's struggle. No one among the inhabitants knew who she was, but the people crowded around and cheered loudly as I sang along with her a spontaneous rendition of "500 Miles." A hot meal of *tortillas* and beans then followed, and, finally, a meeting with a small group of women from the center.

Mary wept silently as I translated the tragic testimonies from Spanish into English, and when she departed later that afternoon, she tore a page from her notebook and wrote the following words, asking that they be shared with the women with whom she had met:

Your children are beautiful
Your food was warm and good
We are women and mothers together
I share your sorrow
And I cry with you
We reach out to each other
I wish it were a lovely day
And your children and your world were at peace.

– Mary Travers

By 1983, I had become consumed by the desire to end the suffering of a people I had come to deeply love and decided to join the struggle in the war zones north of the capital city. I had done many things over the years in Central America that had generated fear and discomfort in my Salvadoran wife, Ana, but nothing could compare with this frightful decision.

By that year, over 30,000 civilians had been killed by death squads and government security forces. Close to a thousand casualties a month were being reported by the Archdiocesan Human Rights Office, and Ana had lost countless treasured friends to the struggle already. She had hoped that the guerrilla organizations of the Farabundo Martí National Liberation Front would deny my request to join their ranks, given that I was a North American. She tried to convince me that I was being overly influenced by an adventuresome spirit, but, in the end, she relented, understanding the love and deepening anguish that had become my driving force.

Looking back on that moment today, I am forced to admit that I was moved, to some degree, by Hollywood illusions of heroism and perhaps even a trace of martyrdom. I had visions of massive guerrilla camps filled with civilian women and children in need of my protection. I saw myself facing down oncoming battalions and government aircraft to defend the peasants from imminent slaughter. I had little idea about what my actual role might be or how long I would stay. My decision had little to do with reason at all. It was a simple matter of the heart.

The climate of repression at the national level and the constant danger of government informants made it impossible for me to speak openly about my decision with the population of Betania or others, beyond a small circle of trusted friends. On my final day in the refugee center, I struggled to construct a credible tale about returning to the United States, feeling embarrassed and robbed of the opportunity to bring two years of intense human warmth and love – one of the most meaningful experiences of my life – to a satisfying close. The population gathered in the late afternoon on a hillside where we had toiled together so many days and gazed at the stars by night. There was shock and bewilderment in the eyes of all at my contrived version of why I was leaving. The women wept, and I fought back my own tears. I burned with the impulse to share the truth. I wanted to shout it out – to tell them all at the top of my lungs how deeply I loved them and that I would never abandon them.

But I kept to my original plan and fumbled with the lies about going home to the country that had brought them such suffering and pain.

CHAPTER FOUR

The Roots of Rebellion

When talking about the root causes of poverty and exclusion in Central America and the underlying motivation for the people's prolonged and tenacious struggle for democracy and social justice, analysts frequently go back to the Spanish Conquest. The levels of inequity, desperate poverty and authoritarianism suffered by the vast majorities of the region can only be explained by examining this history.

The story begins in 1522 when the first European eyes gazed upon El Salvador from a Spanish ship anchored off the Pacific coast in the Gulf of Fonseca, known at the time as the Gulf of Conchagua. It must have been an impressive site, with raging surf crashing upon the dark volcanic sands of pristine beaches, a large expanse of coastal lowlands rising slowly towards the high valleys and volcanoes to the north and the towering mountains of the Sierra Madre. Several large volcanic lakes, later known by their indigenous names, Ilopango, Guija and Coatepeque, might have been dazzling the sun that day with the reflection of its own bright rays, and large rivers carrying clear waters from the northernmost regions of the country would have been charging uninhibited toward the sea.

El Salvador's inhabitants at the time were Pipil and Lenca people with some remnants of Maya Chortis and Pocomam. The Pipil formed the dominant ethnic group. Descendants of the Teotihuacanos from central Mexico, they had migrated south between 900 and 1200 AD, settling primarily in the western regions of El Salvador. By the time the Spanish arrived they occupied almost all of the central and western portions of the country between the Lempa River in the east and the Paz River in the west. They established densely populated settlements in the valley of Chalchuapa, along the upper Acelhuate and lower Lempa Rivers, on the lower slopes of the San Salvador volcano, in the regions around Lake Guija in Metapan, in the valley of Sonsonate and along the southwestern coastal plains near Acajutla.

They planted communal lands with corn, beans, tobacco, cocoa and squash, fished the rivers and the ocean and hunted in the forests. They made pottery and cloth and traded their treasured green jade with other indigenous groups travelling through the region. They were a warrior culture, unlike their Mayan predecessors who were more skilled in science, architecture and art. Pipil society was organized in city states, the largest and most important called Cuscatlan "the land of joy."

According to historians, it was in 1524 that the Spanish conquistador Pedro de Alvarado, under the orders of Hernan Cortés, marched with his troops down from Mexico through what is now Guatemala, and invaded the lands of the Pipil. His mission was to take control of neighboring Honduras where the Spaniards believed, rightly so, that the rivers flowed yellow with gold.

Alvarado reached the western highlands of Guatemala in the early part of the year with approximately 300 Spanish soldiers, almost half of them on horseback, and a large contingent of indigenous warriors from Mexico. His first important military encounter on Guatemalan soil occurred in the valley of Quetzaltenango where the *conquistadores* met the immense armies of the Quiché kingdom under the leadership of Tecún Uman.

It was only through the military advantage provided by superior technology that Alvarado won the day. The tactical use of horses, hunting dogs, steel sabers and firearms was completely unknown to Mayan peoples. Tecún Uman was killed in the battle, but his surviving followers insisted that he had been seen taking flight like an eagle covered in feathers with wings that sprouted from his body and three jeweled crowns upon his head, a myth that survives among the Mayan peoples of Guatemala to this day.

Alvarado and his troops then advanced to Iximché, the center of the Cakchiquel empire, where they were met with fear and awe, but little resistance. Finally they marched on the stronghold of the Tzutujiles who resisted bravely but were overcome in a final battle along the shores of beautiful Lake Atitlan. To secure the coastal region, Alvarado violently overran the Pipil city of Panatacat in present day Escuintla, Guatemala, then crossed the Rio Paz into what is today El Salvador.

The first military encounter between the historical peoples of El Salvador and the Spanish invaders occurred in the coastal town of Acaxual, known today as the port city of Acajutla. Alvarado was wounded in the leg by an arrow, and the Pipil were ultimately victorious. They began a war of resistance which forced Alvarado to abandon El Salvador for a time, and it required almost 15 years of persistent military campaigns to consolidate colonial rule.

In the years that followed the Conquista, the indigenous peoples of El Salvador became increasingly marginalized and impoverished. Spanish *conquistadores* quickly realized that the wealth of El Salvador consisted not in silver and gold but in its rich volcanic soil, and an agrarian society typical of other colonies in the New World quickly evolved. Large plantations were established for the cultivation of cotton, balsa wood, cocoa and indigo, and indigenous peoples were enslaved or forced to work on these extensive farms. Thousands of workers died of exhaustion, malnutrition and plague so that, by the end of the sixteenth century, the population had been reduced from its original level of 500,000 to fewer than 10,000 inhabitants.

Colonial society was highly stratified with pure-blooded Europeans born in Spain at the top of the hierarchy. They were followed by Creoles, descendants of Spanish *conquistadores* born in the Americas. Under them were the *mestizos*, people with a mixture of Spanish and indigenous ancestry who were permitted to occupy certain mid-level administrative positions, but barred from owning land, horses or firearms. And at the very bottom were the disenfranchised indigenous peasants, whose culture was mocked and denigrated, and their language suppressed.

The Catholic Church preached humility and submission, urging indigenous people to accept the burdens of their present life with the hope of reward in the next. Native religions and traditional celebrations were prohibited, temples were torn down and gods were replaced. The indigenous tradition of communal ownership of land was gradually abolished and huge segments of indigenous lands were conceded to *conquistadores* in payment for their services to the Crown. From these concessions came the *haciendas* and *ranchos*, precursors of the extensive landholdings of the modern era.

El Salvador declared its independence from Spain in 1821 and eventually became an independent republic under the rule of a small economic and political elite deriving its wealth and privilege from the system of land tenure inherited from the colonial years. Coffee was introduced in 1840, replacing indigo as the chief export and further accelerating the concentration of land.

Coffee production required a cool climate found on the slopes of volcanoes and lower mountains where the remaining indigenous population had taken refuge; so, in 1882, the government passed a law abolishing *ejidos*, the last vestige of indigenous communal property, producing with the swipe of the pen an immense and defenseless population of landless peasants and assuring a continuous source of cheap labor for what became one of the most powerful oligarchies in Central America.

By 1890, less than 1% of the population controlled 90% percent of the country's wealth, and in later years the country's first standing army was established to defend the new oligarchy from the growing threat of social unrest. Indigenous resistance to the loss of their lands continued throughout the central and western portions of the country with significant uprisings in Zacatecoluca and San Vicente (1832), Izalco and Atiquizaya (1884), Cojutepeque (1885), and Santa Ana (1898). Then, in 1932, landless indigenous peasants, relegated to the underpaid task of harvesting the precious coffee of the oligarchy, rose up again.

A massive and systematic slaughter ensued with government troops killing close to 30,000 indigenous people over a two-month period. A widespread cholera epidemic finished off many of the survivors. Those who remained went into hiding, quit speaking their native language, Nahuatl, and donned western dress, and the last vestiges of indigenous culture slowly disappeared in El Salvador in what some historians still consider to be the most savage act in the history of the Americas.

General Maximiliano Hernández Martinez was the man selected to carry out this vicious massacre in defense of the landed aristocracy. He was known for his bizarre philosophies, justifying poor children going shoeless by insisting that it was good for them to be in touch with the vibrations of the planet and lamenting the death of ants more than that of human beings because humans had a soul that would live in eternity while ants simply ceased to exist. He also dabbled in witchcraft, for which he was nicknamed *El Brujo* (the Witch).

Hernandez Martinez, like other military dictators of Central America during the period, maintained a fascination with European fascism inspired by Nazi Germany and ruled El Salvador with an iron fist until he himself was overthrown in a coup in 1944. His fall was perceived as an opportunity for countries like El Salvador to break with a past of military rule and introduce a more democratic system of government. The disorganized and dispersed social forces of the country, however, still suffering from the trauma of 1932, were unable to regroup and consolidate. Colonel Osmín Aguirre y Salinas, Maximiliano Hernandez Martinez's chief of police during the 1932 slaughter, came to power, and the list of heads of state over the next five decades was overwhelmingly dominated by generals, colonels, lieutenant colonels and military juntas. The military served the interest of a powerful and deeply entrenched oligarchy, referred eventually as the "fourteen families."

Opposition political parties, seeking an end to almost 50 years of military rule, began to regroup in the 1970s in an effort to promote change through the electoral process. But they were met by electoral fraud sustained through a growing wave of repression bent on eliminating all (even moderate) political opposition.

Colonel Arturo Armando Molina lost the popular vote in 1972, but he took power anyway with military backing, confirming to many opponents of military rule that opposition parties could participate in the electoral process, but they could not gain access to power through democratic elections. Two years later, elections for congress and local mayors were held, but the results were never made public. Corruption within the government and military was rampant. Nothing moved forward without the traditional *mordida* (bribe), and millions of dollars of international aid were channeled into the pockets of unscrupulous government functionaries.

Following assertions by the Salvadoran right that the National University had become a nest of communist subversion, Colonel Molina ordered government security forces to occupy university facilities in July 1972. Professors were arrested and foreign teachers were expelled from the country, contributing to the further radicalization of El Salvador's youth.

At the time of my arrival in Central America in December 1977, most countries of the region were still under military rule and the condition of rural peasants had become intolerable. In El Salvador, an inequitable system of land tenure, with 60% of agricultural lands in the hands of the wealthiest 2% of landowners, left over half of the rural population without access to enough arable land to feed themselves. The income of the vast majority of rural farmers was less than ten dollars a month and the per capita calorie intake of the population at large was considered to be the lowest in the western hemisphere. As a result, over 70% of rural children under five years of age were severely malnourished. One out of ten women died during childbirth. Children and adults alike died from illnesses that could have been easily cured with minimum access to basic healthcare, and only a small percentage of the school-age population had access to formal education. Landlessness produced cyclical poverty. Poverty was producing desperation, and desperation was threatening violence.

By the 1970s, peasants had begun to find new forms of expression through broad-based "popular organizations" with a national focus. The Christian Federation of Salvadoran Peasants (FECCAS), had been formed earlier, in 1965, and the Union of Peasant Workers (UTC), was organized several years later to struggle for land reform and higher wages. By 1977 these two organizations joined forces and were building strategic alliances with industrial workers, students and other key sectors. Their demands were met with increasing repression, and more people around the country began to wonder if non-violent change was possible under the existing regime.

It was in this context that Antonio Rivas, a disenfranchised hard dirt peasant farmer and sugar cane cutter, whom I would come to know and love, struggled, along with his wife, Teresa, and five small children, to eke out a meager existence on the barren hillsides around the town of El Paisnal in the north central province of San Salvador.

Teresa had given birth to four daughters in rapid succession followed by a son. Eva, the oldest, was born in 1969; Victoria, the second daughter was born in 1971; Gladys, the third daughter was born in 1973; and Isabel was born in 1974. The first son, Aníbal, was born in 1978, shortly after my arrival in Central America. Their life, so distant in many ways from my own at the time, was filled with the drudgery and uncertainties of El Salvador's harsh rural countryside in the 1970s, but it was also generously laced with the joy of family, simple living and humble expectations. In Antonio's words, spoken many years later, they were "free, happy and without danger." They were also unaware of the storm that was approaching that would bring us together, but would also rock their world, separating the children from their parents and leaving several family members dead.

The first winds of change blew into the villages around El Paisnal in September 1972. Rutilio Grande, a Jesuit priest born in El Paisnal, who had studied in San Salvador and Rome, had come home. He had been named to head up the parish of Aguilares, of which El Paisnal was a part.

Rutilio was a close friend of Bishop Romero and a strong advocate of the new social doctrine emerging from within progressive sectors of the Catholic Church, influenced by Vatican II and the thinking of Pope John XXIII and developed by figures of the Latin American Church, like Gustavo Gutierrez in Peru, Leonardo Boff in Brazil and Jon Sobrino in El Salvador. The new doctrine was referred to as the "Theology of Liberation." It reflected the growing concerns of the Latin American Episcopal Conference about injustice and violence throughout the subcontinent and introduced new concepts like "social sin," "structural injustice" and a "preferential option for the poor." It called upon the clergy to move beyond the traditional precepts of pastoral action, focused primarily on the sacraments, to a deeper commitment to the liberation of the oppressed.

Shortly after his arrival in Aguilares, Rutilio formed a team of young priests and seminarians to work with him toward the goal of revitalizing the local church through the formation of living communities, referred to as Christian Base Communities and made up of lay men and women working as agents of pastoral action and builders of their own destiny. At the root of Rutilio's methodology was the "praxis" of Brazilian educator Paulo Freire, based on the empowerment of the poor through the strengthening of abilities and tools to objectively analyze their reality and change it. It was based on the conviction that the poor and oppressed must become responsible and committed to their own historical process of "re-creation" and liberation.

Aguilares, at the time, was a growing and bustling city surrounded by 35 large *haciendas* producing cattle, sugar cane, and staple crops. It was located only 20 miles north of the capital city and reflected all of the social contradictions and injustices of the country itself. The parish encompassed an area of approximately 100 square miles with a population approaching 30,000 inhabitants. Its geographical domain included the northern portion of San Salvador province, part of Cuscatlán province and a portion of northern La Libertad. It had a single paved highway, *La Troncal del Norte* (the Northern Highway), extending northward from the capital city, passing through Chalatenango and reaching the southern border of Honduras.

An excessive concentration of agrarian lands in the hands of a few large owners produced an impoverished mass of landless peasants with fewer than 150 days of paid employment per year earning less than 15 cents a day. The largest *haciendas* produced enormous wealth for their owners, while the workers and their families, like Antonio and Teresa, lived a life of deprivation and despair, toiling from sunrise to sunset in a semi-feudal existence, receiving starvation wages and paying half of their harvest each year to the owners of the *hacienda* in exchange for the right to a small plot for planting their annual staple of corn and beans for their families.

The worker/owner relationship was one of domination and exploitation with little protection under the law. The labor code of El Salvador was designed to address the rights of full-time employees only, and agricultural workers were generally employed seasonally or on a part-time basis. Labor practices common to more industrialized societies, such as minimum wage and the eight-hour workday, were relegated to the whims of the *patrón* (owner).

The plantation owners, or their fierce *capataces* (foremen), ruled their workers with absolute impunity, frequently firing them without recourse after years of dedicated service, or evicting them and their families with little notice from homes they had occupied for decades. Protest up until that time had been futile, given the growing reserve of available labor. And rural workers lived in a permanent state of debt, leaving them vulnerable and tolerant of inhuman levels of exploitation. The lifestyle of rural peasants was frequently unstable, unhealthy and laced with violence. A system of exploitation and oppression was assimilated and internalized by the workers and their families as if it were a normal state of affairs. The brutal treatment of men, women and children on the *haciendas* was reenacted in the home where Latin *machismo* rendered even the most destitute man king of his castle and the woman his obedient, and frequently abused, servant. Peasant women were treated as beasts of burden throughout their lives. Children were overworked and severely punished for the slightest offense or for being even a bit negligent in the performance of their household duties. Marriages were seldom formalized with religious or civic ceremony. Domestic relationships were made and unmade around the need to migrate in the constant search for work, and those who re-

mained at home generally lived in the shambles and squalor of
people uneducated in basic hygiene.

Abandonment by husbands overwhelmed with hopelessness
was common. A large percentage of households were headed by
single women. The birthrate was among the highest in the western hemisphere, and so was the level of mother and child mortal-
ity. Decent housing, electricity, running water and sanitary facilities were all luxuries beyond the wildest dreams.

It was a world filled with fatalism, fear and superstition, the
macho rites of passage and the blindness as well as the beauties
of tradition. A permanent cycle of poverty, vulnerability and exploitation produced a self-image that often lacked the most minimal elements of human dignity and self worth, and malnutrition,
disease and violence left those who were "lucky" enough to reach
their forties with an undeniable sense of living on borrowed time.

This was the explosive and chaotic world into which Antonio, Teresa and many others like them were born, where they
were challenged to build a meaningful and productive livelihood.
This was the world that Rutilio Grande and his team of Jesuits
entered at a moment when the social contradictions of El Salvador threatened to send the entire nation into chaos. It was the
ultimate challenge for priest and lay workers alike, committed to
change through nonviolent Christian witness.

Teresa and Antonio were drawn to the vision and the promise
of Rutilio Grande's pastoral message and were elected by their
community to serve as Delegates of the Word, or Catequists as
some called them, meaning that they would provide leadership
and service to their communities in coordination with the local
pastor and his pastoral team, conducting religious ceremonies
when a priest was not available and serving as a bridge between
the community and the parish. Their efforts were described as
a "mission" in order to use a terminology harmonious with the
people's previous experience within the Church. In practice,
however, the work had little in common with the traditional mis-

sions of earlier years. Its fundamental objectives were more am-
bitious, more revolutionary: to construct a new world, without
oppression or oppressors, in accordance with God's plan.

By the end of 1973, 18 months after the arrival of Rutilio
Grande, over 300 Delegates of the Word were working throughout the parish, and over 50 Christian Base Communities had
been organized in the villages around El Paisnal and in other
municipalities. For the long dormant and poorly organized peasantry, it was an awakening. They had discovered the subversive
gospel message that called upon the poor to confront injustice.
They were gaining confidence in themselves and in their ability to act. They discovered that they had a voice and that they
could make their opinion heard. They were beginning to develop
a sense of their own dignity and, in so doing, were becoming indignant over the enormous injustices imposed upon them.

It was not a surprise, therefore, when that same year 1,600
cane cutters on the sugar plantation La Cabaña went on strike
to demand unpaid wages. Rutilio was not involved in the organization of the strike, but the central message of his pastoral work
had clearly provided the necessary impulse.

Antonio, like many other Delegates of the Word who worked
as seasonal laborers on La Cabaña, helped organize and participated in the strike, and Rutilio was called in to mediate. In a
heated meeting with the plantation owners from the wealthy de
Sola family, part of the famous fourteen families ruling El Salvador, Rutilio sided with the workers, insisting that "the Church is
on the side of truth, and truth, in this case, lies with the workers."
The strike was resolved without violence in favor of the workers,
but those who participated or supported the effort would be remembered by the owners and their local henchmen.

Rutilio became a visible symbol of a religious movement
with economic and political dimensions that was taking hold
at the local level and beginning to threaten the interests of the
wealthy landowners throughout the parish. His Delegates of the
Word and other strike leaders began to experience the first wave
of repression to hit this region of the country when right-wing
death squads, closely tied to the military, began arriving in their

villages at night, pulling men from their beds and carrying them off, never to be seen again.

A second and more prolonged strike of sugar cane cutters from the plantation, La Cabaña, followed, and the Delegates of the Word of El Paisnal were again among its leadership. Teresa and her young daughters, Eva, Victoria and Gladys, provided moral support, food and medicines during the 15 days of the strike's duration in compliance with Rutilio Grande's orientation to "sing and bring joy until the struggle was won." Fear was spreading among the peasants, keenly aware of their own vulnerability, but growing solidarity and a deepening conviction about the justification for their struggle kept spirits high.

Following the second strike, La Cabaña refused employment to suspected organizers and known participants. From that time on, most of the Delegates of the Word were left with only the meager earnings of subsistence farming to support their families. Repression increased significantly. The visits of the death squads became more frequent, and the men of the parish were soon forced to sleep at night in the nearby hillsides around the villages. In their absence, their women and children quickly became targets as well, and entire communities were soon abandoning their villages with the approach of nightfall to sleep huddled together under the stars in clandestine sites scattered throughout the countryside.

No one was safe from the death squads, and no one who fell into their grip ever lived to tell about it. Their calling card became the grotesquely mutilated bodies with the tell-tale tiro de gracia (gunshot wound to the head) that began appearing with disturbing frequency along roadsides and in other public places in warning to all who might dare confront the established powers that be.

The death squads began as loosely knit and highly motivated right-wing citizen groups. Their membership was generally made up of people from the middle class, supported by a few sympathetic soldiers and police officials. The oligarchy and its military allies quickly realized their utility as a tool for demobilizing political opposition, however, and more sophisticated organizational structures were soon built across the country, directed by high-level military and police intelligence officers and operating with complete impunity. Much of their financial support came from the upper echelons of Salvadoran society and from wealthy Salvadoran exiles residing in Miami.

They were by no means an isolated phenomenon. They were a form of organized terrorism that was eventually integrated into the formal structures of the State, either through commission or omission. For two decades in El Salvador, groups with names like the White Hand, the Union of White Warriors, the Secret Anticommunist Army and the Maximiliano Hernandez Martinez Anticommunist Brigade threatened, captured, tortured, assassinated and "disappeared" thousands of innocent citizens, mainly among the poor and working classes. The local newspapers became filled with the grisly reports of their nightly activities, referring to them as "well-armed men dressed in civilian clothing," "illegal armed groups with political motives," or, as they came to be known in popular street jargon, the "squash."

Prior to the formation of Christian Base Communities in the area of Paisnal, there was little organization among peasants. When the Christian Federation of Salvadoran Peasants (FECCAS) began to establish bases there during the first six months of 1974, however, the people from the Christian Base Communities joined en masse. During that same year, the Union of Peasant Workers (UTC) was formed in the southern provinces of San Vicente, La Paz and Zacatecoluca. It began by organizing seasonal workers from the coffee and cotton plantations, but rapidly spread to include agricultural cooperatives and the Christian Base Communities of the northern province of Chalatenango. Shortly thereafter, the two organizations became allied as FECCAS/UTC, and then finally fused as the Federation of Peasant Workers (FTC). All of this was perceived by the owners of La Cabaña in Alguilares, and by El Salvador's military and wealthy elite, as a threat to their self-interests, and provoked a further increase in repression by death squads and government security forces.

It was in this tumultuous political context that El Salvador was selected to be the sight of the 1975 Miss Universe pageant. The government and the private sector saw the event as an opportunity to promote and strengthen the country's incipient tourist industry, and invested over 30 million dollars in preparations. They were also intent on projecting an image to the world of social harmony and political stability. But that image was far from reality, and the increasingly combative social forces of the nation were not collaborating.

A public protest by university students in the western city of Santa Ana was violently dispersed by the National Guard. Then, on July 30, students from the National University in San Salvador, marching in solidarity with their comrades from Santa Ana, were surrounded and fired upon by the National Guard, leaving 37 dead and dozens kidnapped and "disappeared." In November of the same year, peasants struggling for land in La Cayetana in San Vicente Province were fired upon by national guardsmen and police, leaving six peasants dead, 13 "disappeared" and 25 arrested.

In spite of the repression, the popular organizations continued to grow. In 1975, the process took a giant leap forward with the formation of the Popular Revolutionary Block (BPR), joining the peasant organizations of the FTC with organizations of industrial workers, students, market women, teachers, church activists and other groups. It marked a dramatic departure from the social dispersion of the past. It introduced a new kind of political organization built upon strategic alliances among a wide variety of social sectors capable of building consensus, and it offered an alternative to traditional, and ineffectual, political parties.

The Popular Revolutionary Block and other broad-based coalitions formed during the period began to have an enormous impact on the political life of the country. They were well organized; their membership was politically astute and highly combative; their capacity for personal sacrifice in the name of *la lucha* (the struggle) permitted them to overcome the obstacles related to increasing government repression and, over time, they demonstrated an enormous potential for political action.

Their initial tactics included large demonstrations, strikes, the occupation of factories and agricultural lands. They were quickly radicalized, however, in response to the repression and were soon occupying the National Cathedral and other churches, occupying embassies, burning buses and taking over radio stations. They eventually came to assume a place of unique historical importance in the defense of popular interests in El Salvador and generated panic among the oligarchy at the prospects of a repeat performance of the uprising of 1932.

Rutilio Grande and some members of his pastoral team were slow to accept the new broad-based popular coalitions that were evolving, fearing that they would eventually lead to violence. The peasants of El Paisnal, including Antonio and Teresa, were eventually swept up by the momentum, however, and were soon participating in the activities of the Popular Revolutionary Block at the local level as well as traveling to the capital city for increasingly massive demonstrations.

In response to the repression, the Popular Revolutionary Block began forming "security commissions" in rural villages and urban barrios. Given his long years of leadership and service to his own community as a Delegate of the Word, Antonio was invited to form part of these new commissions. It meant carrying a gun for the first time in his life, a small .38 caliber revolver which he kept hidden at all times. It was his first step in the direction of the increasingly probable option of armed struggle.

His membership in the security commissions was clandestine. No one was to know that he was armed, and he kept his secret on many a tense journey by bus to San Salvador and back with the unsuspecting civilian population of El Paisnal. He was called upon to use his weapon only once, in a shootout with National Police in the capital city after a group of workers and peasants had been fired upon while trying to carry several comrades, assassinated days earlier, to the National Cemetery for burial.

On February 13, 1977, members of the Catholic clergy gathered in the town of Apopa to denounce the growing repression against the poor, and the persecution of the Church at large. A Mass was celebrated and Rutilio Grande gave the sermon, later described as a powerful and angry homily which placed the final seal on his own death warrant:

"...it is dangerous to be a Christian in the world in which we are living!.... It is practically illegal to be an authentic Christian in the world in which we are living! Precisely because the world around us is built upon an established disorder which sees the mere proclamation of the Word of God as subversive....

...I greatly fear, my beloved brothers and friends, that very soon, the Bible will not be able to enter through our borders. Only the cover will arrive, because all of the pages are subversive....if Jesus of Nazareth were to return, as in those times, coming down from Galilee, that is to say, from Chalatenango to San Salvador, I dare say that He would not get as far as Apopa...they would stop Him there, somewhere near Guazapa. There they would take him prisoner and send Him off to jail. They would carry Him before many Supreme Juntas and accuse Him of being unconstitutional and subversive...they would accuse him of being a rebel, of being a foreign Jew, of promoting exotic and strange ideas contrary to democracy, that is to say, contrary to the minority...and they would crucify Him again."

Almost one month to the day after pronouncing these words, Rutilio Grande joined the growing ranks of martyrs in the struggle to build a new and more humane El Salvador. For the military government, who had recently taken power in the country, and for El Salvador's economic elite, Rutilio Grande was the inspirational source for the growing unrest of the peasantry, and his death was a price that they were willing to pay in order to turn back the pages of history and retain the country's future in the hands of the ruling oligarchy.

At 5:55 pm on Saturday, March 12, 1977, Father Grande was in his jeep bouncing down the dusty road that weaved through the cane fields of La Cabaña en route to the town of El Paisnal. He was accompanied by 72-year-old Manuel Solórzano, 16-year-old Nelson Rutilio Lemus, and several small children. He was accustomed by now to the death threats, and Antonio remembers many occasions when he would remind his peasant flock of Jesus' message that "man should not fear those who kill the body, but rather those who kill the soul."

In the town of El Paisnal, a large group from the surrounding villages awaited his arrival to celebrate Mass for the Novena of Saint Joseph. Antonio had been called away by family members to search for the body of a cousin who had fallen into the Lempa River and drowned while fishing. Teresa was at home in their village of Amayo caring for the children.

As Rutilio approached the halfway point in his journey, a truck which had been following them during most of the trip began to pull closer. A second vehicle was parked on the roadside just ahead, with several men standing alongside. Among them was a police officer from Aguilares.

As Rutilio passed, the group of men raised their weapons and fired, sending bullets into the throat, ear, skull, pelvic area and left foot of the priest. Subsequent blasts killed Manuel Solórzano and Nelson Rutilio Lemus, while the young children accompanying them were miraculously left unscathed. A medical exam, performed by a forensic physician, disclosed that the shots had been fired from three different directions and that most of the bullets that penetrated Rutilio came from a weapon used by the National Police.

The news spread quickly, and reached Teresa before nightfall. She left her four children with their grandparents and rushed to El Paisnal in time to accompany a group of mourners to the site of the slaying. They then carried Rutilio's body to the church in El Paisnal, where it remained until the following day.

Throughout the night and the next morning, peasants continued to flood into the town, stunned and dismayed at the loss of their beloved pastor. Antonio returned late that evening with the cadaver of his cousin, swallowed by the raging river and recovered four miles from the point at which this hapless peasant, unable to swim, had slipped and fallen into its treacherous waters. The search had been long and arduous, and an exhausted Antonio wept when Teresa broke the news of Rutilio Grande's death.

The corpses of Rutilio, Manuel Solórzano and Nelson Rutilio Lemus were transferred to the National Cathedral in the capital city on the following Monday morning, where the Papal Nuncio celebrated Mass. The crowds that accompanied the ceremony were unprecedented, cramming into the gigantic cathedral, spilling out onto the street, and filling the central park. Later that day, the funeral procession returned to Aguilares in a slow chain of passenger cars and cattle trucks loaded with peasants. From there it proceeded on to the little church of El Paisnal where Rutilio had attended Mass as a boy and where Antonio and Teresa had been married. The three corpses were buried together near the altar of the church while rustic guitars accompanied peasant voices lifted in mournful song.

Rutilio Grande was the first in a long list of priests and nuns who were later assassinated or "disappeared" for their accompaniment of the poor in El Salvador. A campaign of slander and accusation by public media controlled by the oligarchy had prepared the way for his slaying, but his death symbolized something larger and more important than the silencing of a radical Jesuit. It was an attack on the pastoral work of the Catholic Church, on the Church's preferential option for the poor and on the solidarity of its priests and nuns with the growing numbers of victims of repression.

The Christian Base Communities and members of FECCAS were deeply shaken by Rutilio Grande's death, but they remained determined that his voice not be silenced and that his mission not be in vain. In mid-1977, Antonio and Teresa, along with their four children and other peasant families of El Paisnal, occupied the *hacienda* San Francisco. The action was planned to protest its owner's refusal to lease uncultivated lands to the peasants for the planting of corn and beans, their staple diet without which they risked starvation.

The occupation was named in honor of Father Grande, and the peasants placed a large portrait of the slain priest in the center of their temporary shanty town of cardboard and zinc huts. They planted their corn and beans on the surrounding hillsides and resisted eviction for two months until government troops finally drove them out in a pitched battle of hand-to-hand fighting as the first crops were coming up.

The soldiers pursued the peasants into the surrounding villages, searching and then burning houses and arresting women and children, many of whom were never seen or heard from again. From El Paisnal, the troops marched on to Aguilares, reinforced with tanks and armored cars. They machine-gunned the church in the center of the city, where Rutilio had once preached and where a number of peasants had now sought refuge. They then carried out a house-to-house search, beating and arresting anyone found with a photo of the "subversive" priest. The final toll of the day is still uncertain, but eye witnesses speak of 50 dead and over 300 jailed or "disappeared."

Later that same year, the peasants of El Paisnal, including Antonio and Teresa, occupied the *hacienda* San Antonio Grande, where they blocked the tracks of the local railroad and successfully resisted eviction for 22 days. Centuries of desperate poverty and repression were driving the local population into more radical and confrontational action in the effort to advance their struggle for survival and for basic human rights. It wasn't long thereafter that small cells of armed guerrillas began to establish a presence in the area of El Paisnal. At night, heated gun battles could be heard from Antonio's and Teresa's village of Amayo as the first guerrilla units of the modern era, descendants of Pipil warriors, began attacking nearby military positions or "cleansing" the countryside of death squads. Most of the fighting took place during the dark hours of the night when the guerrillas controlled the countryside. By day, the guerrilla fighters blended into the civilian population and moved about undetected.

Jimmy Carter was President in the U.S. at the time, intent on burying the collective memory of Watergate and Vietnam and trying to convince the world of the unique moral fiber of his government. He introduced an impressive human rights agenda in his foreign policy, curtailing military aid to Guatemala in response to gross human rights violations in that country. But the sincerity of his rhetoric and the coherence of his policies were severely tested in El Salvador.

The U.S. was concerned about growing government repression and the political unrest it was generating. But the logic of the cold war still dominated in the minds of policymakers. The Soviet Union had invaded Afghanistan and was exercising considerable influence in Cuba, and Carter ultimately accepted the imperative that Central America remain, at all cost, within the United States' sphere of influence, even if that meant turning a blind eye to blatant and ongoing human rights violations.

Repression in El Salvador became institutionalized in November 1977 under the newly elected president, General Carlos Humberto Romero. The oligarchy was pressing for more drastic measures against the popular organizations, and the military regime of General Romero responded with the "Law for the Defense and Guarantee of Public Order."

The new measures outlawed all criticism of the government and restricted free association, communication and the exchange of information. Most importantly, it emphasized the punishment of political crimes over the punishment of common crimes, a paradox for a government arguing that it was combating totalitarianism. In juridical terms, the law was an aberration, since it gave lip service to the defense of democracy and human rights while legalizing the physical elimination of any dissident voice, person or group considered a threat to the government.

The underlying intent of the new law was to inhibit the spiraling organizational process occurring within the political opposition and to block the flow of news and information on human rights violations to the exterior. It was of little help in controlling the growing violence and slowing the rapid decline of economic conditions, however. The roots of the crisis lay in the deteriorating social, economic and political system, but Romero's policies lacked any suggestion of reform and became squarely focused on repression. The lists of the assassinated and "disappeared" continued to grow in a deepening vacuum of civic, moral and institutional values.

The law was ineffective at weakening social protest. In the sixteen months that it was applied, there were over 40 strikes throughout the country. The wealthy families of El Salvador's oligarchy and their military clients began to calculate out loud how many lives it would take to maintain the status quo, and estimates began to circulate that from 20,000 to 100,000 deaths would be required to hold back the raging sea.

During the same year that General Carlos Humberto Romero took office, another Romero appeared on the political scene and was soon challenging the general's power. He was Archbishop Oscar Arnulfo Romero (now Saint Romero), perceived originally as a meek and conservative influence within the Church, but dramatically changed – in his own words, "converted" – by the events of his time. He was deeply moved by the assassination of his colleague and close friend Rutilio Grande, and by the growing repression against priests and lay church workers.

Named by the Vatican just weeks before the electoral fraud that brought General Romero to power, he admitted later having been assigned the task of reining in radicalized priests supporting revolution. Following the assassination of Rutilio Grande, however, an enraged Archbishop Romero openly opposed the new law for public order, defied the state of siege in effect at the time, closed the Catholic schools for three days, demanded a government investigation and boycotted all government functions during the rest of his tenure.

A man once more inclined to seek harmony among the economic classes of El Salvador, he now began to denounce the injustices that blocked reconciliation. His words, which had once tended to remain in the realm of generalities and abstraction, began to acquire a poignant quality in his increasingly clear and painful analysis of concrete reality. He became known as "the people's bishop" and the "voice of the voiceless." His sermons became fiery and informative, providing a weekly analysis of current events for the impoverished and illiterate masses of El Salvador. They offered a sense of hope and solidarity that attracted the poor in hordes, who packed the National Cathedral each Sunday morning and rewarded his message with frequent applause.

By mid-1977, Archbishop Romero, and the Catholic Church as a whole, had been targeted by the oligarchy and the government as a source of ideological "contamination" and the architects of much of the country's growing unrest. During the first six months of that same year, two more Catholic priests were assassinated in El Salvador, two were imprisoned, two others tortured, one was beaten, four were threatened with death, and seven were refused entry to the country. Through it all, flyers circulated in the wealthy neighborhoods of San Benito and Escalón exhorting the citizenry to "Be a Patriot, Kill a Priest."

The government and its U.S. backers in the Carter administration struggled to hide from the world a reality all too well known by six million Salvadorans. But, by the end of 1977, the reality of the country had begun to seep through the cracks and flow into the world's consciousness. A surprise visit to National Guard headquarters by a United Nations Human Rights Commission in January 1978 turned up clandestine cells and torture chambers. The U.S. State Department had to admit, in a report released in February 1979 that El Salvador was among the "most serious violators of individual freedoms in Latin America and the Caribbean." Then, in May of that same year, a massacre of civilians on the steps of the National Cathedral was caught on film by a CBS cameraman, and El Salvador became front-page news.

Repression continued to grow throughout the decade of the 1970s under the principles of the U.S.-inspired National Security Doctrine. This doctrine, developed by the United States military during the war in Vietnam, introduced the concept of the "enemy within" and focused on government efforts to defend the State from its own citizens. The Salvadoran version of this doctrine meant the systematic elimination of any person or group that opposed the power of the oligarchy.

On January 20th, 1979, a contingent of National Guard and other government security forces attacked a parish retreat house, *El Despertar*, in San Antonio Abad on the outskirts of the capital city. An artillery blast from a government tank severed the head of the parish priest, while a young nun accompanying him, a teacher and 34 young students were arrested and carried away.

On May 2nd, the Popular Revolutionary Block occupied the National Cathedral and three embassies in San Salvador demanding that the government release five of its leaders captured during a march on the previous day. Antonio and Teresa were not present on this occasion, but hundreds of other demonstrators from urban and rural communities flooded the front steps of the National Cathedral in solidarity. Security forces arrived and opened fire with machine guns, killing 25 people and wounding over 100. Then, on May 22nd, security forces fired upon a group of students gathered in front of the Venezuelan embassy with a toll of 14 dead and many more wounded.

That same month, President Romero met with the leadership of El Salvador's economic elite to analyze the growing threat of revolution. The message was: "you better take care of yourselves, because we (the military) can no longer defend you." For those present, this statement represented an abdication by the military and an assertion that it was time for the oligarchy to arm and defend itself. It symbolized a historical weakening of an alliance that had lasted 47 years, and marked the beginning of a new wave of death squad slayings.

It was gradually becoming clear to the United States that American interests in the region were no longer being served by General Romero's regime and the 17 military dictatorships that had preceded him. The political center, around which alternatives might have been built, had been systematically decimated or driven into exile by a crazed far right alliance of wealthy land barons, military leaders and their death squads. Its space had been filled by the popular organizations and a growing guerrilla force talking openly of socialism and led by teachers, workers and peasants proposing armed struggle. Washington's tactics gradually became more focused on neutralizing this combined force and building a more acceptable substitute to military rule.

The solution they found was a group of young U.S.-trained military officers with close ties to the State Department and a shared conviction that some level of reform was necessary. On October 15th, 1979, these young officers, with U.S. consent, staged a successful coup and drove General Romero into exile.

They installed a junta with civilian and military participation and spoke of a new era; but an attack a few days later on striking factory workers, in which 18 people were killed and 78 others detained, left many Salvadorans wondering how much had really changed. A later report by Amnesty International stated that, within its first week of office, the new government had been responsible for the death of over 100 demonstrators and striking factory and farm workers.

The National Guard continued to harass the peasantry while the National Police and Treasury Police, all under the control of the Armed Forces, attacked public demonstrations in the cities. During that same year, President Jimmy Carter sent a mobile training team to teach riot control to the security forces of El Salvador.

It was soon obvious that the real power within the junta remained in the hands of the military, and civilian members resigned in protest. Determined to build a political model capable of neutralizing the threat of leftist insurgency, military leaders quickly assembled a second junta in early 1980, assigning a central role to the once-credible Christian Democrat Party and its historical leader, José Napoleón Duarte. But the Christian Democrats had lost much of their former support from the middle class, as well as from the rural and urban poor, and the Carter administration found itself again trying to paint a civilian face on a military in clear control of all strategic areas of government.

The new pact between the military and the Christian Democrats allowed the latter to initiate certain reforms as long as it did not intervene in military matters. In this way, the Christian Democrats, with the support of Washington, were allowed to initiate a program of agrarian reform and the nationalization of banking and international commerce. But the military was granted a free hand in its campaign of extermination against the popular organizations.

It was during this period that Antonio's older brother, Angel, was caught by the death squads in Aguilares and shot four times.

A year later, a second brother, Eduardo, who had worked with Antonio as a Delegate of the Word in the missions of Rutilio Grande, was captured and tortured to death. Antonio found his body in an open field with a bible at his side and a large bloody cross sliced into his stomach and chest.

Death squad members caught and killed three other Delegates of the Word on a small mountain path just outside El Paisnal. A member of the Christian Base Community in the village of Las Araditas, where Antonio's wife, Teresa, had spent her childhood, was shot in the head. And five members of the Christian Base Community in the village of Serradera were machine-gunned in their sleep.

The counterinsurgency model evolving in El Salvador combined modest socio-economic reform with violent repression, and the U.S. government provided the economic and technical tools for both. Land reform was based on a model from Vietnam and designed with counterinsurgency rather than structural reform in mind. It affected less than 30% of agricultural lands and left untouched the fertile coffee farms of the oligarchy. It was also accompanied by a second state of siege in which all forms of public protest were again outlawed, public media was censured and, within the first three months of 1980, over 600 people were killed.

During the previous year, Archbishop Romero had become more vociferous and adamant in his opposition to the junta and the repression that formed the core of its domestic policy. In early 1980, he pleaded in a personal letter to Jimmy Carter to curtail U.S. military aid in the face of growing human rights violations. He also encouraged the remaining civilian members in the junta to resign, arguing that they were providing a mask of legitimacy to a corrupt and repressive government.

The pretensions of the Christian Democrats to somehow salvage a program of reforms under the control of an unconvinced military were illusory from the start. The project was doomed to failure by the lack of political will within the governing junta to oppose the power and influence of the oligarchy. The alliance between the military and the country's economic elite had been weakened, but the army was not prepared to take the process to the ultimate consequences.

The announcement and promulgation of the reforms by the government junta brought another increase in the levels of repression against the popular sectors, those same sectors that were supposed to benefit from the reform package. As this irony became increasingly clear, ministers of government and one of the civilian members of the second junta resigned in response to the request of Archbishop Romero.

In an effort to strengthen the political opposition, The Popular Revolutionary Block joined forces with other broad coalitions in the second week of January 1980 to form the Revolutionary Coordination of Masses (CRM). The first action of this body was a massive demonstration held on the 22nd of that month, generating panic within an oligarchy already intimidated by token government reforms and the growing strength of the popular sector.

The night before the march, security forces machine-gunned the buildings of the National University, where young protesters arriving from the countryside had gathered. That same evening, the offices of the Popular Revolutionary Block and the labor federation, FENASTRAS, were also attacked. On the day of the march, buses filled with protesters from small towns and villages around the country were refused access to the capital city, and concentrations of people waiting for the march to begin were sprayed with insecticide.

In spite of these measures, over 200,000 demonstrators took to the streets in the largest manifestation in the history of El Salvador. The march was attacked along its route by security forces positioned on the rooftops of public buildings, and a massacre of men, women and children ensued. It marked the beginning of an open war of extermination against the country's growing popular movement.

In its Third Pastoral Letter, the Episcopal Conference of El Salvador took a major leap in legitimizing the growing popular insurrection, justifying this option "in exceptional cases of evident and prolonged tyranny that gravely threatened human rights and impeded the general well-being of a country whether it originates in a single person or in evidently unjust structures." Then, in a sermon on March 23, 1980, the beginning of Holy Week, Archbishop Romero addressed the growing crisis in the country, directing his final message at the nation's security forces:

"Brothers, each one of you is one of us. We are the same people. The peasants you kill are your own brothers and sisters. When you hear the words of a man telling you to kill, remember instead the word of God, 'Thou shalt not kill.' God's law must prevail. No soldier is obliged to obey an order contrary to the law of God. It is time that you come to your senses and obey your conscience rather than follow a sinful command. The Church, defender of the rights of God, the law of God, and the dignity of each human being, cannot remain silent in the presence of such abominations. We should like the government to take seriously the fact that reforms stained by so much blood are worth nothing.... In the name of God, in the name of our tormented people who have suffered so much and whose laments cry out to heaven, I beseech you, I beg you, I order you, in the name of God, stop the repression!"

One day later, while celebrating Mass, Archbishop Romero was shot through the heart by a hired gunman. It was an attempt to silence the "voice of the voiceless"; but tens of thousands of El Salvador's poor, accompanied by a vast array of international delegations, attended his funeral in the National Cathedral on March 30 and vowed to keep his memory and message alive. Antonio and Teresa had planned to attend the ceremony, but their oldest daughter, Eva, had fallen desperately ill and they were unable to make the trip to the capital city. Had they gone it is possible that they wouldn't have survived, for the blood of the poor would again flow on that day.

The government, in a desperate attempt to deliver a final blow to the Romero mystique, placed security forces and sharp shooters on the rooftop of the National Palace adjacent to the Cathedral. As the funeral Mass began, they opened fire on thousands of unsuspecting worshipers gathered in the streets and in the central park below. There was mass panic as bodies began to drop. People fled in all directions with no clear route of escape, trampling each other as they ran. Twenty-six people were killed and over 200 were severely wounded. Unmoved by the violence, the U.S. Congress and the Carter administration ignored Romero's final request, and, on the following day, approved an additional package of military aid to El Salvador.

The Christian Democrats and the U.S. government were searching for a solution someplace between two extremes, but they ultimately chose sides and opted for the path of repression. Instead of resolving a complex political dilemma with profound historical roots, they exacerbated the existing contradictions: rendering, on the one hand, a threatened oligarchy more desperate and dangerous while, on the other, providing fodder and fury to the strengthening cry for revolution.

The situation of El Salvador was not only tragic; it had become a box canyon with no easy exits. It was not just a problem of growing conflict; it was a problem with no feasible solution. The margins were being narrowed while the problem was expanding. The positions of opposing social forces were becoming more radicalized. And, in this process of political polarization, the most talented minds of the country, those with a political will for finding a workable medium, were being systematically silenced or forced to abandon the country at a moment when they were most needed. Hope was waning, and the stage was being set for a bloody civil war.

CHAPTER FIVE

Going to the Mountain

From the time of the Spanish conquest, when the Pipil and the Lenca people were driven from the fertile valleys and southern plains of El Salvador, the mountains had served as a refuge. In later years, when coffee, cotton and sugar barons began grabbing up peasant lands for the cultivation of export crops, the people spoke of "going to the mountain" in search of a piece of unwanted soil to scratch out a living for their families. In the vernacular of the 1980s, however, "going to the mountain" meant joining the armed struggle.

The phrase did not refer to a physical space, but rather to a political option. La montaña could include the towering peaks of northern Chalatenango province or the southern coastal plains of La Paz and Usulutan, the lowlands of Guazapa or even the suburban municipalities on the outskirts of the capital city. Nor was it a matter of distance. El Salvador is one of the smallest countries in the western hemisphere: slightly over eight thousand square miles in area and only 168 miles in width between its farthest points. With the highest population density in the Americas, no region is isolated or remote. "Going to the mountain" was more a matter of dimension, a move from one world into another.

In 1983, the Farabundo Martí National Liberation Front (FMLN) was consolidated throughout the country and had launched its second major offensive at the national level to "cleanse" the countryside of death squads and government military forces. They attacked the rural bases of the National Guard and drove the army out of the larger towns. By the end of the year, almost a third of the country was under their control.

They set up their own democratically elected municipal governments, called Local Popular Powers, and began to build a new social and economic order based on equity, solidarity, collectivity and self-sufficiency. Large contingents of government troops could enter the "liberated zones" for brief periods, during which they destroyed housing and crops and often massacred civilians. They were constantly harassed by the growing guerrilla army, however, and were unable to maintain a permanent presence.

There was enormous collaboration with FMLN forces by civilians living within or on the fringes of the liberated zones. Often at risk to their own lives, they informed the guerrillas of government troop movements, supplied food and other basic necessities and maintained silence about the location of guerrilla camps in the area. Over the years, I would move frequently between the two worlds, and my life often depended on the skills and dedication of these daring and deeply committed people.

The U.S. State Department had originally predicted a military victory in El Salvador by 1983; but, by January of that year, presidential advisor Jeane Kirkpatrick, along with the head of the CIA and the Pentagon, were warning that a significant increase in military aid and U.S. advisors was necessary to halt the FMLN advance. President Reagan went before Congress with an urgent appeal, backing his request with the overblown notion that the U.S. faced a special threat to its national security in Central America. Then, several days later, he tried to reinforce the growing fear in the American public by describing El Salvador as being on the front line of a battle aimed at the very heart of the western hemisphere.

I entered the liberated zones under the control of the FMLN for the first time in August 1983. The world I found there was indeed filled with horrors, with levels of deprivation and with dangers far beyond my worst initial fears. But I also found surprising levels of joy and a degree of human solidarity unknown in more comfortable settings.

I found the clandestine warriors of the guerrilla forces – referred to as "terrorists" by my own government – to be determined in their mission, yet humble and highly respectful in their

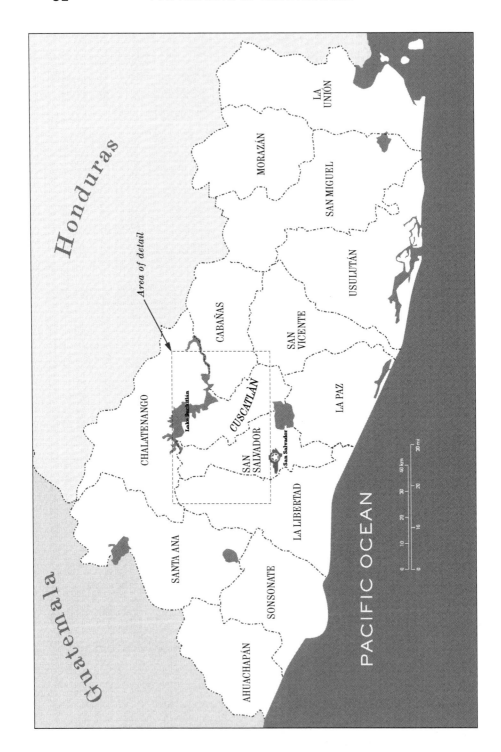

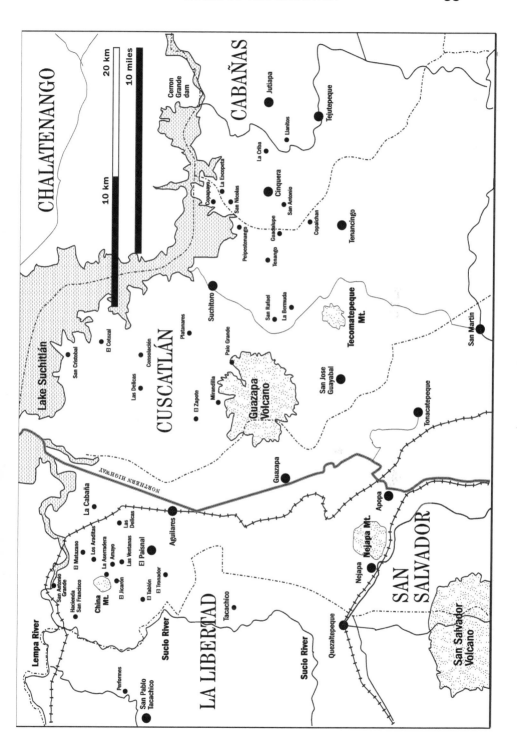

manner. Most of them came from the ranks of El Salvador's rural poor and underprivileged, pushed to the limits by an unbending oligarchy and the blindness of American arrogance. They were the true patriots and heroes of their generation, sacrificing their youth and the pleasures of today for the promise of tomorrow, faceless and hidden from society at large, like flowers that blossom in the shadows.

My first visit took me to the Felipe Peña Front in the north/central part of El Salvador (see map), one of the most highly contested war zones in the country at the time. All five guerrilla organizations making up the FMLN maintained some level of presence in this area, as it was deemed to be the "point of the lance" in the drive towards the capital city and final victory.

It was controlled primarily by the Popular Liberation Forces (FPL), with whom I was affiliated, the largest member organization of the guerrilla coalition. Their leadership was made up of staunch anti-imperialists, highly distrusting of North Americans, but I was received with confidence and warmth into this clandestine world.

Entering guerrilla-controlled territory from the capital city could be a dangerous and terrifying experience. On August 17 I was met in a small restaurant in central San Salvador by a middle-aged man who had been instructed to look for a young *gringo* with a Newsweek magazine under his arm. After "finding" each other, he took my back pack and instructed me to return to the same restaurant at noon that day. With some time on my hands, I decided to visit the tomb of Archbishop Romero in the National Cathedral and prayed there for a considerable amount of time asking for his protection, his guidance and, most of all, his strength to be faithful to the cause of a people for whom he had dedicated his life and accepted the inevitability of his own death.

At mid-afternoon, I returned to the restaurant and ate a simple meal, unsure when I might see food again. At the established hour, my contact person returned with an old pickup truck and we departed from the restaurant together. We drove east along the Pan American Highway for slightly more than an hour and finally stopped just outside the town of San Martin to pick up another young man. We then continued our journey heading north on a smaller paved road and I watched with expectation as the small suburban towns abruptly gave way to the rural countryside. It was dark when we arrived at our destination along a lonely country road where my companion and I were let down and then waited in silence, listening to the sounds of night.

My companion suddenly pointed to a nearby hillside where six silent shadows slowly wove their way down a winding mountain path in single file, headed in our direction. As I watched, I felt a sudden surge of excitement and a degree of trepidation at the realization that I was standing at the doorway to that other dimension – far from everything I had known in my previous life.

The small column consisted of five men of varying ages and a young woman in her late teens, all dressed in black and heavily armed. They greeted us warmly in silent whispers, and then we shouldered our backpacks and headed off into the night.

Our journey took us through miles of countryside and several small villages where loudly barking dogs protested our presence, but nobody stirred from their houses. We stopped at one point just outside of one of the villages to rest and drink water from a small stream. In my inexperience, I was travelling without a canteen, so the young woman in the column offered me a drink from her own. Not knowing my name, she referred to me simply as *compañero*, a term, I would later learn, widely used in the liberated zones to mean companion or comrade, instilling an immediate sense of acceptance and belonging in this new and alien world.

We continued our march and finally arrived at the guerrilla camp in the subzone of Cocal shortly after midnight. We slept almost immediately on the cold and lumpy dirt floor of a collapsing adobe hut, and I awoke with the first light of the following day to the realization that we were in an abandoned coffee farm of the Salvadoran oligarchy.

The other *compañeros* in the camp were already moving about in whispered conversation with steaming tin cups of coffee warming their hands and a variety of weapons slung from bony shoulders or stuck into back pockets or belts. A makeshift lean-to served as a kitchen, and lookouts were posted around the camp a short distance away. I could tell from their manner that most of those present were of humble peasant extraction, rough and rugged in their appearance but disarmingly respectful. My *nom de guerre* (war name) was Alcides, given to me by members of the Guerrilla Army of the Poor years earlier in Guatemala, but everyone was addressed here simply as *compañero*, or *compa* for short, even when names were known.

Like most guerrilla fighters I would meet over the years, those in Cocal were short of stature, thin and muscular. "Pure fiber," as a friend once described them. At five-feet-eleven and a well-fed 180 pounds, I was a giant among them, but I would quickly learn that their strength and endurance were things that I would never be able to match. They could move over the rugged Salvadoran countryside with the silence and agility of a cat, and they could march ten miles through the night, attack a military position before dawn and then march ten miles back to their base camp before the army knew what hit it.

They had been prepared for their struggle by the very system of exploitation and oppression they were intent on destroying. The ability to tolerate extensive periods without food or water was forged in the cruel circumstances of the *hacienda*s in the days of their youth. The ability to overcome the fear of battle and the dangers of war came from a lifetime filled with uncertainty. Tracing their footsteps over the mountain paths of the liberated zones of El Salvador would become, for me, a source of enormous pride.

I remained in Cocal for two days awaiting the arrival of additional supplies from the capital city for transport to the camps further north. I had little to do during this time and anxiety began to build, so I was relieved when we finally departed on the third evening. Life in the camps on the margins of the liberated zones was stifling due to the constant threat of attack. Conversations were carried out in whispers; movement was restricted and there was no civilian population to distract one from the daily stress of war.

As the last afternoon light waned, we gathered in a heavily-armed column of 20 men and women of varying ages carrying large bundles of clothing and boots. The camp commander gave last-minute instructions regarding the need for silence during our journey, since it would take us through areas frequented at night by government patrols. Finally, we were given a *consigna* (password) to be used in case anyone became separated from the column in the darkness, and well-wishers shared their hopes that we not encounter *el enemigo* (enemy troops) along our intended route.

Darkness fell shortly after our departure and, to my great dismay, it rained incessantly for the next several hours. We walked in silence, in single file, headed north along the narrow muddy pathways that wove through the countryside, each of us lost in our own private thoughts and hypnotized by the endless rhythm of marching feet. It was difficult terrain and, in my inexperience, I suffereqd a number of humiliating falls, tumbling over unseen rocks and tree stumps or slipping down the muddy ravines hidden in the darkness along the way.

Three hours into our journey, we stopped briefly to rest in a small mountainside clearing from which the city of Apopa could be seen in the distance. A light rain continued to fall as our column dispersed over the open hillside, and I sat alone on the damp grass, gazing down on the bright city lights, missing my life with Ana Eugenia already and trying to ignore a sudden yearning for the warmth and comforts of home.

We resumed our march north and arrived several hours after daybreak at our final destination near the town of Cinquera. We had walked for 17 hours. My stomach was queasy, and my clothes were caked with mud. But I fought to keep my spirits high as I rested my aching body in a worn hammock strung from the wooden beams of a small adobe hut.

The main guerrilla camp was located in the village of San Antonio, a small hillside community whose highest point offered a view of the surrounding countryside. To the west, China Mountain spread its shadows over the communities of el Paisnal, where Teresa and Antonio Rivas lived. Also to the west lay the Guazapa volcano, a symbol of popular resistance throughout the war. The towering peaks of Chalatenango rose to the north and, to the south, the distant lights of the capital city – so near yet so far away.

The village itself had been largely abandoned by the poor dirt farmers and their terrorized families who once humbly called it home. Many of the houses had been leveled in a long chain of search-and-destroy missions by government soldiers; and the small fields used for planting corn and beans were pockmarked with craters from 500-pound bombs dropped daily by U.S.-supplied A-37 Dragonfly jets.

There were no sprawling camps filled with helpless civilians for me to heroically defend, as I had once so equivocally envisioned during my last days in the refugee camp of Betania. In fact there were few open spaces at all. Small concentrations of guerrilla combatants were dispersed throughout the area in deep muddy ravines where the sun seldom shone, and the civilian families that remained lived in the bombed-out shells of their former homes in a state of permanent anxiety, suffering from a trauma that I had not yet begun to truly comprehend.

We were in the Felipe Peña Front, a war zone. The Felipe Peña Front was named for one of the early founders of the Popular Liberation Forces, killed, along with his girlfriend Gloria Palacios Damián, in a gun battle with the National Guard in August 1975. Felipe was 24 years old and the second-in-command of the FPL. Both he and Gloria had participated in the revolutionary struggle since the 1970s as student leaders in the National University until the army closed down the university in 1972. When the National Guard surrounded an FPL safe house in the capital city, Felipe ordered the evacuation of his comrades and organizational files while he covered their escape. Seeing him wounded, Gloria returned to his side and was shot dead trying to drag his bullet-ridden body to safety.

The Felipe Peña Front extended from the town of Jutiapa in the east to El Paisnal in the west, and from Lake Suchitlan in the north to the capital city in the south, encompassing the provinces of Cabañas, Cuscatlán, San Salvador and northern La Libertad.

It was divided into five smaller areas called "subzones," each with its code name in an effort to confuse army intelligence. The area around the town of San Martin, where I had entered the liberated zones several days earlier, was given the name of *Cocal*. The area around the town of Cinquera, where I was currently camped, was called *Radiola*; the area around the Guazapa volcano, including the town of Suchitoto, was called *Guazapa*; and the area further to the west was divided between the communities of El Paisnal, referred to as the subzone of *Piedra*, and the communities just north of the capital city near the town of Nejapa were referred to as *Chapin*.

In 1983, the civilian population in the villages of the Felipe Peña Front was war-weary but leather-tough and essential to the armed struggle. It was the lifeline of the revolution, providing food, clothing, intelligence information and other vital services, including recruits, for the guerrilla army. U.S. designed counterinsurgency measures, therefore, called for its forced displacement. In the descriptive language of low intensity warfare, the policy was referred to as "scorched earth" or "drying up the sea to kill the fish."

My experiences over the years in the war zones of El Salvador brought me in close and frequent contact with these civilian communities and I increasingly found myself committed to efforts designed to making life more viable for them in order to slow the "draining of the sea." This process began early in my first visit, when it was agreed with FMLN commanders that, given my past experience in community development, I would work with other political cadres to fortify a "war economy" throughout the Felipe Peña Front. I spent each night surrounded by armed combatants in guerrilla camps for my own safety, but I would spend my days with civilian farmers and their families designing projects for agricultural production, small-scale industry and commerce. With no official currency available, our medium for exchange was based on the barter system.

The initial idea was to take advantage of the strengths and compensate for the weaknesses of each subzone within the Felipe Peña Front. Where soil was fertile, we would concentrate on the production of basic grains and vegetables. Where fruit trees were plentiful, we would produce mangoes, jocotes, oranges and other fruits to enrich the local diet. We also constructed beehives that could be moved or hidden during government incursions. Where families had access to nearby towns for the purchase of basic materials like cloth, thread, leather, rubber, glue and zinc, we would plan cottage industries for the production and repair of clothing, shoes and cooking utensils. My previous experience in Liberia, Guatemala and in Betania provided the technical elements for this new task, and I initiated my work with the enthusiasm and satisfaction of one secure in the belief that he had something important to offer.

The subzone of Radiola presented the greatest challenge to our plans, given the levels of instability caused by frequent incursions of government troops and constant aerial bombing. Also, it was a region with little tradition of cultivating anything other than corn and beans. But some of the other subzones offered promising opportunities for productive and commercial enterprise. In Guazapa, well-hidden peanut farms, mobile beehives and cheese factories, all difficult to detect, already flourished throughout the subzone, while brown sugar and molasses were produced from sugar cane on a smaller scale. The subzone of Piedra was more suited to small-scale industry, given its proximity to the town of El Paisnal. Massive incursions of government troops and the indiscriminate bombing of civilian villages destroyed all of these initiatives with frequency. But they were quickly rebuilt in a tenacious David and Goliath struggle between an army with unlimited resources and a people of iron will.

Whenever word reached a civilian village that government troops were approaching, the inhabitants evacuated while FMLN combatants held the soldiers at bay. In an effort to sustain morale, the guerrilla leadership referred to evacuation as a "tactical retreat", but the civilian population, in a more accurate reference to the panicked flight that it was, called it *guinda*.

Guinda was a way of life in the subzone of Radiola in 1983. My first experience occurred only three days after my arrival.

Late in the morning on August 24, I was meeting with the civilian population of San Antonio when government artillery began shelling the village. The mortar fire continued throughout the day, and by mid-afternoon government troops had been sighted advancing from several different directions. It was clear that a full-scale military incursion was under way.

The men, women and children from the village scrambled to hide scarce food supplies and the heavier household possessions that would have to be left behind. Emergency food provisions, readied days earlier, were collected and quickly thrown into worn gunny sacks. The younger children ran to gather small domestic animals and were then mounted on the shoulders of their parents readied for flight.

By nightfall the civilian populations of San Antonio and several surrounding communities had rendezvoused in Guadalupe, a small abandoned village whose inhabitants had been massacred by the army several months earlier. From there, they headed off in a slow silent column, supporting themselves on crude walking sticks and the bony shoulders of family members and neighbors. They were accompanied by the popular militia and local guerrilla units, who would guide them in their desperate search for a break in the enclosing circle of government troops.

I was ordered to remain with a smaller unit of FMLN political cadres to which I had been assigned, including a handful of combatants and a Salvadoran Catholic priest-turned-revolutionary named "Chele" David Rodriguez. We walked for 12 grueling hours through the night, at times in the rivers to avoid leaving tracks. I took frequent and serious falls, due to my inexperience and the treacherous muddy footpaths we were following. At one point during the first night, while scaling a muddy embankment, my right leg slipped into a deep hole with tremendous force, causing the ligaments to snap forward over the knee and preventing me from bending my leg. I knew that I couldn't walk in this situation and that our column had to keep moving; so, as the young combatants of our unit watched in consternation, I bent my leg with all my force until the ligaments snapped noisily back into place, and we continued on in the darkness.

By the second day, my body was bruised and swollen from so many falls, and I drew laughter by insinuating that we might have sustained more injuries in our small unit than the guerrilla combatants who were engaged at that moment in a fierce gun battle a short distance away.

We continued moving, always at night, in ten-hour spurts in an effort to outmaneuver the battalions of government soldiers sweeping the countryside for any signs of our presence. It was the height of rainy season, so with each evening's march we were soaked, and caked with fresh layers of mud. We rested during the day, hidden among trees or thick underbrush and feeding on a small daily ration of ground cornflour mixed with sugar.

By the end of the fifth day, our maneuverings had brought us full circle to a grassy hillside overlooking the town of Cinquera. San Antonio was a short distance away, and hope sprouted that we might soon be returning to our base. Our radio had gone dead early into the *guinda,* so we were unable to communicate with other units. We had not had contact with the civilian population since the rendezvous in Guadalupe, and we had no information on the location of army positions.

We hid ourselves in the tall elephant grass and were analyzing our next move when the shouts of government soldiers suddenly sounded nearby. Their relaxed tone told us that our presence had not been detected, but their voices were growing louder, a clear sign that they were moving in our direction. Without radio, we had unknowingly stumbled into the midst of a small contingent of soldiers and electrical workers who were taking advantage of the large-scale incursion to repair power lines cut by guerrilla units several weeks earlier.

My heart began to pound with the prospect of facing my first combat. I felt confident, given the presence of experienced guerrilla fighters, and was comforted by the conviction of being in a cause worth dying for. I was less certain about taking the life of another, however, keenly aware of being a North American in a conflict that pit Salvadoran against Salvadoran – sometimes brother against brother – and that those doing the fighting on both sides were extracted from the poorest sectors of Salvadoran society. The United States was providing the impetus, the strategies and the means for waging war, but it was the poor of El Salvador who provided the bodies.

Military service was required by law in El Salvador, and the favored method of recruitment by the army was to surround rural villages and grab every able-bodied male. New "recruits" were taught that they were battling communist subversion, and many firmly believed, as they went into battle, that they were defending their nation from an invading Soviet force. The issue was not resolved for me at that particular moment, nor was it resolved in future combat situations in which I found myself with a troubling degree of frequency over the next six years.

As the voices grew louder we dropped to the ground and began crawling through the tall elephant grass on our bellies as quickly and quietly as possible, lifting the grass behind us to conceal our trail. We found an area of thick underbrush a short distance away and hid there in silence for the remainder of the day, listening to the conversations of the soldiers nearby and hoping that we would not be spotted by the helicopters now flying back and forth overhead.

Later that night, under the cover of darkness, we slowly abandoned the area, moving in the direction of San Antonio. After several hours of walking we stopped to rest. It rained heavily again, but exhaustion overcame us and we all slept briefly on the wet muddy ground. We were on the move again before daybreak, and by mid-morning were within a few miles of San Antonio. Two of the younger combatants in our unit, Joel and Santiago, were sent off to explore the area around the village and search for a large bottle of honey hidden prior to the *guinda*. We had not eaten anything substantial in five days and our bodies were in dire need of high-energy food.

Around noon, the daily commercial flight from San Salvador to Miami passed overhead, and visions of cushioned seats and cold Bloody Marys tormented my mind. It was a flight I had taken many times in the past, looking down on the war zones from the security and comfort of a large Boeing aircraft, and I began to miss again the comforts of a previous life. My spirits were quickly lifted, however, with the return of the young combatants, a large bottle of fresh honey in their hands and a smile upon their faces that told us that government troops were finally withdrawing from the area.

I had been in the war zones for less than two weeks, but the return to our base camp in San Antonio felt like coming home. We were all fatigued and caked in a week's worth of sweat and mud, but we were relieved and jubilant that this *guinda* was finally over.

The long column of civilians was returning home as well, and we spent that night in the one-room mud hut of a middle-aged woman and her five children. There was little food to go around, and the clay tile roof of their house had been destroyed by government soldiers during the incursion. It provided sufficient cover to protect us from the persistent rain, however, and we felt thankful for the small luxuries of life as we lay down to sleep on the hard and lumpy dirt floor.

With the arrival of FMLN health promoters from the guerrilla units the following morning, the house was quickly converted into a community clinic. Young children and elderly men and women who had been walking barefoot for the past five days appeared in a steady stream throughout the morning and into the afternoon to heal their torn and bleeding feet. Many of the civilians were suffering from acute stages of malnutrition and I was informed that three young children from the village had died of starvation two days into the *guinda*.

I had witnessed the worst of life in the war zones within only weeks of my arrival and was to relive the experience of *guinda* many times over in the years that followed. In the first week of September 1983, I was meeting with the civilian population in the picturesque mountaintop village of Azacualpa, a four-hour walk from our base in San Antonio, when the silence of the late afternoon was suddenly shattered by incoming artillery and heavy ground fire nearby. Small children were quickly loaded onto adult shoulders as we headed down the treacherous mountain paths while guerrilla combatants confronted the advancing soldiers. We walked most of the night, but the troops did not follow, and this *guinda* ended quickly with no casualties. A week later I endured a third and more prolonged *guinda* which left me thin and weak and in a state of undernourishment approaching that of the people around me.

The large-scale incursions by government ground forces were highly disruptive of life's routine in the liberated zones and devastating to the exhausted civilian population. But the ever-present air war was even more frightening. The U.S. government had provided the Salvadoran Air Force with an impressive array of deadly aircraft, including A-37 jet bombers, Huey helicopter gunships, Hughes 500 helicopters, Cessna Push and Pulls, and AC-47s. All had been utilized by the United States in the war against Vietnam. All were particularly suited to counterinsurgency warfare in a setting such as El Salvador. And all were designed to confront a lightly armed or defenseless population.

Over the years, many of the aircraft were nicknamed by the civilian population in accordance with the special characteristics they possessed. The agile Hughes 500 helicopter was referred to as the *abispa* (hornet). It could fire five thousand rounds per minute from Gatling machine guns mounted on each side of its fuselage and was perfectly designed for the rugged, mountainous terrain of El Salvador. It appeared suddenly and without warning, swooping into the deep ravines where the civilian population generally hid during *guindas*.

The Cessna Push and Pull was called the *gradilla* or *pushanpú*. It was armed with deadly rockets able to destroy targets, large or small, at short range. Perhaps its only advantage, from the standpoint of the civilian population, was its tendency to reduce power before each rocket was fired, warning its victims and providing a few seconds to throw oneself to the ground before the rockets hit.

The AC-47 was known as the *paciencia* (patience) because of the slow lumbering circles it could make for hours above its target. It was armed with 50-caliber machine guns that could riddle an area the size of a football field in seconds, and was referred to by U.S. military advisors as "Puff the Magic Dragon."

As time went by, the air war began to dominate the military strategies of the United States and Salvadoran governments. The use of landmines by the FMLN and the increasing effectiveness of guerrilla ambushes rendered largescale incursions too costly in terms of dead, wounded, and troop morale. Government aviation, on the other hand, could hit the FMLN and their civilian supporters deep in controlled territories, generating an environment of permanent tension among the *compañeros*.

The constant bombing, combined with the continued incursion of ground forces, eventually became intolerable for the exhausted civilian population and generated a steady trickle of elderly, women and children north to the more stable zones in Chalatenango, to refugee camps run by the UN in Honduras and to the United States. Others went south to church-run refugee centers like Domus Mariae and the Catholic Seminary, San José de la Montaña; to Betania, where I had worked, and to other Central American nations, primarily Nicaragua, Costa Rica and Panama. The displaced population of El Salvador eventually attained one million, one sixth of the country's inhabitants. In 1983, however, there was still a sizable civilian presence in the Felipe Peña Front, suffering stoically at the loss of sons and daughters in a battle that seemed to have no end, but still prepared to sacrifice all in the ongoing war effort.

By late September 1983, I began to perceive a dramatic buildup of guerrilla fighting units in the area of Radiola. Military plans were highly guarded secrets, but the continual flow of combatants down from the Apolinario Serrano Front in the northern province of Chalatenango signaled that something important was in the making. It also forewarned the civilian population that there would be some difficult months ahead.

The military units in the subzone grew to close to 600 combatants, joined by another 200 support troops, including medical personnel, cooks, and a communications unit to which I was temporarily assigned. My original role in support of agricultural production, small-scale industry and commerce continued to be a priority, but when major battles came, everyone in the war zones participated. Communications offered the best alternative for a foreigner with little practical knowledge of war and as yet inexperienced in combat.

Word finally spread that we would be attacking a large military contingent of the elite Cobra Battalion stationed in the town of Tenancingo, on the outskirts of Radiola. At the time, the town had a civilian population of approximately 5,000 inhabitants dedicated to farming, small commerce, and traditional arts and crafts. They were living under the close scrutiny of over 300 government soldiers, however, and the attack was designed to "cleanse" the town of the military presence and broaden the area under guerrilla control. The specific responsibilities of our communications unit included meeting with the civilian population once the town was secured, distributing our materials calling for a negotiated settlement to the war, and helping with the transport of captured weapons, food and medical supplies back to our camps after the fighting.

The Vanguard Units in Radiola

In the early afternoon of September 23, guerrilla combatants from the vanguard units (elite guerrilla forces) of the FPL and several columns of fighters from the sister organization, FAL, gathered in a small clearing in San Antonio. The first to depart for Tenancingo were the scouts with their young faces darkened with charcoal. An hour later, the guerrilla battalions departed, followed shortly thereafter by the support units.

We marched in silence through the humid night in a winding column along the steep and narrow mountain paths leading south from Radiola. There was a bright full moon to light our way and I was left in awe each time we ascended an open hillside by the size and the silence of our column. This was my first experience in a guerrilla attack, and I was keenly aware that I had taken another qualitative leap in my involvement in El Salvador's civil war.

Two and a half hours into our journey we forged a wide and turbulent river where we drank our first water. I had a severe case of diarrhea that was getting worse as our march continued, so I found a discreet place to quickly relieve myself, and was left laughing silently at my own embarrassment as our column pulled out and wound up the steep mountain slope on the other side of the river.

It was late evening when we finally stopped on the outskirts of Tenancingo to await the hour of attack. The first sound of gunfire was heard shortly after midnight. The attack had begun at the exact hour planned, a sign that the scouts had done their job well and that the Vanguard Units had not been detected during their approach. With rifle fire crackling in the distance, we arose quickly in the darkness, hoisted our backpacks and continued our own journey in the direction of the fighting.

Several minutes later, we reached a small clearing on the outskirts of the village of Copalchán, and the *compañeros* of the health unit began setting up a field hospital while the rest of us tried to get some sleep. Government helicopters were quick to respond to the attack, however, and sent us scurrying for cover each time the fiery red glare of tracer bullets rained down in our direction.

By daybreak the skies were filled with government aircraft. Cessna Push and Pulls launched rockets over our positions while A-37 Dragonfly jets dropped 500-pound bombs that rocked the earth around us and filled the air with razorsharp shrapnel. From our trenches we learned late in the morning that several bombs had fallen on the town itself, the first in the central plaza of Tenancingo and two others in residential areas on the edge of the town.

By mid-afternoon, government troops were in flight and we entered the town greeting the exhausted guerrilla combatants now scattered about in small groups and resting from their fearsome ordeal. Their young faces beamed with the pride of victory, and we all shared a profound sense of triumph.

The scene we encountered as we moved towards the central plaza, however, replaced our joy with increasing horror. Twisted bodies of young children lay strewn about the main thoroughfare in dark pools of blood. A girl I judged to be no older than seven lay like a discarded doll on the sidewalk, a gaping hole in her lower abdomen. A small boy lay beside her, his right leg bloodied and twisted. The charred corpses of men and women with

missing limbs lay in heaps. A young male with skin like charcoal writhed in pain seconds before dying. Houses, stores and offices lay in shambles, with smoke still rising from the burning timbers.

A quick count revealed that 35 civilians had been killed in the bombing. Eyewitnesses informed us that, with the first light of dawn, Green Cross volunteers had begun gathering the town's inhabitants for evacuation. When the planes appeared overhead, they placed a large white sheet in the street where civilians had been concentrated and waved Green Cross flags at the government aircraft; but the jets began to dive immediately, dropping their payload with murderous accuracy on the incredulous civilians below.

While some of the *compañeros* began preparing captured weapons and other supplies for transport back to our camps, our communications unit busied itself pasting our prepared materials on the walls that remained standing throughout the town. Several representatives of the International Red Cross arrived a few hours after the fighting had ceased, and close to 60 government soldiers captured during the battle were released into their care.

The surviving townspeople moved about in shock, examining the damage and collecting their dead as we readied our own departure. The heavy stench of death began to fill the air, and dark ominous rainclouds approached overhead, adding a final touch to the sense of doom that had begun to descend over the town. Through it all, I kept to myself, feeling weary and disconcerted as Bob Dylan's ominous song "Knocking on Heaven's Door" kept running though my mind. I could find no satisfaction or joy in the victory of this day.

Guerrilla units continued to occupy Tenancingo for several days after the bombing and I almost returned the day after the attack to help in the ongoing process of transporting captured weapons and supplies back to our camps. Had I done so, I would have seen my wife, Ana Eugenia, who worked at the time with Catholic Relief Services in El Salvador and was accompanying an international delegation on a tour of the damage. Neither of us knew until many months later how close we had been, and I am uncertain about how I would have reacted had we met under those circumstances, since acknowledging our acquaintance could have left her in extreme danger.

In the days that followed, the civilian villages of Radiola were subjected to constant bombing. Harsh criticism from international human rights organizations poured in from around the world protesting the unnecessary carnage at the hands of government aircraft, but it didn't stop the military from venting its anger at its embarrassing defeat.

Large numbers of soldiers who had fled the fighting days earlier continued to roam the subzone, lost, armed and desperate. On more than one occasion, they came upon civilians or unsuspecting guerrillas and killed them outright or carried them away as captives. One *compañero*, surprised while defecating one night, was stabbed five times and had his throat cut. Special security measures were adopted throughout Radiola, including an evening curfew with orders to fire upon anything that moved after 7 p.m., and night watch was carried out in pairs. Civilians stayed close to their homes, toasted corn and ground it into flour for emergency food rations. Everyone knew that it was just a matter of time before a massive incursion of ground troops would force us into *guinda* again. And we didn't have long to wait.

On September 27th, just 4 days after the battle for Tenancingo, close to 8000 government troops invaded the subzone of Radiola from several different directions. As I read over the journal that I kept at the time, I am reminded in detail of the nightmare that followed:

September 28, 1983

Yesterday afternoon, several battalions of government troops entered the subzone through the village of Guadalupe, an hour's walk from our base in San Antonio. Our unit, together with the civilian population, immediately began to hide all non-transportable items and prepare for evacuation. We left our base camp late that afternoon under heavy artillery fire and with ground fighting only a few hundred yards away. Incoming mortars whistled over our heads and crashed around us in thunderous explosions as we ran down the narrow mountain paths leading out of San Antonio.

By nightfall, we had managed to skirt the government's advancing line of fire and rendezvous with other support units in a small clearing just outside the village of San Antonio. Twenty-five wounded guerrilla combatants from the battle of Tenancingo lay scattered about on the ground. Hammocks had been tied to bamboo poles in order to transport them, and several of us were recruited as bearers.

We walked through the night under a driving rain in a silent column of approximately 50 men and women. The small mountain trails were slick with mud, and the presence of government troops made it impossible to light our way. Many of us took frequent falls under the heavy weight of our human cargo, inflicting considerable pain on our wounded comrades.

The compañero I am transporting (and with whom I have fallen several times) was shot in the chest during the fighting in Tenancingo and is in tremendous pain. He is approximately

A worried father transports his wounded young daughter

*my size, and his anger and desperation deepen with each fall
that we take. After sliding on a muddy hillside and losing our
balance for the fourth time, he demanded that we give him a
weapon and leave him to confront the enemy alone, saying that
he would rather risk death in combat than continue battering
his body with us. I laughed quietly to myself at this through
much of the night, but by early dawn the skin of my shoulder
had been rubbed raw from the weight of the bamboo pole,
and my strength was failing. Our clothing was caked with
an odorous mixture of sweat and mud, and I was beginning
to seriously worry that I might not have the strength and
stamina to make it through this guinda. Not even the sudden
appearance of blue skies and a new day this morning could
bring relief from the horror of this experience.*

September 30

*Yesterday afternoon, as we rested by the banks of a small river,
we suffered our first casualty. He was a young combatant with
wounds too serious to sustain the pace of the previous night. We
buried him with little ceremony a short distance from the river,
then headed north towards Lake Suchitlan where we hope to
find enough small boats to transport the remaining wounded to
FMLN field hospitals in Chalatenango.*

We walked for nine hours, rotating the wounded among our pool of bearers, and arrived just before midnight at an abandoned chapel in the village of La Criba. The wounded were placed on the cement floor inside the chapel to protect them from the incessant rain, and the rest of us slept for a few hours on the ground outside. Before dawn this morning, we were on the move again, headed for the village of Yanitos and, at the Aseseco River we finally found a safe spot to rest the wounded and wait for daylight.

I had been separated from the compañeros of my unit on the first night of the guinda and was pleased to find Ruben [the head of our unit] waiting when we arrived. The young guerrilla combatants, Joel, Santiago, Chico, and the middle-aged Angel, along with Mama Elena, an elderly woman who cooks for our unit, were also present, and we greeted each other with joy and laughter. I was later deeply saddened, however, to learn that the eldest son of Mama Elena, a young combatant who had been fighting the oncoming battalions of government troops, had lost his leg to mortar fire during the first day's battle and, out of extreme disillusionment, had taken his own life.

October 1

We left the river in Yanitos late yesterday afternoon, heading for the small community of Almendra where we hoped to find food and shelter for the wounded. We were intercepted midway, however, by two guerrilla scouts with the news that a large contingent of government troops was headed in our direction along the same path we were following, so we turned our long column around and headed back towards the river. The rain continued to fall in angry torrents and turned the mountain trails into raging rivers.

At one point during the night, as the incessant rain began to erode the muddy hillsides around us, a sudden flash flood came roaring down the mountain, crossing our path and carrying my good friend Mundo into a deep ravine. Mundo is an intellectual from the capital city working in communications and, like me, he has limited skills for walking in El Salvador's rugged

*countryside. He was carrying all of our weapons at the time of
the flash flood and they went with him into the ravine.*

*It was too dark for us to see him and we couldn't use our
flashlights, but after a short wait, we heard the clatter of metal
and saw a single white hand reach out of the muddy darkness
in a heroic effort to pull himself and the weapons back up onto
the trail.*

*It was still raining with tremendous force when we reached
the river's edge. The river itself had risen, and we were unable
to cross, so we left the path and went into the heavy underbrush,
with the wounded on our shoulders, to search upstream for
another safe place to hide. We wrapped the wounded in plastic
sheets to protect them as best we could from the rain and cold
night air, then sat our own weary bodies on the muddy ground
to wait for morning.*

*There was a young male civilian, approximately 11 years
of age, among the wounded, and by the third day of guinda he
was delirious and out of control. His skull had been fractured by
shrapnel from a government mortar and he suffered from severe
muscle tremors in his right arm. His mother had also been
wounded, but she had somehow been evacuated to the subzone
of Guazapa. The boy cried out constantly for her, and finally
had to be quieted with a heavy dose of sedatives lest he give our
position away to government troops nearby.*

*At times like this, I often wonder to myself if the compañeros
around me are suffering as much as I am, or if their lives of
hardship and deprivation prior to the war have somehow
prepared them better for the sacrifices of the revolution.*

October 2:

*Yesterday morning the rain subsided briefly. The bearers were
fed half of a tortilla, our first food of the guinda, then told to
prepare the wounded for departure. Government troops still
blocked our access to Lake Suchitlan, so we returned to the
village of La Criba via a shorter but more torturous route, and
took shelter in an abandoned schoolhouse on the ridge of a small
mountain looking down on the lights of Jutiapa. After attending*

*to the wounded, we tried to sleep, but the evening winds in
our mountaintop shelter turned unbearably cold, so, with wet
clothing and a hard cement floor as a bed, I remained awake
through most of the night.*

*Just before dawn today, another of our wounded died. She
was a young female combatant. Her death brought a certain
sense of relief to us all, however, as she had been in excruciating
pain since leaving San Antonio.*

*On the fifth day of the guinda, Ruben and the other
compañeros of our unit found me again, still accompanying the
wounded, and gave me the news that I had been yearning for.
The army was withdrawing from the subzone. The column with
the wounded would continue on to Lake Suchitlan, but I was to
rejoin Ruben and return to our base in San Antonio.*

Knowing of the incursion of government forces into Radiola,
the civilian population in the subzone of Guazapa had raided
a large poultry farm near the city of Aguilares belonging to a
wealthy government sympathizer. They "confiscated" 9,000 thor-
oughbred hens and sent the greater part to Radiola. The subzone was soon carpeted with white feathers, reminding me of
snowy days in my home town of Boston, as starving civilians and
guerrilla combatants from Radiola voraciously devoured the first
meat we had eaten in over a month.

By 1983, the FMLN controlled almost one third of the rural
countryside in El Salvador, chiefly areas where landlessness and
rural poverty were most pronounced and where massive incorporation into the revolutionary organizations had taken place
in the late 1970s. Popular organization was widely promoted in
these liberated areas, and organizations of farmers, women and
even children emerged with the goal of building unity and social
force, as well as providing critical support to the war effort.

The liberated zones were controlled politically by collective
leadership among FMLN cadres like Ruben, but local popularly

elected governing bodies were also established among the civilian population in the country's first experiment with popular
rule. They were called Local Popular Powers, and were considered to be the building blocks of a new democracy, built from
the grassroots and guided by a logic that emphasized majority
interests over elite privilege.

Their geographical jurisdiction roughly paralleled existing
municipal boundaries, but their responsibilities responded to
the special concerns of a population at war. Each Local Popular
Power had at least six members, including a president, equivalent
to a mayor; a coordinator for juridical affairs, responsible for recording births, deaths and marriages; a coordinator for economic
development, responsible for promoting agricultural production
and small-scale industry (with whom I coordinated my work); a
coordinator for social welfare, responsible for health, education
and recreation; a coordinator for information and communication and a coordinator for civil defense.

The local economies that emerged were mixed. Collective
forms of production were introduced to provide adequate food
and supplies for the war, but peasant farmers insisted on their
own individual plots as well to provide annual harvests of corn
and beans for their families, in accordance with Salvadoran
peasant tradition. "People's stores" were established to provide
articles of basic consumption and offer a market for surplus production. Boots, cooking utensils, clothing and simple tools were
manufactured and repaired in small cottage industries when raw
materials and essential equipment were available. What couldn't
be produced locally was purchased through civilian collaborators
residing in nearby towns and cities.

Prior to the war, few of the peasants residing in the liberated
zones had access to health care or to formal education. By 1983,
however, small health clinics and field hospitals were scattered
throughout the Felipe Peña Front. Almost every village had some
form of health service with trained *sanitarias* (health promoters)
capable of treating common illnesses and minor injuries. More
complicated problems were treated by physicians, many of them
foreign collaborators, based in the field hospitals of the FMLN.

Infrastructure in these hospitals was basic, often with nothing more than a simple lean-to covered by plastic sheeting to provide shelter from the sun and rain. Surgery was often performed by candlelight, and razor blades or knives sometimes served as scalpels, especially in the initial years of the war. Anesthesia was normally available, but antibiotics were frequently in short supply, making post-surgical infection a serious problem, given the unsanitary environment of the countryside.

Schooling for the children and literacy classes for adults were widespread. Because of the constant threat of air attacks, classes were often held outdoors under the shade of large ceiba trees or in deep ravines. The children normally sat on the ground, and large slabs of wood served as blackboards. Trained teachers were scarce, so men and women with any education at all were recruited to fill this role. Those with a third-grade education taught second grade. Those with a second-grade education taught first grade, and anyone with basic literacy taught adults to read and write.

I have regretted during most of my post-war lifetime the fact that I did not join these educational efforts in a more systematic and personal way. My experiences in Liberia would have

A young teacher with his students

provided me with the necessary skills to make a meaningful contribution, and I felt a calling in this direction. I was working with the Local Popular Powers to improve local production, however, and in 1983 the political leadership of the Felipe Peña Front was prioritizing this area of work.

Life in the liberated zones was not all austerity, drudgery, danger and death. Hardship and pain were ameliorated by astonishing levels of human solidarity, and interlaced with frequent moments of laughter and joy. When conditions permitted, evenings were spent around the cookfires in relaxed conversation, listening to the news of the day on a small battery-operated radio or playing guitars and singing. It was during one such evening that I was handed a crude guitar and asked to play.

I knew only a few songs in Spanish, so I took a risk and sang several rock and roll tunes from my youth. Little did I know at that moment of the fame that this would generate for me throughout the Felipe Peña Front. I introduced the *compañeros* to Elvis Presley, Ricky Nelson, Little Richard, Fats Domino and Chuck Berry, and, from that moment on, whenever a guitar appeared, I was asked to sing my *rokirol*.

During periods of stability, one could experience the more alluring attributes of life in rural El Salvador. Women cooked

Women grind corn for tortillas

traditional dishes of *tamales, pupusas, chilate y nuegados* (a meal of large doughy balls of cornflour dipped in molasses), and *chuco* for all to share. The young men fished in nearby Lake Suchitlan, and we appeased our exaggerated appetites with endless quantities of *tilapia* and *guapote*. "Revolutionary *fiestas* (parties)" were frequent, especially when the moon was full, and young *compañeros* would dance the night away to the sounds of local musicians and the clanking rhythm of ever-present weapons slung loosely over their shoulders.

The day's catch from Lake Suchitlan

It was during such a pause in this abominable war that I attended the "revolutionary wedding" of two young combatants in the village of Guadalupe. The ceremony was duly registered and presided over by the president of the Local Popular Power. Dozens of family members and friends gathered just after nightfall in the center of the village to witness the simple but formal event in which the young couple was reminded that their love for each other "should serve to strengthen their commitment to their people and to the revolutionary cause," and that the marriage should be considered by all as "sacred, permanent and binding."

Alcohol was strictly prohibited in the liberated zones. Tobacco was the main vice, and the unadorned art of simple conversation remained the principal form of passing time. Conversation was incessant, whether sitting under a shady tree, walking through the countryside, bathing or waiting for sleep at night. With the high illiteracy rate among El Salvador's peasants, books were not an option. Information, passed by word of mouth, was the only history text available to the rural population, and it was through this art of conversation that the unwritten biographies of the war's heroes and martyrs were created and kept alive.

It was during these quiet moments of recurrent conversations that I began to better understand the psyche of the Salvadoran guerrillas and the life experiences that had driven them to their struggle. As in the case of Teresa and Antonio Rivas, who I would meet in the months to come, few had looked for the war. The war had overtaken them and drained their lives of options. Personal goals had been put on hold, and friendships and family had been sacrificed for the cause.

Claudia was a young *compañera* who I met one morning in a meeting with the civilian population of Radiola in early October 1983. She couldn't have been more than twenty years old, but she held a position of immense responsibility as president of the local chapter of the Salvadoran Women's Association in the bordering subzone of Guazapa. She had been assigned temporarily to Radiola to strengthen the organizing efforts among women in this area. Her strength of character as well as her physical appearance reminded me of my youngest sister, Amy, and her eyes sparkled with delight when I told her so. She then laughed and announced jokingly that we would be brother and sister from that day on.

I had taken her humor lightly, but later that same morning I overheard her talking with another young *compañero* about her family in Guazapa, where she had lived before the war in a small village on the slopes of the volcano, along with her mother, father, younger brother and four sisters. Their life had been fruitful and they had little thought of war until a contingent of government soldiers patrolling nearby captured her brother and shot him several times in the head. Her father had found him eight hours later, just in time to trade the love and joy of a lifetime for a brief and final embrace before the young boy died. It was clear from the sadness in Claudia's voice as she told her tale that she had felt a special attachment to her brother, and our brief exchange of earlier that morning came back to mind in a more sobering light.

Ruben was a member of the FMLN political leadership of the subzone of Radiola and, while he talked incessantly about the war, he tended to give few details about his personal life. He had participated in the struggle since the early 1970s, when the first small guerrilla cells began appearing in the rural areas of El Salvador, and when the only weapons had been small hand arms or hunting rifles. He often described the countless battles he had had with the National Guard, but I had never heard him speak of a woman.

One night, as we lay on the hard dirt floor of our sleeping quarters in San Antonio, I asked him if he had ever been married. His normally lighthearted demeanor turned serious as he told me of his marriage to a young *compañera* serving as platoon leader in the guerrilla army. She had been caught in an ambush and killed by government troops just four months prior to my arrival in the war zones. Ruben then acknowledged how good it had been "to have someone to share the intimate things of life" in this harsh and dangerous environment, and that the "enemy" had dealt him a serious blow on that day.

Chico, Joel and Santiago were all young combatants in Ruben's unit, and each had lost their families and homes to government repression in the late 1970s. Roque, who worked in communications, had been a university student in the capital city until the military occupied the campus, killing many of his fellow students, and shutting the institution down. Alex, a political cadre in the subzone of Radiola, had been shot and wounded by death squads in 1980, and had lost his wife and children to government bombing. The young males serving as messengers throughout the war zones during the first years of the war, before more sophisticated communication devices became available, had lost parents and homes in early childhood. All had stories that could chill the soul, and their lives followed a common thread through poverty, exploitation, repression and war.

It was also during those quiet moments that the *compañeros* shared their views on the complicated issues related to the use of violence for advancing an agenda for change in El Salvador. Many were obviously driven by hatred for an enemy that had killed family members or repressed civil liberties beyond tolerance. Few questioned their own life choices, seeing them as the inevitable result of a lack of non-violent options, but all hoped that the war would quickly be resolved through dialogue and negotiations.

Unlike the young guerrilla combatants around me, I had no previous experience with war prior to entering the liberated zones in 1983. My inspiration came more from love for the Salvadoran people than from hatred of their enemy. I never received military training and, at 40, was too old to be a combatant. I frequently found myself over the years in combat situations, but it became increasing clear that my contribution to the war effort would be in non-military areas.

I did not resolve, in my head or in my heart, the troubling issues related to the use of violence until after the war when I became an aspiring pacifist and celebrated the fact that I had done no bodily harm to another human being. But in 1983 I

The author (left) with Joel, Angel, Chico and Santiago

was travelling in one of the most fiercely contested war zones in the country, facing a military bent on our annihilation; so, for my own defense and that of the innocent women, children and elderly with whom I spent my days, I frequently carried a weapon. I supported the heroic efforts of the United Nations and international human rights organizations to guarantee the rights of civilians and non-combatants residing in war-torn areas in accordance with the Geneva Convention, later referred to as "humanizing the conflict," but in the early years of the war, there were no holds barred in the liberated zones of El Salvador.

In mid-October 1983, I left Radiola and traveled to the bordering subzone of Guazapa to continue my efforts in support of the Local Popular Powers and local communities in the design of projects for agricultural production, smallscale industry and commerce. The trip to Guazapa can be made by land, but the *compañeros* preferred the less exhausting route by small boat, westward across Lake Suchitlan.

As we paddled out onto the lake's still waters in the approaching darkness of the late afternoon, I was astounded by its exquisite beauty. Large white flocks of egrets flew silently overhead like clouds, dipping occasionally in elegant formation to glide over the lake's mirror-smooth surface, then swooping up again towards the heavens, leaving me feeling more like a tourist than a guerrilla collaborator in a fiercely contested war zone.

Halfway through the journey, now in darkness, we passed the lights and sounds of the city of Suchitoto on the southern shore, and the order for total silence was passed among us, since the government maintained several patrol boats with 30-caliber machine guns in Suchitoto. Two hours later, we entered the waters off the liberated zone of Guazapa. It rained lightly for short periods of time during the four-hour trip, but we arrived safely and relatively dry, and slept with a peasant family in the lakefront village of Corasal.

I was accompanied by Marta, an attractive but shy woman who, like Ruben, formed part of the political leadership of the Felipe

Peña Front. She had been with the FMLN since the war began and had traveled many times to Guazapa. It was my first glimpse of this area and I was amazed upon waking the following morning at how its terrain differed from the harshness of Radiola. The northern lowlands were flat and fertile, unlike the hilly and broken landscape of Radiola. The Guazapa volcano to the south rose towards the clouds, and China Mountain stood alone among the low-lying hills to the west, overlooking the communities of El Paisnal.

The large extensions of flat and fertile lands of the subzone were planted primarily with sugar cane, as they were prior to the war, but also now produced an abundance of food, including rice, beans, corn, peanuts and vegetables. There were goat cheese and milk, mangoes and breadfruit, and beehives dripping with fresh sweet honey.

Honey production in Guazapa

The civilian population resided primarily in the lowlands. Guerrilla camps were scattered about on the lower slopes of the volcano, and government troops occupied the highest peaks, from where they were rotated and supplied by helicopter. Military incursions were less frequent than in Radiola, but more problematic, as there were fewer places to hide.

On our first day in the subzone, Marta and I headed for the village of Mirandilla on the northern slopes of the volcano where a meeting was scheduled with the FMLN's local political leadership. En route, we stopped briefly in the village of Consolación where I met Lito, a middle-aged leader of the civilian population. He wore a cowboy hat, had a contagious laugh revealing the absence of most of his teeth, and carried a pearl-handled 45 automatic pistol on his hip as he received us generously with a breakfast of *tortillas*, dried fish and a large gourd of fresh honey. I consumed the honey without taking a breath, recognizing for the first time the demands of an undernourished body now screaming for sources of energy.

Following our meal, Marta and I continued south, buoyed by the breakfast, Lito's contagious laughter and the vast sea of sugar cane that extended endlessly in all directions. As we slowly walked along, we chomped noisily on juicy cane stalks enjoying the peace and beauty of the morning. As our journey progressed, the humidity from the previous night's rain and a blistering sun began turning the day into a virtual sauna, and both of us were sweating profusely when we stopped briefly to rest and drink water at a small communal store on the outskirts of Mirandilla.

Our conversation wandered as we resumed our trip up the open slopes of the volcano when, suddenly, out of nowhere, a Hughes 500 helicopter and a rocket-launching Cessna Push and Pull appeared on the near horizon, and we were quickly returned to the realities of life in the war zones. Both aircraft were flying low, following the contours of the volcano, so the sounds of their engines had been muffled. They caught us without warning and with no place to hide other than a small dried cornfield nearby. We ran to it and knelt among the brown papery stalks, hearts thumping, as the aircraft made their first pass low overhead.

Knowing that the next approach would easily reveal our position, we threw our backpacks to the ground and searched frantically for more significant cover. In my panic, I lost sight of both Marta and the aircraft, but within seconds heard her shouting that they were coming towards us again. In that instant the machine guns began to roar.

I ran for the cover of a small cluster of rocks about 30 yards away, curled up behind them, then waited for what seemed like an eternity, drowning in a sense of absolute helplessness and the humbling realization that I was completely out of my realm. No experience that I could remember in life had prepared me in any way for this moment. The rocks were too small to protect my entire body, so I covered my head and chest as best I could and kept my protruding lower limbs completely still, assuring myself that I might lose my legs, but I wouldn't die.

The aircraft made a second pass overhead, but the direction of their firing revealed that we had still not been seen. On the third pass, they swerved just below our position, gained altitude and began to circle. In this brief interval, Marta reappeared and we ran side by side as fast as we could up the slope of the volcano to a patch of trees 100 yards away. The two aircraft then flew off toward the lowlands where Marta and I had shared breakfast with Lito earlier that morning. As we gathered our backpacks and resumed our journey, large white whiffs of smoke announced the launching of rockets against the civilian villages below.

We spent several days in Mirandilla, then I left Marta and the guerrilla leadership to return to Consolación in the lowlands and begin planning my work with the civilian population in the subzone. The sun beat down intensely as I traveled by horseback down the winding trails, astonished again at the physical beauty around me. A slight breeze blew off Lake Suchitlan, caressing the endless green sea of sugarcane and forming perfect and gentle waves with their tassels, momentarily hushing the fiercer winds of war that haunted this otherwise heavenly place.

As I had done during the previous months in Radiola, I would be helping to develop an overall plan for agricultural production, micro enterprise and commerce with the Popular Local Power of the subzone, this time with the participation of the Federation of Peasant Workers and the women of the Salvadoran Association of Women. We would first lay out a general vision for the subzone, then develop specific objectives. After that, we would analyze for hours the activities and resources necessary to implement the plan and develop together the necessary budgets

Making molasses in the
lowlands of Guazapa

that would be required by international funding sources in solidarity with the struggle.

Between meetings with the civilian leadership, I took advantage of the temporary stability of the subzone and its relative abundance, eating all that I could in an effort to augment my near skeletal body. The peasant families, intrigued by the presence of a North American, invited me frequently to eat *chilate y nuegado*, fresh vegetables, wild honey, fresh cheese and, of course, the staple of rice, beans and *tortillas*. On several occasions I accompanied the men to their hidden sugar cane presses where juice was extracted, boiled in large iron vats and transformed into molasses and brown sugar.

These projects, part of peasant life before the war, were small and underequipped operations with antiquated and heavily rusted machinery and tools, but they provided a life-sustaining source of energy for the civilian population during the frequent *guindas* that this subzone, like Radiola, experienced.

I was approached one day, during one of my visits to observe sugar production, by a young *compañero* who gave me a teasing grin and asked if I had "fallen into any rivers lately." I didn't recognize his face at first, but soon realized that it was Emilcar, one of the wounded I had helped to transport in Radiola after the battle of Tenancingo, and with whom I had fallen into the river at Yanitos, soaking myself and almost drowning him. His injuries from the fighting had left him with no feeling in his entire left side, and he told me that his lips frequently got stuck over the upper part of his teeth when he laughed or yawned. He was also blind in his left eye and partially deaf in his left ear from previous battles, but he was preparing to rejoin his unit in Radiola after a brief visit with family.

We talked at length about the *guinda* we had shared and the tremendous suffering among wounded, bearers and civilian population alike. I then asked about the others we had transported and was saddened to learn that the young boy whose skull had been fractured by mortar fire had died in a field hospital in Chalatenango.

Air raid shelters in Guazapa

Guazapa, because of its sparsely wooded slopes and lowlands, offered excellent targets to government aviation, and attacks were almost daily. The most dangerous hours were in early morning, at midday and early evening. Warplanes came looking at those hours for the smoke of cookfires, and the *compañeros* began to refer to their predictable ration of bombs three times a day as "breakfast," "lunch" and "dinner." The A-37 Dragonfly jets were the most dangerous. They came swooping out of nowhere, roaring across the lowlands in an effort to pinpoint guerrilla camps and civilian communities and drop their deadly payloads. When they had a target in sight, they rose high into the clouds, circled and then dove. The horrific sound of a jet in a nosedive was the warning that 500 or 1000-pound bombs were on their way. These aircraft brought terror to many a day during my stay in Guazapa.

In the same way that ground incursions of government troops proved so devastating to the civilian communities of Radiola, the air war wrought havoc to the population of Guazapa. During my first trip to the area, I frequently visited civilian villages where homes had been completely leveled, killing large numbers of inhabitants and where surviving women and children sought safety in dugout caves or ditches. I walked through a countryside scorched black and littered with uprooted trees where government bombs had fallen. And I spoke with peasant families whose lives, like their homes, had been left in shambles. Some of them were demoralized beyond remedy, and were searching for the energy to pick up the pieces and somehow continue on with their lives.

In one essential way, Guazapa resembled all of the subzones of the Felipe Peña Front: In spite of being subjected daily to all of the horrors that the government and its U.S. backers could conjure up, it remained sparsely populated by a tenacious civil-ian population determined to assimilate its losses and carry on the struggle. As the war continued, some of these civilians would remain in the liberated zones among the ashes of their homes and the unmarked graves of their loved ones, but many others would eventually pick up and leave for the refugee centers in Honduras, San Salvador or Betania.

Late in October, I held my final meeting with the leadership of the civilian population of Guazapa and prepared to travel that night to the subzone of Piedra, near the town of El Paisnal. It began to rain shortly after our departure, but the evening skies eventually cleared to reveal a breathtaking bright full moon. It lifted our spirits but also lit our path with more light than we would have preferred as we moved with caution over the flat and open terrain. We walked steadily for hours in a silent column through the muddy fields heading west from Guazapa towards the ever present summit of China Mountain, passing en route through the seemingly endless green sea of the La Cabaña sugar cane plantation.

These were the fields where Antonio Rivas and other peas-ant farmers of El Paisnal had toiled away their young manhood in a desperate effort to support their families on 15 cents a day. These were the fields where Father Rutilio Grande had been ac-cused of subversion and brutally killed. And these were the fields where deeply religious but desperate men and women eventually found no alternative but to go to war.

The extensive plantation, once owned by El Salvador's oligar-chy, was now controlled by the country's National Institute for Agrarian Transformation, and was heavily patrolled by government troops. We reached the Acelhuate River at approximately eight in the evening and crossed it in the darkness in a silent column, alert for the slightest movement in the shadows of the opposite shore.

Two hours later we were approaching the Northern High-way, running from the capital city to the southwestern border of Honduras, and our movements again became deliberate and vigilant. The highways were often patrolled by the army, and crossing them was dangerous at any time, day or night. There were no patrols that evening, however, so we ventured into the open, quickly crossed over the hard asphalt surface, and disappeared into the continuing expanse of cane fields on the other side. It was a brief but exhilarating moment for me. The physical contact with pavement, following months of muddy hillsides and foot trails, was like touching a bloodline to a more familiar and comfortable world – and to Ana Eugenia, by this time asleep in our small apartment in the capital city.

Just before midnight we entered the subzone of Piedra, stopped briefly to rest, and eased our hunger with a few pieces of brown cane sugar that we had brought from Guazapa. We were bathed in sweat and covered with mud from the fields of La Cabaña. I had also developed a painful blister on the ball of my right foot, a large boil had formed on my left ankle and my shoulders were aching from the weight of my backpack as we sat and slowly cooled in the evening air.

We arrived in the village of Amayo half an hour later, peeled off our soaked outer garments and slept on the rough cement floor of a small warehouse used by the guerrillas of this subzone for storing supplies channeled into the war zones from the capital city and surrounding towns. It was a cold and lonely welcome for an area that would later embrace me so warmly and bless me with treasured friendships.

In the early afternoon on the day following my arrival, a wiry middle-aged *compañero* came to meet me and guide me to the sub-zonal headquarters in the village of Las Ventanas, an hour's walk from Amayo. His name was Santos and he was the coordinator of the civilian population in the subzone of Piedra. I would learn as well that he was the older brother of Teresa Polancos de Rivas, the catequist-turned-revolutionary who had married a local soccer star, Antonio Rivas, at the age of 15 and now organized women in the war zones in the Felipe Peña Front.

Santos helped me gather my belongings, strewn wildly about drying in the morning sun, then led me up the small mountain path en route to his village. In the midday heat, I was quickly bathed in sweat as we climbed the steep incline, my body still exhausted and suffering from the previous night's journey. We stopped briefly to rest halfway up the mountain en route to Las Ventanas, and gazed over the rugged horizon. China Mountain rose like a defiant fist in the distance, but I knew little of the heroic struggles fought in its shadows. I knew of Rutilio Grande and his assassination at the hands of death squads in 1977, but I had not yet learned the histories of the brave catechists who had battled injustice in the cane fields of La Cabaña, or the men and women from this region who made the difficult decision to take up arms against injustice and repression.

I was thankful when we finally arrived at our destiny, and began immediately to learn about life in Piedra before the war as I sat on the ground in the midst of Santos and his family, shucking beans for the evening meal. Santos was a humble and unassuming man of approximately 40 years of age. He was slightly nervous in the presence of his new guest, but he had an easy laugh, reminding me more of an Iowa farmer than a militant revolutionary. His wife Fidelia, whom I would later learn was the sister of Antonio Rivas, was lightskinned and unusually large of stature for a peasant woman, but her gnarled and calloused hands and unschooled manner reflected the history of poverty and toil from whence she had come. The children were all very beautiful, and excited with the presence of a foreigner in their midst, and it felt enormously good to be in the company of a family again.

Among the children of Santos and Fidelia who still remained in Piedra, 12-year-old Patrocinia was the oldest. She had been named for her grandmother and, like the old woman, was serious and quiet by nature. She had a disarming grace and a sense of humor reserved for a chosen few, and an unequivocal way of reminding this guest of the harshness of life in her world.

Several days into my visit, I was watching her as she worked silently amidst the raucous of her younger brothers and sisters.

Patrocinia (center) with Rosita and Moises

She was grinding rice into flour in preparation for the next *guin-da*, when she suddenly looked up and, with disarming candor, said: "when you leave here, you will never return." Not knowing how else to respond, I laughed, and asked her why she would say such a thing, but she returned to her work and fell silent again until I pressed her for a reply. She responded this time without raising her eyes: "you'll forget about this place when you leave."

I was caught completely off guard by her directness and in-sisted that I would never forget her or her family and that I would certainly return. I was highly moved, however, by this stunning young peasant girl, so fully aware of the circumstances that distin-guished her life from mine, of the fickleness of my socio-economic class and of the burden of struggle that rested on her shoulders.

Next in line came Rosita, age nine and the cutest of the brood. She was curious and playful and equally adept at girlish games with dolls and the tomboyish antics required for compet-ing with her brothers. She became my constant companion dur-ing my stay in Piedra and was the first to "adopt" me as a full-fledged member of the family.

Moises and Vladimir, ages six and seven, were typical young peasant boys, cheerful and rambunctious and seemingly unaware of the constant danger and hardship of their environment. They wore ragged oversized trousers with no belts, so their pants were constantly falling down around their knees. Moises' only shirt had several large holes in the front, so, he frequently wore it backwards. Little Alvaro followed. He was one year old and spent most of his time in his mother's arms.

The two oldest daughters, Blanca and Consuelo, were off in Radiola at the time of my arrival, working as radio operators with the guerrilla units. The children that remained were too young for such commitments, still wild and carefree, bathed in love, and with little notion of life in a world without war.

The subzone of Piedra was particularly vulnerable to government incursions due to a paucity of forests in which to hide, so the civilian population dug large underground tunnels around the villages and in the surrounding countryside. When the situation was "normal," families lived in their homes and filled their days with the routine of peasant life. When government troops invaded, however, they spent their days and nights in the cramped muddy darkness of these underground *tatús*. On such occasions, ground cornflour mixed with sugar provided the only source of food. Physical necessities were performed in plastic bags and the stagnant air quickly became rank and foul. Small bamboo shoots penetrating the roof of the tunnels served as the only source of clean air, and the need for prolonged silence challenged the patience of children and adults alike.

Between military incursions, the population remained vigilant. The subzone was small, and large towns occupied by the army were close by. There were few guerrilla fighting units in the area, so the role of the popular militia, under the command of Antonio Rivas, was key to survival. Militiamen were posted around the periphery of each village, armed with hand guns and homemade explosives called *papas* (potatoes). These explosives could be detonated by throwing them against a rock or other hard surface, serving as a signal for miles around that a military incursion was under way.

At nightfall families would gather together in "safe houses," much as they had done to protect themselves from the death

Fidelia and her children return from their "safe house" in the morning

squads in the years leading up to the war. Most of these were small one-room adobe homes abandoned by their original owners, with few walls still standing and only small sections of roofing still intact. The "safe house" where Santos and his family slept at night had only three walls and a small roofing area of clay tiles to keep out the seasonal rains at night. But when the family huddled together on the hard dirt floor, it became a warm and inviting shelter.

Soon after my arrival in Piedra, Santos departed for Radiola to attend a meeting of political cadres from throughout the Felipe Peña Front. I then began to focus my own efforts on my work with the scattered villages of the subzone to plan and develop small-scale agricultural initiatives and micro-industry.

The first of such meetings was held in the village of Corriente, located on the periphery of Piedra, but in the midst of our planning, as we sat on the ground under a large shady tree sharing information on the potential for improving production levels, a portable radio playing softly in the background suddenly announced that U.S. troops had invaded Grenada. And I was confronted again with the special challenges of being a U.S. citizen in love with a people at war with my own government.

Grenada is a small island nation forming the last link in the chain of the Lesser Antilles just north of Venezuela. Its surface area is a mere 340 square kilometers and its population numbered less than 100,000 people at the time. It had close ties to Cuba, however, and, in 1983, was perceived by the Reagan administration to be a strategic threat to the security of the United States.

As the radio continued to give details of the invasion, I sat quietly in awe. I had often heard the *compañeros* voice their concerns about the threat of a direct military intervention by the United States in El Salvador, but hadn't truly assimilated this possibility, confident that the lessons of Vietnam had not been wasted on the American public, and hopeful that there were enough good and courageous hearts in the U.S. to prevent a recurrence of this tragic experience. The invasion of Grenada, however, made it all more plausible.

The elderly peasant men listening to the radio report with me were not so shocked, and one by one expressed their readiness to combat the "Yankee aggressor" when he invaded their country. I felt discomfort and shame and was again appalled by the arrogance of a government prepared to topple any nation or people who questioned its hegemony. I was also shocked at the cowardliness of the United States and wondered at the unjustified satisfaction and pride derived from attacking militarily such a defenseless foe as Grenada. I was deeply gratified, however, when the old men around me, one by one, expressed their acceptance and appreciation for my participation in their struggle in pursuit of ending centuries of poverty and oppression in their country.

Several weeks into my visit to Piedra, Blanca, the oldest daughter of Santos and Fidelia, arrived in the subzone on temporary leave from her duties as radio operator in Radiola. She was stout, strong and quick-witted with an outgoing and confident nature, the resilient product of a childhood of irrefutable hardship who had found a redeeming sense of pride in the revolutionary struggle.

At our first meeting in Piedra, she grinned broadly and recounted an evening we had shared together months earlier in our camp in Radiola, playing and singing *rokirol*. In all honesty, I couldn't remember our meeting. Nevertheless, later that evening, while waiting for sleep together with the entire family on the hard dirt floor of our "safe house," she requested that I sing some *rokirol*. I sang several revolutionary songs that I had recently learned instead, and she sang several more. Not to be outdone, little Patrocinia joined in with a song that she had learned a year earlier during the horrible *guinda* to the Feliciano Ama Front, and the silence of the night was suddenly transformed into a raucous song fest in the dark.

The next morning, as Blanca helped her mother toast *tortillas* for breakfast, they talked about the early days of the struggle. Taking turns, they told of Father Rutilio Grande and his persistent struggle for more just and dignified working conditions for rural peasants on the large *haciendas* and sugar cane plantations around El Paisnal. According to Fidelia, Rutilio knew that his death was imminent and frequently instructed his parishioners to rejoice rather than succumb to sorrow or to fear at the moment of his "final conquest." Talking about more recent times, Blanca and Fidelia told of the tragic *guinda* the civilian population had suffered during the previous year when a massive incursion of government troops forced the population to evacuate their villages and flee, en masse, to the Feliciano Ama Front in the western province of Santa Ana. The *guinda* lasted 15 days, and many of the weaker members of the population did not survive.

The villagers of Piedra had been joined at the time by close to 500 civilians from the subzone of Guazapa, forced to flee several days earlier from their villages by the same government forces. With the guidance and protection of the popular militia, under the command of Antonio Rivas, they crossed the Sucio River headed west on the first night and were able to sneak through army lines. They walked by night and hid by day with no food and little water to sustain them.

They were moving through unknown terrain for the first three days, and parents spent much of their time keeping their exhausted and sleepy children on the narrow foot trails, lest someone get lost and be left behind in the darkness. Early into the *guinda*, two of the elderly died of exhaustion. Two younger women gave birth along the way, but neither baby survived. The breasts of nursing mothers dried up, and young infants were kept alive by being forcefed green mangoes, the only available food.

But the saddest tragedy of all occurred in the afternoon of the third day while the people rested in a shallow ravine. The Popular Militia detected a large contingent of soldiers moving in their direction and, as they searched frantically for an escape route, the population of almost 1,000 elderly, women and children sat in helpless silence watching the soldiers approach. A four-year-old boy in his grandfather's arms began to cry and the old man, in panic, placed his hand over the young child's mouth and nose and unwittingly suffocated his grandson to save himself and the others from certain death. The population eventually escaped without being detected and made it to the subzone of Feliciano Ama, but the old man and the young boy's parents carried a burden heavier than death for the remaining days of the *guinda*.

Blanca was used to sleeping on the ground in close proximity to male *compañeros* in the guerrilla camps of Radiola, and she always slept close by my side during her visit to Piedra. We would lie in the darkness talking for hours, usually about the war. One evening we shared stories about the tragic bombing of Tenancingo by the Air Force in September of 1983, during which so many civilians from the town had been killed. She told me that she had been operating the radio for the guerrilla command, listening to the conversations between pilots and government ground forces at the moment when government troops were being surrounded by the guerrilla units. And she overheard the specific orders of army officers on the ground to bomb the town in spite of the dense civilian presence.

She was a restless sleeper, and I was frequently awoken by her frantic movements in the night. When I teased her one morning about a slight kick to the stomach she had given me, she laughed in embarrassment, fearing that I might take it as a romantic advance. She told me, however, that she was suffering from recurrent dreams in which she was either in *guinda* or in battle, with her friends lying dead all around her. I tried to explain to her the little that I remembered about war-related stress syndrome from my days as a psychology major at Villanova University. But later that night I felt her tossing again, and I knew that I had done little to ease the anxiety and trauma of this combative but still vulnerable young peasant woman.

I spent a great deal of time with Fidelia, Blanca, Patrocinia, little Rosita, Vladimir, Moises and Alvaro during my first trip to the subzone of Piedra. And it was through this family that I came to meet Teresa and Antonio Rivas along with their five beautiful children. My work with the civilian population brought me in contact with Teresa first in her role as head of the local chapter of the Association of Salvadoran Women.

She was in her mid-thirties at the time of our first meeting, stood approximately five-feet-four inches tall, was slightly stout, as peasant women tend to be, and wore short curly black hair. She had a resplendent smile and big bright eyes that widened into dark intoxicating moons when her enthusiasm overcame her. She was not a woman of extraordinary physical beauty, but she was an impressive figure of obvious intelligence and spiritual strength, qualities that she often tried to camouflage with a heavy dose of modesty. Among the women of the subzone, she was a natural leader, orienting and encouraging without dominating.

She had been a fighter from birth, overcoming obstacles that would have demoralized and debilitated a weaker spirit: the death of her mother at childbirth, the harsh upbringing by her grandmother Patrocinia, the responsibilities of a married woman at 15, and now the task of incorporating the women and young girls of Piedra into the revolution. She was generous with her smile and laughter, but it was easy to perceive the serious and determined woman that lay within.

The children of Santos and Fidelia lured me frequently down the mountain from Las Ventanas to visit their uncle Antonio and Aunt Teresa in the village of Amayo. At that time, Antonio was called by his *nom de guerre* (war name) of Tiburcios. Teresa had taken the name Orcircs. They lived on the plot of land that Antonio's father had lent them at the time of their marriage, and planted a small amount of corn, beans and squash for their yearly sustenance.

Seven years after their marriage, Antonio had finally been able to build a simple adobe structure with a clay tile roof to replace the grass hut in which their first four children were born. They had lived in their new home for only three years, however, when an incursion of government troops left it in shambles.

The house had served also as a school where Teresa, ever adamant about the importance of education, taught the young children of Amayo to read and write. Soldiers had found the crude benches and tables where the young students sat, and burned them, along with the house itself. In tenacious defiance, Antonio had quickly rebuilt the walls and repaired the roof as best he could, and school sessions resumed. But the dream of owning a fitting home would not be realized again for many years.

When the war first began, Teresa and Antonio, like the other Delegates of the Word in the villages of El Paisnal, knew little about armed revolution. Following the FMLN offensive of 1981, however, the rural areas of El Paisnal had been laced with guerrilla camps, and contact with the armed organizations became inevitable.

Because of his widespread popularity as a community leader and his experience in the security commissions of the Popular Revolutionary Block, Antonio had been recruited to serve as head of the Popular Militia. He continued to farm and attend to the daily needs of his family, but he also began to train in the use of weapons and simple explosives. He was not a man inclined toward violence. He was simply the product of too many years of degradation and despair who had come to accept the burden of struggle that came banging on his door.

Antonio had 45 men under his command, and it was their responsibility to ensure the safety of the women, children and elderly in the dispersed villages of this increasingly warlike subzone. He ensured that lookouts were strategically placed 24 hours a day in order to detect government troop movements. Together with other militia members, he blockaded access roads into the subzone and ambushed government troops when they penetrated the area. He had become skilled at military tactics and was totally convinced of the inevitability of the armed struggle. But he remained a fervent Christian, and still turned to the bible rather than FMLN propaganda for his ideological and political inspiration.

Teresa had been recruited as well to help organize the women of the area. Her role was more political than military. Her responsibilities centered around the formation of women's collectives for agricultural production in an effort to ensure adequate food supplies for the weak and infirm among the civilian population and for the growing guerrilla army in other subzones. She put her love for education to work organizing makeshift schools, like the one in her own home, and designed literacy programs for children and adults.

When the civilian population from other subzones was forced to flee in *guinda* to Piedra, it was Teresa's initiative that assured them sufficient food, water and housing during their stay. On such occasions, she depleted the emergency food stocks of her own family and organized committees among the women of other villages to provide additional supplies to the needy members of the population in flight.

As I spent more time with this family, I began to appreciate what a closely knit unit they were. Teresa preferred nothing more in life than surrounding herself with her children and bathing in their incessant laughter and conversation. They were constantly hanging from her arms, pulling on her dress and vying for her attention. Children for her were a gift, not a chore, and she always shone the brightest when engulfed by her joyful brood. She would correct and scold with gentle gestures and smile at me with embarrassment each time some unintended infraction of etiquette was committed against her foreign guest. But her annoyance was quickly surpassed by the depth of her patience and love.

The family had been blessed and was still intact in 1983. Teresa's youngest brother, Jose Victor, had been shot and seriously wounded by henchmen of the sugar plantation, La Cabaña, in the mid-seventies. Two brothers of Antonio had been killed by the death squads just prior to the war. Even Ranchera, the old family cow that had provided the milk that kept Teresa alive in her first year of life, had been killed by the army in one of its early incursions. But the nuclear family had not suffered a *baja* (loss) as of yet.

The oldest of the children was Eva. Like her mother, she was sprightly and radiant and highly intelligent. At 15 years of age – the age of her mother when she married Antonio – she had not yet joined the guerrilla army, but worked as a *sanitaria*, providing rudimentary health care to the civilian population or to wounded guerrilla fighters. She also cared for the younger children when Antonio and Teresa were in meetings away from the

From left to right: Antonio's brother Felipe, Eva, Gladys, Victoria, Aníbal, Teresa, Isabel, Antonio in front of their home recently destroyed by soldiers

family home. She was her parents' pride and joy, and their greatest hope for the future once the struggle had been won.

Victoria followed at age 13. She wore a perennial smile, was inquisitive and sincere with an aura of wisdom that belied her years. Gladys was next at age 12. Like her cousin Patrocinia, of the same age, she was quiet and serene with a luminous presence that spoke of character and depth. Isabel was 10 and a mischievous little tomboy ready to challenge males of all ages at climbing trees, jumping over rivers or running up hills. And Aníbal was six, the firstborn son, laughing incessantly, oblivious to the war, finding delight in everything around him.

Antonio's parents had both passed on, but Pedro and Patrocinia, Teresa's father and grandmother, lived close by. They continued to have a stressful marriage as a result of Pedro's infidelity many years earlier, but both remained active supporters of the revolutionary efforts of their children, grandchildren, nieces and nephews to the extent that their physical limitations allowed. I felt an immediate affinity for this very special family and visited them as frequently as I could.

Living with the civilian population in the war zones meant celebrating the good and mourning the evil collectively. On November 2, All Souls Day for those of the Catholic faith, we did both by remembering the dead – and, by 1983, there were a lot of dead to remember in the war zones of El Salvador. In the subzone of Piedra, Teresa and Antonio, like the rest of the population, awoke in a somber mood and began to make preparations to visit the graves of loved ones. There was no cemetery to speak of and gravesites were widely scattered, with rustic markings where family members and friends lay buried. At each site the men cleared away overgrown brush and placed new soil on top of the grave while the women planted wild flowers and described in detail the circumstances of each *compañero*'s death. The histories were filled with death squads, ambushes and bombings, and were followed by a moment of silence with clenched fists raised in the air.

At the gravesite of their brother Eduardo, Antonio and his sister Fidelia, took turns describing the young man's work as a catechist with Rutilio Grande, and his later role as an organizer

Fidelia, with her children and neighbors, honor the slain in Piedra

with the peasant farmer's organization, FECCAS. They recalled his ambush by National Police in which he and his fiancée had been wounded and captured. Their bodies were discovered the following day by Antonio and several other men from the village of Amayo. The young woman was found stretched face down over a large rock with the top of her skull blown away. The body of Eduardo was sprawled on the ground nearby with a gunshot wound in his right knee and his abdomen slit open in the form of a cross. It had been a horrible death that brought agonizing memories, and Antonio was unable to hold back the tears as he recalled that tragic day.

After several meetings with civilian leaders of Piedra, my work in the subzone was coming to an end. My departure was delayed, however by a lack of radio contact with the subzones of Guazapa and Radiola, always a sign of trouble. The absence of communication created a growing sense of tension in Fidelia and Teresa, concerned for the safety of Santos, who was meeting with other FMLN political cadres in Guazapa.

In an attempt to ease the tension, I suggested to Antonio that we climb nearby China Mountain. In all his life under the shadows of this dormant volcano, he had never scaled its steep slopes and he responded with enthusiasm to my proposal. Before dawn on the following day we began our journey, along with Eva, Victoria, Gladys and little Rosita.

The outing had its dangers, as there was little coverage to protect us from government aviation should a plane fly overhead during the climb, but we all agreed that it was well worth the effort as we stood on the summit gazing over an amazing panorama with the towering mountains of Chalatenango to the north, the Guazapa Volcano to the east and the San Salvador Volcano to the south.

Word finally reached us on the morning following our climb that the situation had "normalized" in Guazapa. Government troops had been frustrated and angered by another defeat at guerrilla hands, this time in the town of Tejutepeque in the province of Cabañas. In retribution, several battalions had invaded the subzones of Radiola and Guazapa, destroying villages and massacring a large number of civilians, but had finally been driven out by local guerrilla units. Santos returned a day later, looking emaciated and exhausted. He had been with the *compañeros*

The author with Eva, Victoria, Gladys and Rosita on China Mountain.

when they took the town of Tejutepeque and had endured eight days in *guinda* without food.

On the first night of his return, he and I talked for several hours as we waited for sleep in our safe house in Las Ventanas about the recent reports of a buildup of foreign troops along El Salvador's western borders with Guatemala and Honduras. The United States had established the United Command of Central American Armies in the 1960s "to provide joint aid to any Central American government threatened by revolution," and there was constant fear of a coordinated assault directed by Washington. In spite of his weakened condition, Santos remained firm in his convictions, however, and asserted again his determination to battle "any enemy who tried to intervene in the struggle."

Several days later, on a hot clear afternoon in November, I bid farewell with a heavy heart to Santos, Fidelia and their children. I was especially saddened to leave little Rosita, who begged me to "stay forever." I walked alone down the mountain path to Amayo, and people shouted goodbyes from their houses along the way, wishing me a safe trip and asking that I not forget them. The sun was waning and China Mountain turned a hazy blue as I slowed my pace in an effort to savor this unusual moment of peace and beauty.

I spent the next two days in Amayo with Teresa, Antonio and their five children amidst continuous laughter and song. We had been blessed during my visit by a period of calm, without the terror of military incursions, and I was thankful for having avoided the experience of long cramped days in a dark underground tunnel.

The monotonous routine of peasant life becomes an unusual gift and a blessing in the rare moments when the drums of war are silent, providing an opportunity for rest and for healing. Such moments are also opportunities for bonding among civilian families dedicated to the demanding rhythm of the struggle, and forced to spend extended periods of time away from their homes.

During this final visit, Antonio and Teresa's family awoke in the pre-dawn darkness to begin the chores of the day. They ground corn for *tortillas*, much as their Pipil ancestors had done for thousands of years. A small fire was built in the family kitchen to one side of the adobe house, and coffee was soon boiling. Beans, eggs and *tortillas* followed, then Teresa assigned the morning chores and the children scattered with merriment to begin washing the dishes, gathering firewood, sweeping the dirt floor of the house and boiling the big pot of beans for lunch.

When the chores were finished, everyone headed to the nearby river for bathing and washing clothes. A lunch of *tortillas* and beans followed at midday and then a space of free time until the stifling afternoon heat slowly began to wane. This time was used by most of the children for climbing trees, searching for crayfish in the nearby river, trapping iguanas and teasing each other incessantly. Teresa spent the afternoon mending the family's clothing and embroidering, an art learned from her fourth-grade teacher many years prior in the small school of Las Araditas. Dinner was served as darkness began to fall, followed by a short songfest with an old borrowed guitar, and the family, overcome by exhaustion, was asleep before eight.

CHAPTER SIX

In the Valley of the
Shadow of Death

On the night of November 10th, I began the long walk back to Guazapa. Our column was on the periphery of the subzone by sunrise and arrived at Lito's camp in the village of Consolación at approximately eight in the morning, wet from the previous night's rain, sweaty, and exhausted. It had been a grueling trip in which our guides had lost their way on several occasions and a severe case of amoebic dysentery left me weakened and defecating frightening quantities of mucus almost hourly.

We slept in Consolación that evening and I rested most of the following day. Anxious to return to my "home" base in San Antonio, however, I joined a guerrilla column of approximately 30 young combatants en route to Radiola early the second evening. They were all experienced fighters, used to maintaining a fast pace when they traveled – *paso militar* (military pace) they called it – and my weakened physical condition required an enormous effort to keep up. I was always determined to demonstrate my endurance, however, and to never hold up a column, so I pushed myself relentlessly for the next five hours.

We arrived in the mountainous terrain of Radiola before sunrise and rested briefly in the village of Casas Nuevas. We were on the move again as dawn broke, however, and arrived at San Antonio several hours later. The old adobe house where we used to sleep had been destroyed during the recent government incursion, and the *compañeros* from Ruben's unit had moved to a larger and less deteriorated structure nearby. Everyone from the unit was present when I arrived and we greeted each other noisily with warm hugs, heavy backslaps and much laughter. It had been a month since I had seen them last, and it felt like returning to family.

Our conversation quickly turned to the recent *guinda*, and the *compañeros* described in detail how several government battalions had invaded the subzone on the first of November. They had remained for eight days, massacring over 100 unarmed civilians in the villages of Copapayo and San Nicolas. Mama Elena, the old woman who cooked for Ruben's unit, had lost another child during the battles that ensued between the army and guerrilla fighters, this time a daughter.

She was occupying herself nearby with her newly orphaned granddaughter as I approached to offer my sympathies. She wore the same tattered dress she had on the first day I met her, and on her feet she wore oversized work boots with detached soles that I had given her months earlier when I received a new pair for myself. I had never seen her cry or even sigh in desperation during the time that I had known her. But this day her eyes revealed a profound and terrible pain that I knew I could not ease. I hugged her and thought to myself that even a total victory in this war would be insufficient to heal the wounds and return the joy of living to this battered but tenacious old woman.

I was asked by FMLN commanders to travel immediately to the villages of Copapayo and San Nicolas to document the carnage, so, without resting from my previous night's journey and

Mama Elena

with a growing sense of frailty from my incessant dysentery, I forced down a quick bowl of rice and *tortillas,* then set off with Joel, a young combatant from Ruben's unit.

The trip to San Nicolas took two hours, and it was half an hour more to the small adobe house on the outskirts of the village where the majority of cadavers were said to be found. We were warned long before our arrival of the

horror that awaited us by the stench of decaying bodies, perme-
ating the air for miles, and hundreds of black vultures, always the
harbingers of death, circling high overhead.

We were startled upon our arrival by the deafening roar of
wings as a horde of these ferocious beasts took to the air through
a gaping hole in the roof of the house. And the local peasants
who accompanied us stood back in disbelief when I pushed
through the door of this small chamber of horrors.

It was impossible to make an accurate body count once inside the building. Decaying corpses, many without limbs, some
eaten clean by the vultures, lay strewn about the dirt floor, partially buried under roofing tile and other debris. I counted 12
skulls at a glance and determined from pieces of clothing still
clinging to bodily remains that most of the victims were women
and young children.

From the house, we were guided to a grassy hillside nearby
where 12 more cadavers were found. Again, they were in advanced stages of decay and partially consumed by the vultures,
watching impatiently from the treetops above. I photographed
the scene, then continued on to nearby Copapayo, a small village

Assassinated women and children in the house in San Nicolas

Remains of elderly men found on the hillside of San Nicolas

of farmers and fishermen along the southeastern shores of Lake Suchitlan. Another grueling hour brought us to the site along the lake where more cadavers were said to be lying.

As we approached the lake, we came upon the first sign of pandemonium. The hillsides were littered with debris and the personal effects of a people who had fled in panic. Hundreds of pieces of clothing were strewn about the ground along with old gunny sacks, straw hats, little girls' pocketbooks, children's sandals, letters and other personal items.

A small rowboat with a gaping hole in its floor rested at the water's edge, and bloated cadavers bobbed in the water or lay rotting in the sun on the grassy hillsides above. It was the kind of scene that changes a person forever, a scene that lingers in the mind and produces an unconquerable sadness for the rest of one's days.

From the lake, we returned to the village of Copapayo, and I interviewed a 10-year-old boy named Aquilino who had miraculously survived the massacre in the house in San Nicolas. With a blank look and the subdued manner of a highly traumatized child, Aquilino slowly described the events of the previous days:

The water's edge of Lake Suchitlan in Copapayo

On the fourth of November, the elite U.S.-trained Atlacatl Battalion entered the subzone of Radiola in the area of Copapayo, and the civilian population fled. Approximately 150 women and children boarded small rowboats and headed north across Lake Suchitlan, seeking safety in the northern province of Chalatenango.

The local militia accompanying the population was equipped with communication radios, and halfway across the lake they intercepted a communiqué from Atlacatl commanders ordering government troops to withdraw. The civilian population, trusting that the danger had passed, turned the boats around and headed back to the southern shore. It had been a devious but cleverly conceived trap, however. The soldiers were hiding in the low brush on the hillsides above the lake and, when the unsuspecting villagers began to disembark, they opened fire. The defenseless civilians scattered in panic, trying frantically to escape the barrage of bullets raining down upon them, but over 50 men, women and children were killed during the first minutes of the attack.

Survivors were rounded up and marched off to the village of Escopeta, approximately half an hour away. At noon the following day, they were transferred to nearby San Nicolas where the soldiers divided them into two groups. The first group consisted of married women and children, and a second group consisted of younger women and men. The married women and children, numbering approximately 34, were then ordered into a small adobe house while the second group was led into the nearby hillsides. Those in the house were told that they were being transported to the capital city, but, within minutes, a soldier appeared in the doorway, armed with a 30-caliber machine gun, and, without warning, opened fire on the civilians.

Aquilino was the only person in the house not hit by the roaring blast, but he fell to the floor with the others and pretended that he was dead. Another young boy, eight years of age, was wounded in the shoulder. A third boy, 12 years of age, was wounded in the leg. Like Aquilino, both dropped to the ground and lay motionless under the bodies of the other women and children. The troops then climbed to the roof of the small house and smashed the tile with their weapons in a futile effort to hide from the world their grisly deed, while the three boys remained silent and still.

Several hours passed after the troops had departed before they worked up the courage to lift themselves from beneath the layer of bodies and roofing tile. The 12-year-old boy was too seriously wounded to walk by himself, so Aquilino and his eight-year-old companion went to fetch water for their friend in an old shoe pulled from one of the corpses. They then carried the 12-year-old to a nearby ravine where they all spent the night. On the following day, the two youngest boys hid their wounded friend in the tall grass and went to look for help.

All three of the boys survived and were being treated by guerrilla *sanitarias* for their physical wounds, along with several other small children who had been left for dead by the soldiers at the lake. I thought to myself as we finished our interview, however, that the physical recovery would be the easy part for all of these children. The less visible emotional wounds would take longer to heal. In the case of Aquilino, it would surely be a difficult process. He had lost his mother and 10 brothers and sisters in the small house in San Nicolas, and his father had been killed on the hillside nearby.

Joel and I left Copapayo late that afternoon and began the return trip to our camp in San Antonio. We started at a fast pace, but after several grueling hours of scaling hillsides and ravines my strength began to wane. I had been walking for over 24 hours without sleep or rest, and my dysentery continued to worsen. A painful urinary tract infection had also set in from a lack of drinking water and the long hours of sweating, and an old knee injury from my high school wrestling days burned from inflammation. Joel, with all of his youthful strength and endurance intact, showed little pity, and I was literally staggering when we finally walked into our camp shortly after dark. The *compañeros* prepared a large gourd of natural *suero* (serum), containing water, salt and ground jocote leaves, to purge my system and help me to rehydrate my body. Then I collapsed on the ground over a thin plastic sheet to sleep.

I arose several times in the night with vomiting and heavy diarrhea. Crouching in the darkness, the only word I could think of to describe my physical as well as mental state at the moment was "traumatic." My body was in a process of complete breakdown in the absence of the natural defenses and resistance required to survive the harsh countryside of El Salvador, and I was reminded again how far I had journeyed from the comforts of my accustomed habitat.

I left San Antonio to return to the capital city with the film and interviews documenting the massacres at Copapayo and San Nicolas in late November 1983. The U.S. embassy in El Salvador was telling the world that the massacre had not occurred. They argued that it was part of a propaganda scheme to discredit the current regime, and that troops trained in the United States, or within country by U.S. military advisors, were incapable of such a grievous and flagrant violation of human rights. I carried on film, and deeply engraved in my heart and mind, the evidence to the contrary, and would later turn it over to Maria Julia Hernandez, the valiant and persistent director of the legal aid office of the Archdiocese of San Salvador, appointed years earlier by Archbishop Romero to defend the human rights of the poor.

Maria Julia had learned of the massacre at Copapayo soon after it occurred and had publicly accused the United States of partial responsibility, since U.S. advisors had trained the troops who perpetrated this horrible deed. This had won her a harsh response from the U.S. ambassador who accused her in return of spreading "subversive propaganda" and making false accusations designed to discredit the United States. The photos and testimony that I presented to her would provide the necessary evidence to establish the credibility of her case.

My personal involvement in the revolutionary struggle of El Salvador had taken another dramatic leap. My allegiances were now firmly aligned with the forces opposed to the policies of my own government. I was suddenly in direct, if not open, confrontation with my own embassy. Many of my fellow countrymen and women would perceive my actions as subversive and unpatriotic. The friends of my youth and my own family, all people of good hearts and strong moral fiber, would be appalled at the horror of the massacre and the loss of human life, but they would have a difficult time understanding the path that I had chosen.

The bough had broken and the cradle had fallen, and there was much innocence lost in the process. I felt suddenly cut off from my culture and my past and from a country I no longer knew. I would realize in the months that followed that my heart had begun to harden in the face of such insane and inhuman violence. And I was finding it increasingly difficult to attribute to America any human values at all.

Much of the anger I felt toward my fellow countrymen was of course unfounded. Committed Americans battled throughout the 1980s to halt the policies of the Reagan administration. And polls at the height of the conflict in El Salvador put 68% of the public in opposition to U.S. involvement in the war. Solidarity groups nationwide were lobbying Congress, holding workshops, forums and protest marches against intervention, while in

El Salvador itself, growing numbers of young Americans worked alongside peasant, women's and human rights organizations in accompaniment of the people's struggle.

Leaving the *compañeros* from Ruben's unit in San Antonio was a wrenching experience, as I knew that some of them might not be alive when I returned. The day of my departure they gathered around to wish me well and ask that I remember them while I was away. I assured them that I would and pleaded jokingly that they delay the final victory in the war until I had returned. Marta, the young guerrilla leader with whom I had experienced my first serious brush with death on the slopes of the Guazapa Volcano a month earlier, turned my request around and exhorted me not to delay my return until they had won the final victory.

I left our base camp in the early afternoon of November 16 and arrived in the village of Tenango two hours later. From there, I departed with a column of about 40 guerrilla combatants travelling to the subzone of Cocal, near the town of San Martin, where I had entered the Felipe Peña Front a lifetime ago. Our path was lit by a bright three-quarter moon and the eight-hour trip would conclude without incident.

Once outside the liberated zone of Radiola, we passed through several heavily populated villages, but the people paid us little notice as we moved silently in single file through the night. My time in the war zones of El Salvador had left me almost oblivious to the destruction and decay around me. The bombedout shells of houses and rugged overgrown terrain where farmlands once existed were part of a landscape that no longer produced shock or dismay. I was amazed instead by the warm and snug appearance of the small adobe houses that we passed that evening, simple structures of clay and bamboo, lit only by candlelight and cookfires, yet such a comfortable contrast to the bombed-out villages of Radiola, Guazapa and Piedra.

We arrived in the small subzone of Cocal at midnight and slept immediately. I was pleased the next morning to see all of the same *compañeros* who had welcomed me to the war zones several months earlier, but there was little time to visit. I was told to prepare myself for an immediate departure to the capital city.

Without the benefit of a mirror, I cut my scraggly hair and beard for the first time since entering the zones, changed into clean dry clothes and traded my boots for a pair of city shoes. Then I left the camp in the company of a civilian collaborator on her way to purchase supplies in the market of nearby San Martín.

We passed through several small villages without incident, although I was keenly aware of the curiosity that my presence provoked among the inhabitants of the area. At one point, as we approached the last village before the main highway, we heard several loud bursts of machine gun fire, and two women who obviously knew the *compañera* with me approached us to warn that several truckloads of soldiers had been sighted on the road ahead. I was anguished by the prospects of having to turn back, and the *compañera* was intent on completing her mission. So, in spite of the danger, we decided to proceed.

I was carrying personal letters from many of the *compañeros* of Radiola to family members and friends in the capital city and my heart ached at the thought of destroying the only word some of them would receive in years. But if I were captured and searched they would have surely been found, revealing the nature of my presence so far from the normal "tourist trail," so I tore them into small unreadable pieces and cast them into the brush.

The woman then resumed her journey while I waited behind, having agreed to keep a distance of 30 meters between us. She carried her large basket balanced on her head and informed me that she would lower it if soldiers were sighted, recognizing that I was in much greater danger than she at the moment. We continued walking and the small path gradually became a larger dirt road. At one point, we passed an intersection with fresh tire tracks indicating that heavy trucks had recently passed, but no soldiers were sighted.

As I caught my first glimpse of the Pan American Highway, my heart began to pound. If all went well, I would be with Ana Eugenia that evening in our small rented apartment eating with a knife and fork instead of my fingers, illuminating the night without fear, bathing with running water instead of a cold mountain stream and sleeping in a soft secure bed. I would also be searching for the necessary words to describe the previous months to Ana and help her comprehend a world too far from urban reality to be easily understood.

Without looking in her direction, I thanked the *compañera*, wished her well and said that we would perhaps see each other again one day. She said goodbye and wished me a safe trip, pointed discreetly to a spot ahead where I could catch the bus to San Salvador, then continued on her way along the edge of the highway, mingling with the stream of local women on their way to market.

I had lost almost 20 pounds during my visit to the liberated zones of the Felipe Peña Front and, for the first several weeks in the capital city, I had no clothes that fit. Explaining my weight loss required great creativity until the cooking of Ana's mother and a cure for my dysentery slowly returned my body to its normal weight.

The experiences that I had lived could be shared with only a few as I tried to blend in with the routine of urban life. Trust was a gift extended to a small circle of friends, and the common wisdom of the day was "the less one knows, the better." Foreigners in El Salvador were all highly suspect at the time as there was no tourism to speak of. Military intelligence knew that we were all there for political motives, on one side of the war or the other.

In the city, the death squads and government security forces waged a massive campaign against suspected dissidents. Their rage was focused primarily on urban youth, and I listened with great concern during my first day back as Ana Eugenia shared the details of the month prior to my return, when her own family had joined the ranks of innocent victims targeted by an authority gone mad.

Her parents continued to reside throughout the war in their modest threeroom home in the densely populated working class neighborhood of El Palmar, in the western province of Santa Ana where Ana Eugenia, her six brothers and sisters and three cousins had grown up. Her mother sold shoes in the central market and her father was a retired policeman who had worked several years in Guatemala as a bodyguard and driver for the Salvadoran ambassador to that country. He believed in authority and had taught all of his children to respect the law. But he cast off his illusions the night in October when four heavily armed plainclothes detectives came barging into his house at gunpoint demanding that he hand over his grandson, Juan Carlos.

Juan Carlos was a high school student at the time, dedicated to his studies and with little interest in politics. It was later learned, however, that 12 of his schoolmates had been arrested by the police several days earlier and that one of them, after several hours of torture, had named Juan Carlos as a member of a student organization supporting the revolution. Ana Eugenia's father, Salomon, identified himself to the detectives as a former police officer and asked why Juan Carlos was being arrested, but he was warned to stay out of the way as the four armed men grabbed his grandson, loaded him into a waiting station wagon with tinted windows and drove off into the night.

Ana's mother spent the following days in tears and horror while Salomon struggled to recover from the shock of such abuse at the hands of the authorities that he had once served. And it was Ana and her mother who finally pulled themselves together and began the determined and dangerous search for Juan Carlos.

Fearing the worst, they visited local hospitals, morgues, jails and sites where the death squads frequently left the tortured remains of their victims. They received news at one point that several cadavers had been located in an area known as *el Playón* (the big beach), a large flat expanse of terrain at the base of the San Salvador volcano, covered with lava from centuries of eruptions. It was a favorite dumping site for the death squads since the darkened lava made the white sun-bleached bones of their victims easier to find, sending a deadly warning to anyone who might consider getting involved in the struggles for change in El Salvador.

Upon arriving, Ana, her mother and several other women searching for disappeared sons and daughters found the bodies of four youths, all with signs of torture, dressed only in under-garments and with their hands tied behind their backs. It was a gruesome scene, but they reviewed the bodies carefully one by one, relieved with each new face at not finding Juan Carlos among the dead. One of the women in their group, however, let out a spine tingling shriek as they were readying to leave and collapsed to the ground beside the mutilated corpse of her "disappeared" son.

The search for Juan Carlos continued over the next three weeks, assisted by Maria Julia Hernandez from the Archdiocesan Legal Rights Office and by the parish priest of El Palmar. And it finally generated enough publicity and pressure to force the National Police to admit to holding him in a basement cell in San Salvador. With this admission, it was impossible for the authorities to follow through with their standard practice of killing and "disappearing" suspected subversives, so Juan Carlos and the other students with him were sent to the Mariona prison in Mejicanos, San Salvador where Ana and her mother could finally visit him.

He told them during their first visit that he had been blindfolded, stripped naked, beaten and tortured without ever being informed about why he had been arrested. He remained in Mariona for the next three months in a special cell block for political prisoners referred to by inmates as the "Liberated Zone." He was eventually released, however, and we managed to get him out of the country to the U.S., where his mother lived and where he ironically joined the army and served in the Middle East.

The capital city was a stifling environment for me, having become accustomed to the freedom of the liberated zones, where each day began in well hidden and protected camps, with troop formation, the battle hymn of the FMLN and loud shouts in unison of "victory or death." As the days passed, my thoughts frequently wandered back to the men, women and children of Radiola, Guazapa and, of course, Piedra. I wondered constantly how they were, if they were in *guinda*, if they were resting, if there was food, if they were safe. And, as darkness fell each evening, I would gaze off to the north beyond the city lights and imagine the long silent guerrilla columns weaving like ants along the narrow mountain paths of the Felipe Peña Front. I could hear the hypnotizing rhythm of feet moving through the darkness, and I began to long for the day when I would join the *compañeros* again.

Three months passed before I was able to return to the liberated zones. U.S. strategists, by this time, were making reference to a new phase in the war called "clean counterinsurgency" or "low-intensity warfare." It meant, in practice, that the death squads had done their work, holding back the feared urban insurrection key to an FMLN victory. The United States and its allies in the Salvadoran military command would now have the "luxury" of focusing their efforts on a more sophisticated strategy to pursue national security interests while building an image of strengthening democracy and making El Salvador a better place.

The central pillar of the strategy was "nation-building," modeled after America's effort to defeat the struggle for independence in Vietnam. The ultimate goal was to win hearts and minds in El Salvador as well as the United States and weaken support for the FMLN. This was best expressed in 1986 by John Waghelstein, former head of the U.S. Military Group in El Salvador, when he said, "the only territory you want to hold is the six inches between the ears of a campesino."

The plan to accomplish this goal required profound reform in almost all aspects of Salvadoran society and the building of viable political, economic, military and social institutions. American military advisors and intelligence officers, abundant in El Salvador since the first days of the war, were joined by a flood of lawyers, judges, former police officers, legislative experts and social psychologists determined to construct the institutional backbone of a new nation.

The strategy had been detailed in the report of the National Bipartisan Commission on Central America, better known as the Kissinger Commission, issued in January 1984. The report sustained the Reagan view that Cuba and the Soviet Union were behind the crisis in El Salvador, but recognized the political and economic roots of the civil war and advocated a strategy of reform. It called for a continuation of land reform, an end to the flagrant abuse of human rights by government security forces, the termination of the death squads, the establishment of the rule of law and democratic elections.

Five years and six billion dollars later, U.S. government functionaries involved in the counterinsurgency effort in El Salvador would be forced to recognize the failure of their own policies. Representatives of the U.S. Agency for International Development would acknowledge that the U.S.-sponsored agrarian reform, the central pillar in the efforts to win Salvadoran hearts and minds, had ground to a halt. U.S. military advisors would acknowledge debilitating levels of corruption and incompetence within the Salvadoran military.

U.S. Justice Department officials would be overcome with disbelief at the failure to bring a single officer to justice in a military known to be guilty of the deaths of over 75,000 innocent civilians. And State Department officials would admit that El Salvador could not qualify as an institutional democracy capable of insuring respect for the human and civil rights of its citizens.

The essential problem for U.S. policymakers was that the United States was trying to implement its nation-building strategy by allying itself with a recalcitrant and corrupt military that knew only repression, and with a weakened government that had no experience with democracy. Nevertheless, with the new U.S. focus, political murders by the military and the death squads took a noticeable decline.

For those of us living in El Salvador at the time, it was clear that a precipitous change was occurring in the way security forces and military personnel related to local citizens and foreigners alike. At police or army checkpoints, a level of professionalism previously unknown in the country began to manifest itself. It was, in a sense, the confirmation of an assertion that human rights organizations had made for years: the behavior of El Salvador's security forces, whether it was respectful or repressive, was determined at the highest levels of command and heavily influenced by U.S. policymakers.

The new strategy for winning the war did not include negotiations with the FMLN, as this would inevitably result in some form of power-sharing. And this was perceived within the cowboy mentality of the Reagan administration as the equivalent of allowing the guerrilla organizations to "shoot their way to power."

Notwithstanding, in February 1984, the five guerrilla organizations of the Farabundo Martí National Liberation Front (FMLN) presented the first of many concrete proposals for a negotiated end to the war. It called for the formation of a provisional government in which no single political force would dominate. The new government would be an "expression of broad participation of all social and political forces" dedicated to the "elimination of oligarchic dictatorship" and to the "rescue of national sovereignty and independence."

In the area of international affairs, the FMLN called for a "policy of world relations oriented towards the conservation of peace, opposed to the arms race and nuclear weaponry," and defended the "principles of peaceful coexistence, self determination and non-intervention." With regards to the specific relationship with the United States, the plan proposed the celebration of special accords to guarantee the security interests of both nations.

The social, economic and political content of the proposal coincided to a remarkable degree with the Peace Accords finally signed between the warring parties eight years and over 50,000 civilian deaths later. The proposal was supported by the Catholic and major Protestant churches, academic institutions, labor unions, human rights groups and the majority of social forces in the country. In 1984, however, the United States government and their Salvadoran surrogates were holding out for a total victory. In spite of the fact that the war effort was now costing over a million dollars a day, the proposal for a negotiated peace was rejected outright.

In March 1984, FMLN commanders sent a communiqué to the Joint Chiefs of Staff of El Salvador's military in an effort to overcome the resistance of politicians and bring together those who were most actively engaged in fighting the war and shedding blood on the battlefield:

March 13, 1984

Members of the High Command, Chiefs of Staff, Officers and Soldiers of the Armed Forces –

We direct ourselves to you at this historic moment in the life of our nation. Two positions have been clearly put forth, one by those who wish to continue with the war, and one by those who seek a political solution to the conflict.

The battlefield is stained with the blood of Salvadorans in a civil war between families, brothers, friends, companions from work and study. The military solution is unviable, as demonstrated by eight years of war in which thousands of intelligent and brave young people have died for the motherland on both sides of the confrontation. But it is completely possible to find a just, dignified and independent solution among Salvadorans.

It is indispensable that we exercise flexibility, since maintaining a closed position will only prolong this war – which with each coming day becomes a more lucrative business for others at the expense of our lives. The opportunities for peace and the structural changes necessary to build social justice and a lasting peace are in the hands of those of us who possess the weapons, between you and us, we can decide without the consent of Washington or of the oligarchy. In the current situation in which we are living, we both are the real powers of the country....

Let us talk; let us dialogue. We have common enemies in the form of injustice, misery and dependence which we can battle together.... Let us build the peace, applying the warrior spirit inherited by our people from the legendary ancestral heroes, Altacatl, Atonal and Anastasio Aquino, in an effort to consolidate that peace and build a new future. Attaining this goal requires making concessions on both sides, including building a new Armed Forces dedicated to true democracy, social justice and national sovereignty....

Our people want peace, our revolutionary forces want peace and we are sure that the majority of officers and soldiers of the Armed Forces also want peace....[1]

Commanders: Francisco Jovel Eduardo Sancho
Salvador Sanchez Ceren Shafic Jorge Handal Joaquin Villalobos

---

1   Loose translation

In the midst of this changing context, in 1984, I was offered a job with the American Friends Service Committee (AFSC), a highly respected U.S. Quaker organization committed to peace with justice in the world. AFSC had received the Nobel Peace Prize years earlier for its dedicated humanitarian work in North Vietnam during that war. The organization was highly critical of U.S. strategies in Central America and committed to educating U.S. policymakers and the North American people about the complex realities of the region and the war in El Salvador.

My appointment as their Central American Field Representative would mean that the geographical focus of my work would be broadened beyond the borders of El Salvador to include all of the countries in Central America, with occasional speaking tours to the U.S. In conversations with representative of the FMLN, it was suggested that I accept the position, since it would allow me to reach out to the hearts and minds of people and policymakers in the U.S. and help spread the truth about El Salvador and the civil war that was destroying this nation. They assured me, at the same time, that my relationship with the civilian populations in the liberated zones could continue and that I would be able to travel to those regions when necessary.

My specific responsibilities with AFSC in Central America focused on identifying and supporting grassroots organizations throughout the region working in the pursuit of demilitarization, democracy, justice and peace. With these goals in mind, I coordinated closely with peasant organizations, labor movements, indigenous groups, women's organizations, human rights activists, victims of repression, displaced populations, refugees and civilian populations in war zones struggling for their right to remain in their villages of origin. To all of these actors, we offered solidarity, economic support and Quaker witness.

In my new role as regional representative of AFSC, I returned to the Felipe Peña Front in February, 1984, entering this time through the subzone of Piedra. I was carried by jeep from the capital city to a point along the Northern Highway just south of Aguilares, and dropped off in the darkness along with two Salvadoran priests. We were met by a small guerrilla column, along with several civilian families with children, transporting supplies to the camps further west. Some of the children were mounted on horses and gripped each other tightly as they were led off into the darkness along the narrow mountain paths leading into the subzone. Another horse carried the heavier supplies that we had brought from the capital city, including medicines, boots and a large cumbersome plastic bag filled with unconsecrated eucharists for celebrating Mass. All personal equipment was carried on our backs.

I had been away for several months, but my first painful and embarrassing falls brought me back immediately to the humbling reality of foot travel in the rugged Salvadoran countryside. We walked through the night in a long and silent column and I became gradually hypnotized by the tiny bare feet of a young girl in front of me working her way with great agility over the difficult terrain for hours on end without rest or complaint.

We arrived at the main guerrilla camp in the village of Las Ventanas at approximately midnight and found the *compañeros* in the camp asleep, rolled up like cocoons in their plastic sheets and scattered about on the ground. I had grown soft in the capital city and felt exhausted, so I quickly joined them, thankful for the remaining rays of heat still emanating from the sun-blanched earth beneath me and an exhilarating expanse of starlit sky that held my gaze as I slowly gave in to sleep.

Teresa got word immediately of my arrival and came early the following morning to greet me. It was marvelous to see those radiant eyes and that genial smile again. With the humble enthusiasm I had come to know, she invited me to her home later that afternoon, and I accepted with great anticipation at the prospect of seeing this sprightly family. I was also hoping to visit Teresa's brother Santos, Fidelia and their family, although Teresa informed me that Santos was again away in the subzone of Guazapa, in a meeting of civilian leaders.

It was dry season in El Salvador, so the lush green hillsides that had provided cover from government aviation during my previous visit were now scorched and bare. The heat during the day was stifling. Water for drinking and bathing was scarce, available only in stagnant pools in the dried riverbeds. Nevertheless, it felt good to be back, eating *tortillas* and beans with the *compañeros* again.

I visited for several hours on that first afternoon with Teresa, Antonio and their children. Eva, the oldest daughter, continued to work as a *sanitaria*, and I was honored to find hanging from her neck a small cross I had made for her from an M-16 cartridge the previous year. The younger children, Victoria, Gladys, Isabel, and little Aníbal, were all present as well, and they giggled incessantly as I gorged myself with *tortillas*, beans and fresh fruit.

They were all safe, but looking quite haggard and thin with bloodshot eyes and the paleness that malnutrition brings. Antonio was also suffering from a severe case of malaria. They told me that government troops had invaded the subzone a week before my arrival and that the people of Piedra had spent several harrowing days in their underground *tatús* (bunkers) with no food. A woman from the village unable to reach her own family bunker had joined Teresa and the children in their small dark refuge. She had been a problem from the start, however, and had put the lives of all in serious danger.

As the children told it, each talking at once, there had been a moment during the second day of hiding in which government soldiers had approached the bunker and stood for several moments over its shaky roof. One soldier actually knocked over the small bamboo shoot serving as air duct and the woman cried out in panic. Pieces of dirt were falling from the ceiling as Teresa reached out in the darkness, took the woman's hand and began whispering in her ear that all would be well, urging her to remain silent. It seemed like an eternity before the soldiers finally departed, and it was several moments after that before Teresa dared to restore the small bamboo duct to its original position allowing the people to breathe again.

I slept that night in the home of Teresa and Antonio and, on the following day, we attended Mass together, celebrated by the two priests I had accompanied the night before. Their names were Trinidad Nieto and Tilo Sanchez, both convinced revolutionaries and FMLN activists who remained in the priesthood and served the civilian populations of the liberated zones throughout the war. News of their presence had circulated widely, and people arrived from all of the surrounding villages.

As the Mass proceeded on an open hillside using a small table as altar, I stood on the periphery of the large gathering, gazing in silence at the people around me. There were women with small children and adolescents of all ages dressed in their best tattered clothing for the occasion. I watched the dark leathery faces of the old men, *sombreros* in hand and weapons hanging from thin worn shoulders. These were the men of the popular militia under Antonio's command, products of a lifetime of humiliation and oppression, yet filled with the pride of those who struggle. I then turned my gaze to Teresa and her five children, so radiant in their silence, oblivious for the moment to the harshness of their circumstances and stoically assimilating the dangers of their everyday lives.

The sermon of the priests turned into a prolonged dialogue with the people on the meaning of sin within a revolutionary context. It was Liberation Theology at its best. The villagers confidently shared their ideas and analysis, attained from the missions of Father Rutilio Grande, expressing their positions without inhibition. They referred to the sin of injustice as an "insult to God's love for mankind," then Father Sanchez gave a plenary indulgence to all of us present, followed by an invitation to "all of those willing to change their personal lives and struggle for a more just society" to come forth and receive communion.

The Mass was followed by a "revolutionary dance" to the festive songs of local musicians playing guitars, violins and bass fiddles. Fidelia and her children came and I was finally able to see little Rosa and her brothers and sisters again, including the incredulous Patrocinia, who once told me I would "forget this place" and never return again. We laughed and joked late into the evening with the profound joy and solidarity that shared hardship brings, and were interrupted by the war only briefly, dousing candles and cookfires when government spotter planes began to circle briefly overhead.

On the following day, a second Mass was celebrated in the village of Amayo, and I spent that evening again with Antonio, Teresa and their children, playing revolutionary songs on a borrowed guitar and sharing the family's dwindling supplies of rice, beans and *tortillas*, offered generously in honor of my presence.

I held several meetings with the civilian population during the days that followed, and slept wherever night found me. I was interested in learning how the production projects we had designed during my first visit were going, and was frustrated to learn that funding for the projects had fallen short of our projected goals, a chronic problem for the activities of the civilian population in a struggle prioritizing military strategies. What was worse, of the projects that had been initiated, most had been destroyed by government bombing. It was disappointing news, but we all knew that it was part of the reality of this war.

My primary objectives for this trip focused on bearing witness and providing accompaniment to the civilian population, through the documentation of human rights violations, much as I had done during my first visit, so I continued to meet with communities throughout the subzone collecting evidence and recording testimony. As the meetings proceeded, we were constantly distracted by the sounds of heavy bombing in Guazapa and finally received radio confirmation that this subzone had been under heavy air attack for the past three days. More than 70 bombs and rockets had been dropped or fired on the villages of Mirandilla, La Pava and El Zapote on the northern slopes of the volcano, and several *compañeros* had reportedly been killed.

On the evening after receiving this news, I slept outside on the hillsides just above Amayo with several other families with whom I had been meeting. We spent the night in unsuspecting innocence, confident that friends and family in Guazapa were safe. Just before dawn the next morning, however, messengers from Guazapa arrived with heartbreaking news. Teresa's brother Santos and eight other *compañeros* were among the dead from the bombing of Mirandilla.

I was devastated, remembering how I had almost been killed myself on that same hillside the previous year. Santos' family had talked at length during our last gathering about how much they missed him, and we were all anxiously awaiting his return on this day.

Lito, the toothless pistol-packing civilian leader of Guazapa, had also been killed, along with Guadalupe, a special friend from a wealthy Mexican family who had joined the revolution years earlier and worked in communications in the subzone of Radiola. The only other *compañero* that I knew well was Evaristo, the humble and quiet peasant leader from Radiola whom I had met during my first *guinda* on a dark and terrifying night in 1983.

Upon hearing the news, I rushed down the mountain to the home of Teresa and Antonio. The first light of dawn had just begun its slow journey down the slopes of China Mountain, but I found Teresa awake, stunned and bewildered at the cruel and sudden death of her brother. I could only guess at the depth of her pain as we hugged. Then she silently wiped her eyes and tried to regain her calm in a fruitless effort to spare me from having to share her sorrow.

Antonio was deeply anguished as well at the loss of his brother-in-law and close companion, with whom he had shared so many years of struggle, before and during the war, and whom he had loved so dearly. Santos had married his older sister, Fidelia, years ago when Antonio was still a young soccer star from the village of Amayo. He had been encouraging when Antonio first laid admiring eyes on the young Teresa. And he had been a *compañero* in the struggles with local *hacienda* owners, sugar barons and death squads in the 1970s.

We ate lunch together later that day; then I struggled with my own tears as I searched feebly for the words that could ease Teresa's pain. I promised her earnestly to be forever faithful to her struggle, and tried to assure her that Santos' death would not be in vain. I was scheduled to depart that evening for the subzone of Guazapa and wished that there could have been happier circumstances under which to bid my farewells to the families of Piedra. I had learned by now, however, that life in the war zones followed its own special and cruel logic, with little sympathy for innocent hopes and dreams.

I wanted to see Santos' wife, Fidelia, and their children before leaving, so I hugged the bereaved Teresa one last time, said goodbye to Antonio, and climbed the mountain to Las Ventanas. As I walked alone up the narrow rocky path, I was reminded of the first time that I had scaled this grassy hillside with Santos in October of the previous year. I remembered as well the words he had spoken one sleepless night on the dirt floor of our "safe house": "When I leave my house in the morning, I know that here is never a guarantee that I will return to see my family again."

I arrived in Las Ventanas to find Fidelia and the children preparing to go for water at a nearby well, an obvious attempt to overcome their overwhelming pain through the mundane chores of life. With the children in a collective trance and Fidelia bleary-eyed and confused, we all fought to restrain our emotions as we hugged in somber greeting. We talked through the afternoon about Santos and the other *compañeros* who had been killed and of the critical loss to the struggle that their deaths represented. Then we hugged again and bid a tearful goodbye with promises that I would return soon. I knew in my heart, however, that it would be several months before I could get back to this subzone. I descended the hillside with an overpowering sense of sadness and loss. A cool breeze calmed the stifling heat of the day and the beauty of China Mountain loomed in the distance, but there was no lifting the somberness of this tragic afternoon.

I left for the subzone of Guazapa early that evening, accompanied by the priests Tilo and Trinidad and a small column of guerrilla combatants. Our route this time took us south of the sugar plantation, La Cabaña, as it was still harvest season and the plantation was heavily patrolled by government troops. The night was unusually beautiful, with a star-filled sky and a bright crescent moon to help light our path, but my sadness made it difficult to enjoy. We entered the subzone of Guazapa shortly after midnight and found a place to camp among the underbrush, then resumed our march at sunrise, ascending the gradual slopes of the volcano and arriving in Mirandilla four hours later.

In the early afternoon, we were guided to the site where

Santos and the other *compañeros* had been killed. We spoke there with one of the survivors of the bombing and learned that the villages of Mirandilla, La Pava and El Zapote had been under heavy attack by government aircraft for several days in a row, and that, during one of those days alone, 22 bombs had been dropped over civilian communities. On the morning of March 4, the coordinators of the civilian population of the Felipe Peña Front were meeting in a small adobe hut on the slopes of Mirandilla when a Cessna Push and Pull circled overhead for several minutes and then flew off. Later that afternoon, as the meeting continued, two A-37 Dragonfly jets returned and, without circling, swooped down and dropped several 500-pound bombs around the village. The *compañeros* took refuge in a nearby trench, but one of the bombs landed just meters from their refuge, splitting a giant ceiba tree standing nearby. The tree fell directly on the trench and crushed everyone within.

From the hillside in Mirandilla, we traveled to the villages in the lowlands below where bombs had also fallen. We spoke with a family who had watched in dismay from a nearby trench as three bombs blew their house to pieces and killed all of their

Mother and children in the midst of the ruins of their former home

remaining livestock. At a third site we visited the home of an elderly widower that had been completely leveled. The owner was not present at the time of our arrival, but his neighbor, a toothless peasant woman well into her seventies, came running out to meet us. Noticing that I was a foreigner, and perhaps mistaking me for a reporter, she directed her attention at me as she shared the details of the recent bombing. She was still terror-stricken and in shock, and her entire body shook with an uncontrollable rage as she begged me to tell the world what had happened in this village. As we were readying to leave, she came closer and, with a trembling voice, expressed hope that "some country [would] stand up one day and defend the people here before everyone is killed."

In the late afternoon of the following day, A-37 Dragonflies returned, roaring across the lowlands, swooping up into the clouds, circling and, finally, dropping their deadly cargo on the village of Consolación. As we all ran for cover, I recalled, with

a mixture of humor and contempt, a BBC newscast I had heard earlier in the day describing the efforts of U.S. Secretary of State George Shultz to persuade the U.S. Congress of the urgency of increased military aid to El Salvador, asserting that the Salvadoran Air Force was currently out of bombs.

I was later informed that approximately 500 government troops had again invaded the subzone of Piedra from where I had recently departed, and my thoughts

Watching from the trenches
as the bombs fall

went immediately to Teresa and Fidelia, robbed of the opportunity to grieve their recent loss, and of their small children, now hiding in the cramped and suffocating darkness of an underground shelter.

After several days in Guazapa, we departed for the subzone of Radiola under the darkness of night in four small rowboats. Brush fires, ignited by the recent bombings, were still burning on the hillsides around Lake Suchitlan and eerie clouds of smoke rolled down to the water's edge, reminding me of scenes from the movie *Apocalypse Now*. We disembarked before dawn at the lakeside village of Peipeistenango, now abandoned due to the frequent incursions of government troops and heavy aerial bombardment. From the ghostly scene of this once picturesque community, still heavily populated at the time of my previous visit, we traveled to the village of El Sitio, rested briefly, then continued on to the new subzonal headquarters, arriving just after sunrise.

The camp was well hidden in a deep ravine to protect it from the ever-present danger of airstrikes. Lean-tos made from tree branches and plastic sheeting provided the only source of shelter, but water and shade, both luxuries in the sweltering dry season of El Salvador, were abundant. The *compañeros* in the camp heard our noisy approach and came running to greet us. My heart filled with joy at the sight of them again, even in this harsh setting. The young combatants, Joel and Santiago, as well as the older Angel and Ruben him-

Blanca (left) and her sister, Consuelo

self gathered around to welcome me home, and teased me incessantly about the weight I had regained during my months in the capital city.

Santos' two daughters, Blanca and Consuelo, both still working as radio operators with the guerrilla command, learned of my arrival later that day and came to see me. We talked initially of good times and laughter in far-off Piedra, but the conversation quickly turned to the inevitable theme of their father's death. Both daughters were inconsolably distraught at the loss of Santos, and Blanca confessed that she had not yet assimilated the thought of never seeing him again.

I had brought with me a tape recording that I had made of their mother, Fidelia, and brothers and sisters prior to Santos' death, so we found a silent and secluded spot on an embankment overlooking Ruben's camp and listened together to the animated voices of Patrocinia, Moises, Vladimir and little Rosita.

I remained for several days in Radiola meeting with the civilian population, then made the arduous trip by land with a small column of guerrilla fighters back to the subzone of Guazapa, travelling again to Mirandilla and then to the village of Consolación in the lowlands.

In Consolación, a large kettle of freshly caught catfish boiled over an open fire as I walked hungrily into the camp; but before I had settled, three A-37 Dragonfly jets came screaming across the open fields. Someone yelled "avión" (the plane), and plates flew as people scattered in a panicked search for cover. The jets swooped into the air and circled above us for several minutes as we watched from the trenches below, then dropped 10 of their 500-pound bombs throughout the lowlands and the lower slopes of the Guazapa volcano. Three of the bombs fell on Consolación, splintering trees and brush close to where we were hiding, but there were no injuries.

I slept little that night as I had fallen suddenly ill earlier in the day with severe body aches, fever, clogged sinuses and nausea. I knew from the symptoms that it was probably dengue, a viral disease carried by mosquitoes for which there is no rapid cure. The next morning the symptoms were worse, but the stifling heat of the day made resting difficult, and we were sent scrambling for cover again at noon under a rain of machine gun fire from a Hughes 500 helicopter.

March 24, 1984 marked the fourth anniversary of the slaying of Archbishop Romero. While I continued to suffer from severe muscle pains, fever and sore throat, Delegates of the Word and members of the civilian population from nearby communities arrived in Consolación and organized a prayer vigil commemorating the death of their beloved pastor. They filled the night with song and prayer, and with testimony recounting the lives of Romero, Rutilio Grande and other slain priests. Additional prayers for an end to U.S. military aid and a prompt negotiated solution to the war followed, then several young children were baptized.

As the ceremony proceeded, I lay alone in the darkness on the hard cement floor of the small single-room building that once served as Lito's headquarters. My eyes filled with tears as I listened to the sad music and the prayers drifting in from the patio outside. I struggled for composure, lest someone discover my weeping, but I was soon sobbing and shaking out of control. I knew that it was due, in part, to fever and exhaustion, but I was aware as well that the terrible price in human life of this hideous war, and my deepening rage at the policies of my own government, were beginning to take a toll.

U.S. military aid to El Salvador continued to ignore the obvious: that poverty and oppression breed rebellion. The legitimate aspirations of a just people might be deferred through repression and token reform, but the struggle of such people can never be fully defeated as long as the underlying causes persist.

The following morning I continued to feel ill, but I held a final meeting with civilian leaders in Consolación, and returned to the village of Mirandilla to prepare my departure for the capital city. It was election day in those areas of the country still under government control, and a large group of *compañeros* sat on the ground around a small radio, silently listening to news, as I walked into camp.

The Reagan administration, in its efforts to build an image of an emerging democracy, had spent several million dollars to support the electoral process. In spite of heavy U.S. backing, however, the news reports spoke of widespread disarray. In many of the voting centers there was a shortage of urns. In others, the urn attendants never showed up. There were insufficient ballots to go around, and many lists of registered voters were sent to the wrong sites. By the time the polls closed, only 30% of registered voters had been able to cast their vote.

The following afternoon we prepared to depart for the subzone of Chapin near the town of Nejapa. There was little food in the camp, so a small piece of dried *tortilla* for each *compañero* was our only sustenance before embarking on the long and difficult journey. I was travelling, as usual, with a guerrilla column used to moving swiftly. There was a blazing sun overhead, and I felt weak from the outset from my continuing illness and lack of food, but this was nothing unusual for the young combatants and I was shown no mercy.

We crossed the Northern Highway early that evening and were entering the mountainous subzone of Chapin, three hours later. I was now completely exhausted, and each step required a major act of will. We finally stopped to make camp just before midnight, but it was bitterly cold due to the elevation, and I slept very little.

We arose at sunrise the following morning and continued on to the subzonal headquarters from where I departed that same day for the capital city. I was reminded again of the dangers of travel out of the liberated zones, due to the sparse information one frequently has on government troop movements. On the edge of urban areas close to the capital city, like Nejapa, it was especially hazardous. The only solution was to blend into the civilian population as best one could, a difficult task for a tall white *gringo*.

I was accompanied this time by two young women in their late teens carrying messages for the guerrilla cells in the capital city. They were young and very beautiful, but toughened by their years of struggle, and they demonstrated little concern for the foreigner suddenly in their midst. We walked for several hours along the hot and dusty mountain trails, then stopped briefly at the small adobe home of a civilian collaborator. There the two young women swapped their worn jeans and combat boots for elegant city dresses and polished shoes. They applied make-up in tasteful measure and coaxed their straight shoulder-length hair into more urban styles. I watched with amazement at the transformation taking place before my eyes, knowing that anyone catching a glimpse of them on a busy city street would have no notion of the unmerciful setting from which they had come.

We continued our journey, as the narrow mountain paths gradually widened into more traveled dirt roads, and finally arrived at a point where we could catch the bus for San Salvador. There were no goodbyes or well wishes. We boarded separately and did not look at or speak to each other again. As the bus started up, a cassette of loud rock music began to play, and I felt again the surge of excitement at the prospect of returning to the city.

I was exhausted, physically as well as emotionally, and it was only through great effort that I was able to restrain the flood of tears welling up within as we bumped along the country highway. This trip had been short, but filled to the brim with tragedy. I tried to convince myself that this would be my last trip into the war zones. I was, after all, a foreigner from another world, a middleclass *gringo*, a city person. And, at age 41, I was getting too old! I knew, however, that, once I had recovered physically, the memories of hardship would again begin to fade, the pain of loss would eventually cede and the love of the struggle would begin to pull at my heart once again.

I returned to the liberated zones of El Salvador five more times between July 1984 and February 1989. With each visit it became more apparent that the war was taking an enormous toll on the civilian population and guerrilla fighters alike. The Salvadoran government and its U.S. mentors applied with calculated cruelty their counterinsurgency program of reform mixed with repression. But repression was the only part of the strategy to be found in the liberated zones with continuous incursions of U.S.-trained ground troops and the indiscriminate bombing of civilian villages. By 1984 it was beginning to show some successes in terms of "drying up the sea" and, by the middle of that year, there were few civilian families left in the Felipe Peña Front.

Through the tenacious efforts of human rights groups and organizations of communities displaced by the indiscriminate bombing, measures would be adopted in later years to "humanize" the war and permit the "fish" to return to this still tumultuous "sea." Repopulation programs would be designed and implemented in an effort to return displaced civilians to their villages of origin, and international non-governmental organizations, like the American Friends Service Committee, would struggle for the right to attend to their safety and needs. But in 1984, the Salvadoran army was still guided by the logic of extermination.

In July of that year, I was called upon again to document a massacre of civilians in the subzone of Radiola. Sixty-four non-combatants had been killed during an incursion of government troops, half of whom were women and children under 15 years of age. The youngest of the victims was just over a month old.

I arrived in the area of the reported massacre late in the morning on July 29th and interviewed a 12-year-old boy and an elderly man, both eyewitnesses to the carnage who had narrowly escaped death themselves. The elderly man was still visibly shaken and spoke with a trembling voice as he described the events of the previous week. According to his account, the civilian population had been attacked by several hundred soldiers from the infamous Atlacatl Battalion. His wife and two children had been killed and he alluded repeatedly to the "miracle" of his own escape from the hail of bullets that had taken their lives, adding that "someone had to survive to tell the story."

The incursion was part of a massive operation in reprisal for a guerrilla attack on the hydroelectric plant at Cerron Grande several days prior. Reports indicated that the Atlacatl Battalion entered the subzone via Jutiapa in the province of Cabañas on July 18, and that same day killed 39 unarmed civilians from the villages of Yanitos, Azacualpa, Culebrilla, and La Criba, villages I had known while transporting wounded during the horrific *guinda* in September of 1983. The remains of 14 of these victims were later found at the bottom of a latrine near Jutiapa, covered over with sticks and leaves.

The soldiers then advanced to the village of Tortuga and, on July 21, detected a group of approximately 40 women and children hiding in a deep ravine known locally as the *Bañadero del Zope* (Bathing Place of the Vulture). No order to halt or surrender was given when the villagers began to flee in panic. The soldiers simply opened fire, killing 11 people. The following day, the soldiers detected, pursued and overran a second group of civilians along the banks of the Quezalapa River, killing 18 people. Military helicopters later arrived, transporting gasoline, and most of the cadavers were burned. Along with the human toll, 35 civilian homes and vast acreage of corn were destroyed. I was guided to the village of Tortuga and the Bañadero del Zope the following morning, tracing the steps of the fleeing civilians down into a twisting ravine where I came upon the first tragic evidence supporting the previous day's testimony. The corpses of women and small children were scattered about on both sides of the ravine. Many were partially burned. Some were half buried or covered in mud. All were in advanced stages of decomposition, and partially consumed by vultures. Only hands and feet, too heavily callused from lives of toil for even a buzzard's beak, were left intact.

Some of the bones were broken and skulls were crushed, confirming reports of torture. In a few cases, craniums were missing altogether. Female cadavers showed signs of sexual abuse, with undergarments removed and scattered on the ground nearby. Among the cadavers I found my friend Angel, the middle-aged *compañero* from Ruben's unit with whom I had spent many difficult moments in 1983. His face and lower body had been consumed to the bone by the buzzards, waiting anxiously in the nearby treetops for our departure, but my guides identified him from the tattered scraps of clothing that still clung to his remains.

I traveled the next day to the village of San Antonio, the site of our old base camp, in search of more eyewitnesses, and spoke there with 55-year-old Bernabe Hernandez. In a halting and whispering voice, this traumatized peasant described how

his wife and four children had been captured, shot, then burned by soldiers while he hid in the underbrush nearby. According to his testimony, his youngest son was still alive and semi-conscious when the soldiers threw his bullet-ridden body onto the fire. The shaken, old man then recounted with sadness and shame how he had waited helplessly for the soldiers to leave, listening to the screams of his son as his writhing body was slowly consumed by the flames.

In August 1984, the Christian Base Communities of Cinquera, Jutiapa and Tenancingo sent the following open letter to then president José Napoleón Duarte, denouncing the massacre and other acts of repression, and demanding a halt to foreign intervention:

Mr. President
José Napoleón Duarte

We, the members of the Christian Base Communities of the department of Cabañas, disturbed by the acts of violence in our communities in recent days, find it necessary to direct these words to you so that all people can be witness to the gravity of our testimony and demands.

We are, before all else, Christians, brothers and sisters convinced that our country and our people need solid solutions to the problems that we are confronting, and that, to move forward, these solutions must be based on truth, justice, freedom, and respect for human rights.

Our communities are populated by men and women, elderly and young, all peasant workers who, from birth, have earned our daily sustenance with the sweat of our brow, in the midst of enormous sacrifice, and in conditions of endless poverty.

We are the ones who work the land and produce the wealth for our country; we are the ones who perform the tasks that generate our nation's income, leaving our lives behind in the fields and plantations of coffee, sugar and cotton.

In payment for all of this, we have received starvation wages, insufficient for our own subsistence, constant insults, and mistreatment. We have been obligated to live in sub-human conditions; and when, with every right, we have protested and defended that which is just and human, we have been the victims of repression....

Some of our brothers, confronted with the threat of indiscriminate violence, have been forced to abandon the country, to live humiliated, persecuted and impoverished in other lands. But we have chosen the path of dignity and freedom, following the example of Jesus and of our beloved pastor, Archbishop Romero. For this reason we remain on the lands where we were born. Here we grew up and here we have our small plots from which we continue to derive our only source of livelihood....

Now, just sixty days after you took office for a second term, our communities are victimized once more by grave violations of human rights. Among our families and friends, 27 children under 14 years of age have been killed, along with 11 elderly and various pregnant women; a total of 64 human beings, created in the image of God, have been killed without reason. And the authors of this horrible sin remain unpunished....

In December 1984 I traveled to the Felipe Peña Front again and, on the evening of the 24th (my birthday), after several weeks with communities in other subzones, I arrived with a small guerrilla column at the village of San Antonio in time to participate in the Christmas Eve dance of Radiola. There were several hundred combatants and civilians present, and the atmosphere was festive. Antonio's and Teresa's oldest daughter, Eva, was present, along with Blanca, the daughter of Fidelina and Santos. They both noticed my arrival, shouted out my name in unison and came running to greet me with the giggling enthusiasm of their years.

Eva had finally taken the step that Teresa and Antonio had dreaded for so long. Following in the footsteps of her cousin Blanca, she had joined the guerrilla army. Like Blanca, she was assigned to the central command in Radiola as a radio operator. She was only 16, a year older than her mother Teresa when she had married Antonio, but I was amazed at how she had grown in the eight months since I had last seen her.

She still wore the cross that I had given her in Piedra, and she embraced me with confidence as we danced to the music of violins and guitars. A large group of young combatants watched with envy as they waited their turn with this radiant young beauty, but Eva paid them no attention, encouraging me to dance again as each new song began.

I finally rewarded the patience of the young *compañeros* by turning Eva loose, and went in search of Blanca. I located her in another crowd of young admirers and risked my life again by pulling her away. As we talked, I noticed an unusual sadness about her, and she eventually confided that her mother Fidelia and younger brothers and sisters had left the subzone of Piedra a month earlier. They were now living in a refugee camp in the western city of Santa Ana, and Blanca was obviously suffering again from a deep sense of loss. The death of Santos had deprived life of its joy for Fidelia, and the hardship and dangers of Piedra became more than she could bear without his assuring presence. Patrocinia, now 13, had remained behind to cook for the local guerrilla column, but she was quickly recruited as a radio operator and sent to the Apolinario Serrano Front in the northern province of Chalatenango. Blanca missed her family desperately and was frustrated and angered by the decision of local guerrilla commanders to deny her request to travel to Santa Ana for the Christmas holidays. I learned later that she was also pregnant, and I better understood her frustrations at the absence of her mother.

A unilateral ceasefire had been declared by the guerrilla organizations of the FMLN to allow the Salvadoran people an opportunity to celebrate the Christmas holidays in a momentary peace. President Napoleon Duarte was pressured by the international community to reciprocate, but his military commanders refused to obey his orders to halt hostilities. On December 24, as we danced in the subzone of Radiola, government war planes dropped 12 bombs and fired 20 rockets on civilian villages in the lowlands of Guazapa.

Several days later, I travelled to Guazapa to witness the destruction. En route, we were attacked ourselves by government aviation, confirming once again the dominant role of the military in government policymaking and their hunger for death, even during the Christmas season. There were no casualties, however, and we were eventually able to continue our march, arriving late that evening to the lowlands. In the afternoon of the following day, after observing the destruction from the aerial bombing of Christmas Eve, we left Guazapa, headed for the subzone of Chapin near the town of Nejapa.

Our new column included three women civilians and a one-year-old baby, who had been visiting family in the subzone during the Christmas celebrations. The night was beautiful, with an expansive starlit sky. The only sound to be heard was the soft rhythmic crunching of grass under our feet as we crossed the open fields in a westerly direction. Upon our approach to the Northern Highway, however, the explosion of gunfire shattered the silence, and I saw the flames from several gun barrels leaping into the darkness in our direction from approximately 30 meters away. Government soldiers patrolling the highway had detected our presence and had been waiting in ambush behind a small embankment along the edge of the paved road. Their firing was erratic and none of us were hit in the first barrage of gunfire, so I can only imagine that they were panic-stricken at the thought of doing battle in the dark with a guerrilla column whose size and make up were unknown to them.

Those in our group with weapons returned the fire while the women and children retreated in search of cover, but we were all soon sprinting together across the open field with backpacks, bundles, baby and all. The soldiers continued to fire and bullets filled the air, whizzing by our heads like angry hornets. I saw the woman with the baby fall, but she was unharmed and quickly rose with the one-year-old still in her arms. Once out of range, we stopped to rest and the decision was made to set up our own ambush with several young combatants in case the soldiers followed. The rest of us returned to the subzone of Guazapa where we spent a fitful and restless night hidden in a deep ravine.

The following night we tried to cross the highway again in a smaller group consisting mainly of well-armed combatants. We used a different route and approached with great caution, but the soldiers had gone and we managed to cross without incident. We continued on that night to the subzone of Chapin, and I departed without further incident several days later for the capital city.

By the time I returned to the liberated zones in October 1985, the air war had become the government's favored tactical weapon against the guerrilla forces and the diminishing civilian population that supported them. The strategy of the Salvadoran government and its U.S. advisors was to continue to drive the civilian population out of the liberated zones and convert these areas into free fire zones where aviation and heavy artillery could bomb indiscriminately without recriminations from local and international human rights defenders. The Salvadoran military had also finally succumbed to the pressures of U.S. advisors urging the adoption of guerrilla tactics learned during the war in Vietnam, replacing large-scale military incursions with the use of smaller and more agile long-range reconnaissance patrols.

These specially trained twoor three-man units, referred to by their Spanish acronym as the "PRAL," were dropped by helicopter deep into guerrilla controlled territory with the mission of detecting command positions and calling in airstrikes. In response to this threat, the FMLN had dismantled its own large-scale battalions and dispersed its forces throughout the country. Most of the liberated zones were still fiercely defended by FMLN units, but with the civilian inhabitants fleeing en masse and guerrilla forces dispersed, the lines of battle became more obscured.

The civilian population in the Felipe Peña Front, and in other war zones of the country, had been dwindling gradually over the years. At the time of my visit, only a small but hardcore group of leather-tough and determined FMLN supporters remained. The larger part of the population, exhausted by the cruel realities of five years of brutal civil war, had fled in a steady stream to church-run centers for the displaced in the capital city, to Betania, where I had worked, or to the refugee camps in Honduras, run by the UN High Commission for Refugees (UNHCR).

In 1985, Antonio and Teresa continued to reside in their small adobe house in the village of Amayo, but the civilian population in that subzone had been reduced to just a few families. The popular militia, with no one to defend, was incorporated into the guerrilla army, but Antonio refused to join, as it would have meant abandoning his family and assuming an exclusively military role. In spite of his long years of commitment to the struggle, he was still essentially a civilian at heart. His decision was not well received by a new and younger local guerrilla leadership and continued to generate conflict between his family and the FMLN cadres in the months that followed.

October had been filled with guerrilla victories. The military had suffered over 800 casualties on the battlefield and had been profoundly embarrassed by the FMLN's demonstrated ability to concentrate its forces quickly and overrun any military target it chose. Urban commandos of the FMLN had also captured the daughter of President Napoleon Duarte in the streets of the capital city. They later negotiated her release in return for 23 political prisoners and safe conduct out of the country for close to 100 seriously wounded guerrilla combatants. The government was anxious to deal the FMLN a mighty blow in a desperate effort to regain the initiative in the war. Their first opportunity occurred during the early weeks of my fourth trip into the war zones of the Felipe Peña Front.

Early on the morning of October 29, I arrived at the guerrilla command headquarters in the village of San Antonio and sat resting alone on a large rock, still breathing heavily and sweating profusely from a grueling walk the previous night. As I set my backpack on the ground and wiped the sweat from my face, a military helicopter flew slowly overhead in a northerly direction towards Chalatenango. I felt no immediate danger, as the thick foliage of the trees camouflaged our base from the air, and it was common for helicopters to pass in this way. The aircraft suddenly turned, however, and headed south, and everyone in the camp began watching with a bit more interest and concern.

The helicopter flew out of sight, and I had begun to relax again when the skies suddenly thundered with A-37 Dragon Fly jets. The camp came to life as *compañeros* scurried to gather weapons and personal gear and we all headed down the mountainside toward the protection of the ravines below. The jets circled only once, then began to dive, and a quiet sunny morning suddenly erupted with the explosions of 500-pound bombs crashing around us. We ran as fast as we could down the slick mountain path, throwing ourselves to the ground with the sound of each jet's dive. The bombers were then joined by helicopter gunships, flying in low formation over our position, launching rockets and machine gunning the area. In the confusion of the moment, everyone scattered, and I suddenly found myself alone.

I was searching the skies on bended knee for some sign of what was coming when a helicopter suddenly hovered directly above me at the level of the treetops and began launching its rockets at a target somewhere on the near horizon. The roar of the engines and the scream of the rockets were deafening, but I was reassured by the realization that it was not firing directly at me. In that instant, guerrilla commanders Ramon Torres and Facundo Guardado came charging down the mountain path, along with a small contingent of combatants assigned to their security. I had been unaware that they were in the camp until that moment, and it suddenly occurred to me that a PRAL unit on the ground had detected their presence and called in the airstrike.

Upon finding me alone, one of Facundo's bodyguards shouted out in anger, *"qué puta estás haciendo allí? ¡Corre!"* ("what the hell are you doing there? Run!"). I joined the group in full sprint down the remaining mountainside, feeling a bit embarrassed, but with a naive feeling of safety at the knowledge that I was in the company of members of the highest level of the guerrilla command who would surely make it safely through the day.

The bombing eventually subsided and Special Forces units began dropping from helicopters over the guerrilla camp. Additional troops were dropped around us in a wide perimeter, and Hughes 500 helicopters strafed the forests where I had been kneeling just minutes before. We knew that our own safety lay somewhere between the area around the camp, now being strafed, and the circle of government troops approaching from the periphery, so we stopped on a small hillside at a point between the two while Ramon Torres sent out his scouts to explore the surrounding area.

The Hughes 500s swooped into the ravines like the birds of prey that they were, and followed our path up the hillside with machine guns roaring. With each approach, the firing stopped just yards from our position, and on several occasions, as the aircraft swerved above us, I caught a quick glimpse of the young pilot's face.

Minutes later, the scouts returned with news that government troops were headed in our direction, so we risked moving a short distance down the hillside where thicker brush would provide better cover, trying as we did so to avoid the path of the Hughes 500s. We remained in hiding until the skies fell silent several hours later. Huey choppers then began landing throughout the area airlifting the government troops as we moved cautiously from our hiding place and slowly worked our way back to the guerrilla camp.

It was several weeks later, during this same visit in October 1985, that the enormous cruelty of the war came crashing home once again. Ironically, the day had started out in splendor, with a bright blue sky, a cooling wind, sunshine and the promise of a momentary respite from a bloody confrontation now in its fifth year. But the radiance was stolen by the lingering evils still dominating our perilous world.

I was visiting with the *compañeros* of Ruben's unit in San Antonio, still feeling triumphant at the failed attempts of government forces to entrap and annihilate us several days before. I hadn't seen Eva during this visit, but I knew that she was assigned to the subzone and asked about her whereabouts with the hopes of a glimpse at those lucent brown eyes before returning to the capital city. At the sound of her name, the *compañeros* fell silent. Then, at my prodding, they shared the agonizing news that Eva had been killed in April by machine gun fire from a Huey helicopter gunship, the same that had been hovering over my position days earlier.

I was struck with disbelief at first and clung to a small hope that we were talking about different people. The *compañeros* knew Eva well, however, and when they acknowledged that she had come from a village near El Paisnal, I knew that there could be no mistake. I thought immediately of Teresa and Antonio. Surely they knew the horrible news by now and I wanted to flee in that instant to their village of Amayo to share their grief once again.

With a growing sense of trepidation, I then asked about Blanca and received a second blow. Blanca, the oldest daughter of Santos and Fidelia, had also been killed by government aircraft. She was eight months pregnant at the time, about to give birth to her first baby, and had been caught off guard resting in the shade of a large tree while the *compañeros* of her unit finished their morning exercises in the ravines below.

A Cessna Push and Pull had suddenly appeared overhead and, without warning, launched its rockets over the guerrilla camp. The first rocket fell within a few yards of Blanca, and razor sharp pieces of shrapnel flew in all directions. Several large fragments struck her in the mid-section and tore open her protruding belly.

The rest of the *compañeros* heard her screams and came running to find her lying by the tree in a pool of blood, her intestines and unborn baby on the ground beside her. The baby died almost immediately, but Blanca underwent surgery and her recovery seemed hopeful. Several days later, however, there was a major incursion of government troops into the subzone and the guerrilla units were forced to evacuate. Blanca was carried by hammock, but her wounds were too severe to resist the brisk pace and she suffered an agonizing death one evening early into the *guinda*.

I was heartbroken and enraged at the news of both deaths. I had seen nothing but virtue in these bright young women, along with their immeasurable capacity for sacrifice and valor. I had learned much about personal loss during my years in Central America, but I was still naive enough to hope that young souls such as these would somehow be spared the ultimate consequences of their struggle. I had been bolstered by the understanding that the hardships and dangers of the armed conflict were simply an extension of the crudeness and deprivation of normal peasant life, hoping that the same inner strength and spiritual grace that had upheld them in their earlier years would get them through this war.

I did not have the opportunity to talk with Teresa and Antonio about Eva's death until many years later. I learned after the war, however, that it had broken Teresa's indomitable spirit for a long time. As she had done with me when her brother Santos had been killed on the hillside of Mirandilla, she tried at first to hide the enormous depth of her sorrow from her children. She was often found weeping alone in some dark corner of the house, however, in the midst of her daily chores, and Antonio's words were never enough to comfort a heart filled with such longing for one more moment of a first daughter's laughter.

As the war progressed, conditions in Piedra continued to deteriorate for Antonio and Teresa and finally became unbearable.

Repopulation efforts were igniting hope in the war zones around the country, but this couple, worn and ragged from their long years of struggle, was feeling worried and alone and finally decided to send their children to live with civilian families on the outskirts of the subzone. Army incursions were now occurring every 15 days on the average, and they were unable to continue to submit their only remaining treasures to the dangers and hardship of perpetual *guinda*.

Several months later, the children were transferred to the Church-sponsored center for displaced families, Domus Mariae, in the capital city. Teresa suffered enormously from the absence of her remaining daughters and son. In late 1986 she requested authorization from local guerrilla commanders to visit her children, but her request was turned down. After so many years of commitment and sacrifice, she was infuriated by the decision, and subsequent conversations with Antonio led to the wrenching decision to leave Piedra on her own. She was the last civilian woman to go.

Early into the following year, Antonio himself made the difficult decision to leave. He was still committed to the revolutionary effort, but in the absence of the civilian population in Piedra, he saw little role for himself. His relationship with the new guerrilla leadership in the subzone also continued to deteriorate. After so many years as a clandestine warrior, he was fearful of the capital city and the dangers of compromising his family, now living in the refugee center of Domus Mariae. With the knowledge that his family was safe, he traveled to the home of his oldest brother in the distant coastal province of Sonsonate. There, he borrowed some money and purchased a small piece of land, built a simple adobe house, and planted his first crop of corn and beans.

It was six months before Teresa finally found him, and several months after that before the entire family was reunited. I searched for them in vain for almost a year before finally tracking them down in their new home near the town of Metalío towards the end of 1988. My first visit was to be a surprise, but, ever alert, they spotted me from a distance as I climbed the wooded hill leading up to their house. They came running to greet me, and we hugged and laughed wildly, with everyone speaking at once as we slipped easily into the familiarity which had characterized

Antonio with Gladys, Teresa (holding Rosita), Isabel and Aníbal
in their new home in Metalío.

our friendship a world away in war-torn Piedra.

I brought pictures on this first visit that I had taken years earlier, and Teresa and Antonio lingered over them with a mixture of rapture and sorrow. And they paused with remorse at the only photos in existence of Eva, their beloved first child. Towards the end of their first year in Metalío, Teresa had given birth to a fifth daughter, Rosita, and she displayed Eva's picture to the small baby girl, introducing the sister that she would never know.

We ate hot *tortillas* and beans for lunch and again for dinner, and I slept with them that night as I had so many times before in Piedra. It was grand to see them under these new circumstances, with simple but adequate housing and without the fear of government incursions, heavy artillery barrages, or bombing. The war was still raging, but this family had done its part and had made the ultimate sacrifice in the effort to bring the struggle to a victorious conclusion. The only challenge that remained for them now was to reconstruct their lives and somehow reconcile themselves to their enormous losses. The children were attending school and doing well, in accordance with Teresa's wishes. They were still dirt poor, living only on the crops that Antonio scratched from the dry dusty earth, but they had begun to find happiness again.

CHAPTER SEVEN

The Difficult Path to Peace

In 1986, a unique and perhaps unprecedented event in the modern history of El Salvador occurred. Thousands of families driven from their villages of origin by indiscriminate government bombing and scorched earth military tactics began to return en masse in the midst of war. Internally displaced families throughout the country had been returning quietly on an individual basis over the years. But the process begun in 1986 was massive and public, changing forever the dynamic of the war and transforming the role of the civilian population from that of frightened victims in endless flight to staunch human rights advocates capable of defending themselves in face-to-face encounters with the military. And, with increasing frequency, the ones without the guns won.

The displaced population of El Salvador was commonly categorized into three different groups. The first group consisted of dispersed individuals and families who had fled their villages of origin in the countryside seeking safety in towns and cities throughout the country with little organization and support. A second and more visible group resided in centers for the displaced typically run by the Catholic Church, such as the seminary of San José de la Montaña, La Basílica, Domus Mariae and San Roque, all opened in 1980. Centers formed in later years included Fe y Esperanza of the Lutheran Church and the large open-air center in Betania in the province of La Libertad, where I had worked between 1982 and 1983. A third group fled to the United States, Nicaragua, Costa Rica, Panama and Honduras.

There were four large camps in Honduras under the auspices of the UNHCR. All were enclosed with barbed wire fencing in a troubling resemblance to detention centers, with limited mobility and constant harassment from a hostile Honduran military. Mesa Grande, the largest of the camps, located 15 miles from the Salvadoran border in the Honduran province of Ocotepeque, was he preferred destination of fleeing villagers from Chalatenango and the subzones of the Felipe Peña Front. It eventually grew to a population of over 11,000 people. The second largest camp was Colomoncagua, just three miles from the Salvadoran border in the Honduran province of Intibuca, with over 8,000 refugees from El Salvador's eastern province of Morazan. San Antonio was third with a population of approximately 1500 people and nearby Buenos Aires had a population of fewer than 500 people.

The formal process of repopulation actually began in 1985 with the return of displaced families to the town of Tenancingo in the subzone of Radiola, where I had witnessed the slaughter of civilians by government warplanes two years earlier. Resettlement efforts to this town were hindered from the beginning by a paternalistic and top-down process of negotiations among the town's economic elite, the Catholic Church hierarchy and the military, and ended up benefiting only 800 people of an original target population of 6,000. Nevertheless, the project raised national and international awareness of the phenomenon of forced displacement and paved the way for more participative grass-roots efforts to follow.

A smaller but better organized process of repopulation, organized and directed by displaced families themselves, began in June of the following year with the return of approximately 120 people to the town of San Jose Las Flores in the northern province of Chalatenango. One month later, displaced families returned to San Antonio El Barillo in the subzone of Guazapa, Cuscatlan province. Both events were highly publicized with political ramifications that went well beyond their scope in terms of numbers, and their relative successes offered a model that would be followed on a more massive scale over the years to come.

Encouraged by the repopulation of El Barillo, survivors from the horrible massacres in Copapayo and nearby San Nicolas that I had documented in November 1983 decided also to return. The route home involved crossing Lake Suchitlan in the same small launches that were used in their flight three years earlier and brought back all the memories of that horrible moment. To make matters worse, as the refugees gathered in the town church of Suchitoto in the last leg of their journey home, they were surrounded by the military and detained, along with their supplies, for almost a week. In spite of the difficulties, however, Copapayo became another pioneer in the efforts of repatriation in the subzones of Radiola and Guazapa and sparked similar initiatives on the part of communities throughout these subzones.

Up until mid 1987, the repopulation movement had been made up primarily of internally displaced families, but between 1987 and 1990 over 15,000 people returned from the four camps in Honduras in six different repatriation events, frequently facing ardent (and sometimes violent) opposition from the Salvadoran government and its military. The Catholic Church, Protestant churches, international development agencies, media and international solidarity played a key role in the process. A new kind of popular organization also emerged at the national level to defend the rights of returning communities.

The Christian Committee for the Displaced of El Salvador (CRIPDES) and its sister organization, the CORDES Foundation, had been formed in 1984 to struggle for the rights of displaced civilians from the war-torn areas of Chalatenango province and the Felip Peña Front. Between 1986 and 1991, they coordinated the repopulation of communities throughout the country and promoted small-scale development initiatives to make life in these communities more sustainable.

In the years that followed, other nongovernmental organizations began to emerge, including the Association for Social and Economic Development of Santa Marta (ADES), the REDES Foundation and the Association of "Patronatos" for the Development of the Communities of Morazan and San Miguel (PADECOMSM).

The repopulation movement at the national level had a profound impact on the political as well as the military situation in El Salvador's civil war. It raised awareness and brought international attention to the plight of civilians in the war zones. It also brought massive relief and development resources to regions of the country historically abandoned to poverty and despair and which the government and military were attempting to convert into free-fire zones to eliminate the guerrilla threat.

The repopulated communities from the camps in Honduras brought lessons of self-government, democracy and citizen participation, along with job skills, literacy, new levels of self-esteem, social cohesion and a development model that instilled hope for a better life. They were a threat to the counterinsurgency plans of the Salvadoran government and the U.S. State Department, but also presented a new challenge to the FMLN.

They had little in common with the populations who had fled their country of origin years earlier. Some had been born in Honduras or had children who had been born there. They had faced the Honduran military and won on numerous occasions. They had learned about basic human rights and how to negotiate with an opponent, and were experienced in democratic forms of community organization. They were more cosmopolitan and accustomed to dealing with cultures from other parts of the world and they were resistant to any form of manipulation from either side in the conflict. What they still clearly had in common with FMLN fighters, cadres and civilians who had remained behind in El Salvador was the memory of human suffering and loss which continued to inspire a vehement hatred of the military.

Throughout the repopulation process, the army continued to harass and accuse the returned populations of being "terrorists" aligned with the FMLN, and they systematically blocked access for reconstruction materials, medical supplies, food, personnel and visiting delegations from other countries. They harassed anyone working with repopulated communities and required special passes provided exclusively by Military Intelligence for visits by foreigners to conflict areas. In spite of the restrictions, however, the conflict zones of El Salvador began to open up. International solidarity was growing and more foreign eyes were watching. In the process, the modest efforts of my earlier years to build a viable war economy based on agricultural production and smallscale industry in the Felipe Peña Front gradually blossomed into a multimillion-dollar aid and development effort funded and defended by international donors.

Taking advantage of the process of repopulation in the subzone of Guazapa, Ana Menjivar, the courageous leader from San Rafael La Bermuda with whom I had coordinated so closely in Betania, settled in the lowlands along with her children, her mother and several other families from Betania that I also knew well. Their return to Cuscatlan province was motivated by the desire to be closer to her brothers, Herman and Rodrigo, who had joined the guerrilla forces and were camped on the slopes of the nearby Guazapa Volcano. I had known both of them well during my years in Betania and was honored when Ana informed me that her youngest brother, Herman, had taken my name as his *nom de guerre* (war name). I visited all of these families frequently in their new home during the years that followed and often found Herman with them, armed and in uniform, when the army was not present in the subzone.

Ana's husband had been killed in an ambush during our first days together in Betania and her older brother was killed in combat shortly after. The tragedy of the war had always followed this family, but it was still an enormous shock when her younger brother Rodrigo was killed in Guazapa in 1986. Although the family was now nearby in the lowlands, his body was never recovered. Years later, in 1991, Herman was killed and I rushed to Guazapa to accompany Ana and her mother in his burial.

As we laid his remains to rest in an open field behind their home, Ana shared the details of her youngest brother's death. She explained that Herman had come down from his camp on the slopes of the Guazapa volcano two days earlier, along with several other combatants on a reconnaissance mission to determine the movements of government soldiers who had recently penetrated the subzone. He made the mistake that he had frequently committed in the past by visiting his mother and sister, but was surprised on this occasion by a platoon of soldiers who had been undetected by the guerrilla squad. He was shot while running from the house, but fought off the soldiers from behind a large rock until his ammunition ran out. He was then killed and mutilated and the lieutenant in charge was about to set his body ablaze when Ana bravely confronted him and demanded her brother's remains. It was just six months before the end of the war.

Between 1980 and 1987, the United States pumped close to three billion dollars into El Salvador, ranking this country third worldwide among U.S. recipients of foreign aid. Almost 75% of this aid was earmarked, either directly or indirectly, for military purposes or for political efforts to win the hearts and minds of the Salvadoran people. The Salvadoran army was built up from its original size of 17,000 men to over 60,000 troops, battling a guerrilla force estimated, at the peak of the war, at no more than 10,000 combatants.

By 1987, this same army had killed over 65,000 unarmed civilians and would go on to kill 10,000 more before the war was finally ended. Close to a million people – a fifth of the population – had been displaced from their villages of origin as a result of government incursions and indiscriminate government bombing. Most were rural poor, like Antonio and Teresa.

To apply these same percentages to the population of the United States at the time would mean a death toll of 9 million people with 60 million displaced. The total population forced to abandon their homes by the war in El Salvador grew to exceed, percentage-wise, the displaced population of Vietnam. Another 6,000 people, chiefly peasant, labor and student activists, were "disappeared" by anticommunist death squads, and thousands more were held in dark dank prisons, arrested without a warrant, like Ana Eugenia's cousin Juan Carlos, tortured and held without trial.

In the midst of the violence, the Salvadoran government and U.S. counterinsurgency experts continued their efforts to build an image of an incipient democracy and justify ongoing support for the war. Their efforts enjoyed many years of success in the U.S. Congress and among the American population in general. In El Salvador, however, it was more difficult to convince people that they had a government representing the popular will.

More than half the rural peasants were still landless, malnourished, and living in abject poverty. Fifty percent of the population was illiterate. Urban poor were unemployed, with inadequate housing, health and educational services. And all efforts at organization and protest were defined as "communistinspired insurgency" and violently repressed. In 1987, a poll conducted by the Jesuit University in San Salvador found that fewer than 9% of Salvadorans considered that they were living under "conditions of freedom and democracy."

Elsewhere in Central America, a shared history of poverty, repression and U.S. intervention produced massive social protest and generated an agenda for change that coincided with the demands of the Salvadorans. El Salvador was clearly in the vanguard, but no country was left untouched by political unrest.

Honduras became a key player in U.S. efforts to halt the advance of revolution in the region. By the mid-1980s, under pressure from the Reagan administration, Honduras was occupied by three foreign armies, in flagrant violation of its own constitution. Entire battalions of the Salvadoran infantry were trained there, including the infamous Atlacatl battalion, responsible for dozens of large-scale massacres against its own people. The Contra army, built and trained by the CIA to overthrow the popular Sandinista government in Nicaragua, used southern Honduras as its rearguard. And over 1,200 U.S. troops were stationed at the Honduran Air Force base at Palmerola.

The country was described at one point as a "U.S. aircraft carrier in Central America" for lending key air bases around the country to U.S. military strategists. Honduran citizens, indignant at the loss of national sovereignty, began to stage massive protests against U.S. intervention and the increasing levels of militarization within Honduran society itself. Urban women, along with peasant and worker coalitions, teachers and students, produced a steady stream of anti-war propaganda and protest. They called for the immediate removal of American troops and an end to the use of Honduran soil for U.S. military aggression against the peoples of the region.

Between visits to the war zones of El Salvador, I visited Honduras frequently during my years as Field Representative for the American Friends Service Committee and had ample opportunity to observe the impact of U.S. counterinsurgency policies on this once-sleepy and docile "banana republic." To preserve political stability, special counterinsurgency battalions were created within the Honduran military, in spite of the fact that there was little threat of an armed insurgency on Honduran soil at the time. There were opposition armed groups to be sure, with names like the Cinchoneros, the Lenchos, the Revolutionary Workers' Party of Central America (PRTC) and the Morazanista National Liberation Front (FMLN of Honduras), but they were small and isolated, with little chance of articulating a force capable of challenging the powers that be. The real target was, again, the increasingly organized and vociferous civilian population.

Government intelligence bodies began to infiltrate and divide peasant and worker organizations. Key leaders who could not be bought off were assassinated outright. The extensive and awakening indigenous population, allied with the Afro Caribbean Garifuna population in a struggle for land, was violently repressed, and women's organizations defending national sovereignty and demanding demilitarization, like Visitación Padilla, were accused of terrorism and subjected to constant harassment and heavy surveillance.

As air and military bases continued to be built or enlarged throughout the country to meet the needs of U.S. counterinsurgency efforts, peasant communities were displaced and their homes were often destroyed. When I traveled to the rural areas, I would occasionally visit these communities and hear horrific tales of U.S. army engineers bulldozing entire villages.

On one such occasion, I accompanied a delegation of North Americans organized by the American Friends Service Committee to the Aguacate air base in Olancho province. This base had recently been expanded and modernized by the U.S. to supply Contra forces attacking Nicaragua, and the peasant families displaced in the process, now residing on the perimeter of the new airfield, described to us in startling detail how their homes had been demolished and crops destroyed. Their permanent housing had been replaced by temporary shelters of dried sticks, rusted tin, cardboard and plastic sheets, forming a shantytown of one-room shacks. Both children and adults suffered from severe levels of malnutrition. When asked about the availability of food, a gaunt old woman who had welcomed us into her humble dwelling raised a long bony finger and pointed to the new landing strip less than 100 yards from her doorway. Resilient green stalks of rice were fighting their way through the heavily packed earth along the edges of the airstrip, and the woman's voice trembled as she explained that this had once been her rice field and only source of daily sustenance. She then pointed to a nearby sign hanging from a barbed wire fence surrounding the airstrip that read "Trespassers will be shot on sight."

To the south, in bordering Nicaragua, a guerrilla coalition calling itself the Sandinista National Liberation Front (FSLN) had won a military victory in 1979 against a brutal dictatorship which had been placed in office by U.S. marines 40 years earlier. The FSLN later became a legal political party and was eventually voted into power in internationally supervised elections. But the reforms promoted by the new government to eradicate poverty, and its friendship with Cuba and Eastern European nations, were perceived by the Reagan administration as threatening to U.S. interests.

Without ever formally declaring war on the new regime, the United States Government spent millions of dollars to build a surrogate army, called the Contras, in an attempt to overthrow it. CIA operatives mined the country's ports in an effort to curtail trade and aid from Europe and elsewhere while the Contra army, based in Honduras, attacked rural agricultural cooperatives established by the Nicaraguan government, and systematically assassinated young volunteers who were teaching literacy and health in the most remote areas of the country.

In Washington, the Contras were referred to by the Reagan administration as "freedom fighters." But everyone in Central

America – including foreign governments allied with the U.S. – knew that they were nothing more than a well-trained band of paid assassins. When Nicaragua brought a case for damages against the United States before the World Court, this judicial body ruled in its favor, but the Reagan administration rejected the court's jurisdiction, arguing that "vital U.S. interests" were at stake.

The American Friends Service Committee provided educational outreach to North American people and policymakers and solidarity with Nicaraguan NGOs trying to make a revolutionary project work. We focused our efforts, however, on the Atlantic coast in eastern Nicaragua, promoting dialogue and non-violent solutions to a legitimate indigenous struggle for autonomy that the U.S. government was trying to link with the Contra war raging in the north and western regions of the country.

In Guatemala, Mayan people battled against an army unrestrained by international eyes and pressure. The world community was focused elsewhere – primarily on El Salvador and Nicaragua – where U.S. intervention generated intensive news coverage and provoked wide solidarity with the people of those nations. In the meantime, in the highlands and jungles of western and northern Guatemala, a radically applied policy of scorched earth leveled over 440 villages of indigenous people and slaughtered close to 100,000 innocent civilians. I visited the conflict regions of Guatemala in the northern province of Quiché, areas where I had worked years earlier with Catholic Relief Services, and was able to witness the conditions of life for thousands of Mayan families resisting the counterinsurgency efforts of a government bent on their extermination. I traveled into the towering and freezing mountains around Nebaj, where I had once supported indigenous communities involved in the production of honey, and into the steaming Ixcan jungles further to the north, where CRS had once supported a budding cooperative movement. These regions had been sparsely populated prior to the war because of the harsh setting and a lack of access. But they were now dotted with transient communities fleeing an army who viewed all civilians, especially the indigenous ones, as the enemy.

The communities in the war zones of Guatemala were much more isolated and difficult to access than those of El Salvador. There were no roads at the time, and the thick forests and jungles surrounding the communities were filled with government troops. They had little communication with the outside world, and the outside world knew little of the horrors and hardship of their daily struggle for survival.

The soil was good for planting in the northern jungles of the Ixcan, but fields could not be cleared for risk of being detected from the air. As in neighboring El Salvador, frequent incursions by government troops and aerial bombardment were a constant threat, along with poisonous snakes, malaria and a frightening strain of leprosy which took a heavy toll, especially among young children.

From the Ixcan jungles of northern Guatemala to the English-speaking Atlantic coast of Nicaragua, the isthmus rumbled like the chain of volcanoes that marked its every horizon, and its soil ran red with the blood of innocent human beings determined to have their freedom. In the midst of the horror, the American Friends Service Committee pursued its Quaker mission of bearing witness and supporting the cause for justice and peace.

As part of my work with the American Friends Service Committee, I would travel each year to the United States to speak to U.S. church groups, academics, civil society organizations, politicians and public media on Central America. These visits were part of AFSC's ongoing efforts to educate the American public and speak the truth about U.S. policy in the region. For me personally, they also served as an escape from the daily stress of war.

They provided an opportunity to reconnect with my fellow countrymen and women, and it was during these trips that I began to rediscover the goodness in the hearts of the American people, as well as the naive but relentless trust that many still had in their government. Some listeners were bewildered by my testimony when it contradicted the government line or questioned the motives of key national leaders. Many were angered, although they knew not with whom. Some chafed at the thought of having been duped, and more than a few believed what they heard and became staunch and committed advocates for peace.

It was an awakening for me as well, an opportunity to re-evaluate my own stereotypes and prejudices, a chance to open a heart that had become hardened and cold. I realized for the first time how polarized America had become on the issue of Central America, and how many dedicated human beings fought to hold back the tide of a new Vietnam. I rediscovered my roots and received the gift of hope from men and women moved by the same values as mine. We were in a battle together to bring to an end policies built upon arrogance and fear.

Following a talk in 1988 at Harvard University in Boston, I suddenly realized that I was within an easy drive of Hingham, the town where I had grown up but had not seen in almost three decades. I rented a car and made the short trip with ease, amazed at how much smaller the world had become since the days of my youth. I drove down Main Street, past the house where I had once lived, and visited the church where I had attended Sunday services. I found the high school where I had spent my days as a "cake eater," then drove to the harbor where I had lingered on warm summer nights holding hands on the pier with a young blonde cheerleader named Cherrie Rice.

To my visitor's eye, the town hadn't changed a bit in all the years that I had been away. But I was deeply amazed at the neatness and order. The town had none of the disarray of poverty to which I had become accustomed in Liberia and Central America. There were no trash-strewn streets with roving packs of rabid dogs. There was no sense of street crime, no walls with razor wire to protect the homes of the wealthy. There were no heavily armed police and private guards in the doorways of private businesses. There were no marginal neighborhoods with houses built from cardboard boxes and rusted zinc sheeting. There were no hungry children wandering the streets in search of something to beg or steal. And there were no families residing in the filth of extreme poverty struggling in a furious daily battle for survival.

People walked about with a calm that spoke of well-being, and it all left me feeling out of place. I was a bird who had flown too far south for the winter, and was having a hard time finding my nest.

I located some of my old classmates in the phonebook and felt a sense of relief to learn that I was still remembered in my home town. One friend called another in a long chain of announcements that a "long-lost McKinley" had finally come home. And we soon had a house full of aging men and women, drunk with the joys of reunion and dancing wildly to the "oldies but goodies" (the *rokirol*) of our high school years.

The next morning, there was time for more serene conversation, although we spoke mostly of a past that we had shared years ago rather than risk losing the magic of this very special moment. The conversation finally touched upon professions, however, and I fumbled through a description of my career in international development fearing that few would understand the true direction that my life had taken.

Crisp white snow covered the ground and glistened in the morning sun as we talked in the warmth of friendship and a crackling fire about places we had been and things that we had done. Carole was a highly successful executive with Blue Cross. Her husband, Phil, the captain of our high school football team, was retiring from a factory job that he had held for the past 30 years. Greg was an executive on the fast track with a large corporation based in Boston. Lynn had just changed jobs and was now selling cosmetics. Maggie, who used to sing in a rock and roll band with my brother and me, was in management at Delta Airlines. Patsy, a computer expert, was in the process of changing careers and falling in love with a financial analyst. Pat, my older brother's ex-wife, owned and ran a highly successful restaurant called Strawberry Fare. Their career paths responded to a different world and a different logic than mine, and the twain would never meet. But I felt blessed by their friendship and thankful for the reminder of the saner days of my youth.

Returning to El Salvador from the U.S. was a cold reawakening to the cruelty of a seemingly endless war, but I tried in vain during my first days back to hold onto the warmth and the wonderful memories of a past too elusive to recapture. I entered the liberated zones for the sixth time in February of 1989 at the ripe old age of 45. The decision to return was not an easy one. I had been blessed in May of the previous year with the birth of my first son, David Miguel, and my heart was awakening to the discoveries and joys of fatherhood. I had found myself deeply in love with this new spirit in a way that I had never experienced, but the war was still raging and the moment was key, with growing hopes for peace that would bring a better world for my son. So, after much soul searching, I decided to go one last time.

El Salvador was in the midst of an increasingly intense search for a light at the end of the tunnel in a war that had dragged on for more than nine years, taking thousands of lives, destroying the economy and contributing to levels of political polarization that would haunt the country for decades. People in the war zones, as well as in areas controlled by the government, were beginning to show signs of exhaustion. Both sides in the conflict were finding it increasingly difficult to attract new recruits to replace continuing losses on the battlefield. The challenge was especially acute in the liberated zones of the FMLN where humble peasant families who had lost too much in a war that had lasted too long were reluctant to lend their remaining sons and daughters to a cause that offered little hope of victory in the near horizon.

The civilian population throughout the country was pushing for dialogue and a negotiated solution to the war, a position strongly promoted by the Catholic Church, the Central American University (UCA) of the Jesuits and many other important institutions and civil society organizations from all social classes. In spite of this growing demand for peace, however, important actors, some of them in Washington and others in El Salvador, continued to hold out for total victory.

The FMLN had presented a new set of proposals for dialogue and both sides in the conflict were giving lip service to the idea of peace talks, but each side was attempting to fortify its negotiating position by demonstrating its strength on the battle-field, generating immense obstacles to the difficult task of building adequate confidence and trust.

In the early months of 1989, right-wing death squads began to attack key proponents of dialogue, bombing the offices of labor organizations and the homes of important political figures who were speaking out in favor of peace. On February 15, the office of the Union of Salvadoran Workers was bombed by a right-wing paramilitary organization calling itself the "Maximiliano Hernandez Martinez Brigade," taking the name of the military dictator responsible for the massacre of almost 30,000 indigenous peasants in 1932. On the 22nd of that month, another bomb destroyed the offices of the National Federation of Workers' Unions (FENASTRAS), causing the death of ten workers.

Undeterred, the FMLN continued to press for a negotiated settlement, suggesting that upcoming presidential elections, planned for March, be postponed until minimal conditions for assuring an open, participative, democratic process could be put into place. The proposal was ignored, however, and elections were carried out as planned under the watchful eyes of the military, resulting in the election of millionaire businessman and right-wing ARENA candidate, Alfredo Cristiani.

In protest, urban commandos of the FMLN carried out a series of attacks on key figures within the Salvadoran right. Well-known oligarch Francisco Pecorini was assassinated on March 15th. Francisco Merino, recently named Vice-President of the Republic, suffered an attempted kidnapping in his home on April 14th; the country's Attorney General was killed by a car bomb on the 19th of that month and Jose Antonio Rodriquez Porth, a wealthy businessman and Minister of the Presidency, was assassinated on June 13th.

In the midst of the bloodshed, both sides continued to form their commissions for a national dialogue and eventually began talks to end the war on September 13th in Mexico. Then, on October 26th, the death squads bombed the home of the well-known left-wing politician and staunch advocate of dialogue, Ruben Zamora. Five days later, they struck again, bombing the offices of FENASTRAS a second time and killing 26 labor organizers. Among the dead was the highly respected and much loved labor leader Febe Velasquez.

The intent of the attacks was clearly to derail the incipient peace process and, in this, the new wave of aggression was finally successful. The FMLN, in response to the slaying of Velasquez, announced its withdrawal from peace talks on November 2nd, arguing that peace, under the current circumstances, remained an implausible dream. So the fighting continued, while the FMLN moved forward with plans to mount a guerrilla offensive at the national level before the end of the year.

At this complex and turbulent juncture, I had arranged a three-month trip to the liberated zones of northeastern El Salvador, travelling on this occasion to the province of Morazán, under the control of the People's Revolutionary Army (ERP), one of the five member organizations of the FMLN. I maintained my organic relationship with the Popular Liberation Forces (FPL), operating primarily in the western, central and northern provinces of El Salvador, but I was interested in observing and learning from the different styles and strategic vision that the ERP brought to the overall war effort, focusing, as usual, on the role of the civilian population.

Ana Eugenia was out of the country at the moment of my departure, so I left her a short note in our apartment which she kept through the years and shared with me during the writing of this book:

February 15, 1989

My love,

I had hoped to see you and David Miguel before leaving. I asked to postpone my trip a few days, but was told that because of an imminent increase in activity, including work stoppages, Thursday was the last possible day. So I go with a clear mind and a tranquil heart regarding my own decision, but with a burning desire to see the endearing smile and feel the carefree warmth of David Miguel just once more. I love him so deeply....

I plan to return by mid April in order to have some time together before your trip. If something should happen, I want my son, David Miguel, to know that he is the most precious thing I've ever seen, and that he has brought more joy and sense of worth to me in the past nine months than I've known in half a century on this earth. My hope for him is that he will continue to have your character and positive approach to life, and that he will love the people of this country and their tenacious struggle as much as I have.

All my love, and strong hugs to both of you, Andrés

I began my journey in the capital city of San Salvador, from where I travelled with ERP political cadres several hours to the eastern city of Santa Rosa de Lima. From there, we headed north, passing through several small towns and villages and gradually moving into the rural countryside. I was left in the home of a peasant family collaborating with the FMLN where I spent the night preparing for the long and dangerous journey into the controlled zones the following day.

February 12:

In the "campo" (countryside) again, working my way north with the help of the civilian population. I spent last night with a peasant family near the town of Corinto, and slept on the dirt floor of their one-room adobe house, in the company of the husband, his wife, four children, four cows, ducks, chickens and a huge, noisy and belligerent pig.

Saturday, February 18

Yesterday we crossed the Torola River and entered the controlled zones of Morazán. There is reportedly a strong presence of government troops in the area just north of the river, so we have been moving slowly and with great caution. Vast regions of the countryside are charred and burned, some still smoking, from fires set by the military to eliminate places for the guerrillas to hide.

Our destination was the large town of Perquín, where the FMLN maintained an important base in the northeastern part of the country. It took us over two weeks to get there due to our constant maneuvering to avoid government troops. The situation in Perquín upon my arrival was stable, secure, but tense. Northern Morazán province is physically beautiful, with towering mountains covered in thick pine forests. It borders with Honduras and, in 1989, was much more consolidated and secure than the subzones of the Felipe Peña Front. It had certainly seen its share of violence during the war, beginning with the massacre of almost 1,000 civilians in the village of El Mozote in December 1981, carried out by the U.S. trained Atlacatl Battalion. It was much further away from the capital city than the Felipe Peña Front, however, and for that reason was less threatening to military leaders preoccupied with the defense of San Salvador in any major guerrilla offensive. It was also more difficult to access, and was fiercely defended by a well-armed and highly experienced guerrilla army with a decade of strategic victories under its belt.

Unlike other war zones in the country, the displaced communities of Morazán had not returned to their villages of origin, choosing to remain in the refugee camp of Colomoncagua in Honduras, just three miles from the border. There was a sizable civilian population in Perquín and the surrounding villages at the time of my arrival, however, and they had begun to play a new and more strategic role in the dynamics of the war.

As in other repopulated areas of the country, the civilian population from this region no longer fled in *guinda* when government troops invaded the area, but would remain in their communities, demanding their rights as civilians, in accordance with the Geneva Convention. To implement this complex strategy, referred to as poder de doble cara (power with two faces), community leaders had to overcome their fears and learn to relate effectively with whatever "authority" was in place at a given moment in their territory. Authority, in this context, meant whoever had the weapons. When the FMLN controlled the zone, they were the authority, and during the brief and intermittent periods that the military occupied the area, they became the acknowledged authority.

It was a system that never would have been feasible in the bloody years between 1980 and 1986, but the U.S. had finally recognized that the systematic violation of human rights by security forces could not win the hearts and minds of the Salvadoran people. As a result, they had begun to pressure El Salvador's military to be more respectful of civilian rights. International human rights and development organizations, like Amnesty International, the UN, Human Rights Watch, the International Red Cross, the Washington Office on Latin America, Oxfam, American Friends Service Committee, and many others from the U.S. and Europe, had much to do with this important political initiative. National organizations, including CRIPDES, ADES, the Committee for Human Rights, Tutela Legal of the Archdiocese of San Salvador, the Red Cross, the Green Cross, Comandos de Salvamiento and others, also played a key role through their courageous and tenacious battle to defend the rights of non-combatants throughout the war.

As occurred during periods of military activity in the Felipe Peña Front, I was assigned to a communications unit, focused at the time on educating the civilian population in and around Perquín about the threat of electoral fraud in the upcoming presidential elections and demanding a negotiated solution to the war. These efforts were coordinated by an amazing young man named Lito, a highly skilled artist from a famous Salvadoran family of painters. He had been in the war since the early 1980s and was affectionately referred to by the *compañeros* as "el dibujante" (the one who draws).

I participated in his courses on communication in Perquín, along with a new generation of aspiring revolutionaries being trained in this area of work and anxious to define their role in the war effort. Following our training, we toiled together through many a long day and night producing the flyers and pamphlets that combatants of the guerrilla army would leave in the towns and villages they planned to occupy over the coming weeks and months.

Lito and I shared a love for music and art and talked incessantly about politics, culture and history. He was curious and open to my perspectives on the war and we had many a debate in good humor on who was the strongest and most important member organization of the FMLN, the FPL or the ERP. Over time, we built a close and trusting friendship that endures to this day.

Between February and May 1989 I continued working with Lito in communications. When the rhythm of work diminished, I visited the surrounding communities around Perquín, climbed the steep slopes of *La Montaña* (The Mountain) to visit the camp of the clandestine Radio Venceremos and spent time with renowned Catholic priests Rogelio Poncel and Miguel Ventura who, in the spirit of Rutilio Grande in El Paisnal, had been working since the early 1980s with Christian Base Communities in the war zones.

Lito

I was asked frequently during those days by political cadres of the ERP about the potential for a general insurrection in the cities of El Salvador if FMLN forces were able to take and hold important urban regions of the country, as had occurred in the successful Nicaraguan revolution of 1979. I knew why they were asking, as close friends within the FMLN had confided with me months earlier regarding the pending guerrilla offensive planned for November of that year, but I never acknowledged having this information. I simply responded honestly sharing my doubts and arguing that Salvadorans were different from Nicaraguans. My listeners' faces would frown with disappointment each time I shared my analysis on this theme, but I was proven correct months later as guerrilla forces battled in the major cities of the nation while disconcerted urban residents looked on in horror, unwilling to take up weapons and join the struggle.

On the night before my scheduled departure from Morazán province, I arrived in the town of Perquín with a small column of guerrilla combatants following several weeks travel in the towering mountains bordering Honduras. We slept that night on a hillside in the nearby *Escuela Militar* (guerrilla training school). I made the mistake of taking off my boots to sleep, and I awoke in the chill of the early morning with a horrible burning sensation in my right foot. Uncertain about what could cause such pain, I spent the rest of the night with my leg outstretched and leaning against a nearby tree.

The following morning, the pain was worse and my right leg had begun to swell. I was obviously suffering from some kind of animal bite, but no one could identify with certainty what kind of animal it might have been. Opinions included tarantula, black widow spider, poisonous snake and lizard.

Since I was scheduled to depart that day for Cacaopera, a town several days walk from Perquín where I could be met by vehicle and transported to San Salvador, it was decided that I should continue on with the guerrilla column departing that morning for the same destination, in spite of the growing pain. We maintained a fast pace during much of the morning with my leg continuing to swell, and I could feel the poison traveling up my body as I became increasingly feverish and weak.

In the late afternoon, we reached a small village of guerrilla collaborators and it was decided that I should remain there until the swelling and fever subsided. I spent the next few days lying in a hammock, delirious with fever, hallucinating with visions of government soldiers pointing their weapons at me from the nearby trees.

The fever finally subsided, but I was still unable to walk when intelligence reports informed us of a large contingency of government troops positioning themselves just south of the Torola River

In the cave in Morazan

for a massive incursion. The real soldiers were coming, so I had to move. The owner of the simple adobe house where I had been recovering, an incredibly strong peasant farmer, lifted me onto his shoulders as if I were a stuffed doll and carried me for several kilometers to an area where I was lowered by rope down a sheer rocky cliff and told to enter a small cave half-way down the ravine.

Several other *compañeros* were in the cave when I arrived. One had been severely wounded and had lost a lower leg to a land mine. Another had a perforated lung from the shrapnel of mortar fire. He still wore the shirt he had on at the time of his injury, now shredded with small holes where the shrapnel had penetrated his clothing and body. A young *sanitaria* had been assigned to care for us during our stay in the cave.

As the days passed, we were continually reminded to maintain silence, since the military now occupied much of the countryside surrounding our cave. The young *sanitaria* kept our wounds clean and told me on several occasions to "be strong like a guerrilla" as she scraped and scoured the infectious rotting tissue out of my wound each morning until it bled.

When the army finally departed, the young combatant who had lost his leg to a land mine was transferred out of the cave en route to Cuba where he would be given medical attention and a prosthetic. The *compañero* with the perforated lung also finally healed and was sent back to his unit. Only this *gringo* with a mysterious animal bite hadn't been moved.

As days turned into weeks, I became increasingly frustrated with my situation, not seeing any improvement in my swollen leg or the gaping wound which refused to heal on my foot. I was also concerned at the prospect of missing the first birthday of David Miguel, my first son, knowing that Ana Eugenia was away in Costa Rica at the time. I communicated all of this to local commanders and we agreed that it was the right moment to leave the cave and attempt the long and dangerous walk to Cacaopera, where I might find transport to the capital city; so we departed the following morning. I was initially placed on horseback, but my dangling leg began to swell again immediately; so I dismounted and walked for the next three days though the dry hilly countryside, with a tree branch for a crutch. My leg oozed a bright yellow liquid, but I learned that as long as I kept moving and flexing the leg muscles, the swelling was minimal.

We arrived the third day in a small village of Lenca people in the municipality of Sociedad, where we spent the night, then continued on the following day. I tried riding horseback again until the poor animal lost its footing on a narrow mountain path and tumbled into the ravine. I fell backwards over the horse's rump onto the dusty ground without injury and the horse was quickly recovered from the ravine; but I decided to go back to walking the remaining distance to Cacaopera.

We arrived just before noon on the outskirts of the town and realized immediately that it had been occupied by government troops. Soldiers lingered in the streets and parks as the *compañeros* rushed me into the first house we encountered and told me to rest while they hid their weapons and went off in search of transportation to San Salvador. The simple adobe structure where I waited turned out to be the home of a family collaborating with the FMLN and they invited me to lie down on their only bed. Excited at having a foreigner in their midst, several family members came up to greet me and wish me well. It was dangerous to linger, however, and I was told moments later to prepare myself for departure. I practiced walking for several minutes, moving back and forth in the tiny family parlor in an effort to loosen tense leg muscles and then passed swiftly through the door to the patio and climbed into a waiting pickup truck, smiling and waving at the nearby soldiers as I went.

By early evening that same day, I was in the western province of Santa Ana where my son, David Miguel, was entertaining his grandmother, aunts and cousins with the antics of a one-year-old. Seeing him after so many months was like being in heaven, but the joyous moment was cut short by a close friend and surgeon named Victor Umaña who informed me that I had incipient gangrene and needed hospital care urgently. Later that night while scrubbing the wound on my foot, Victor remarked on how clean it looked for someone who had spent the past several weeks in a cave, and I told him about the young and committed *sanitaria* who had scrubbed it twice daily until it bled, urging me each time to be silent and brave, like a guerrilla.

By the end of the decade of the 1980s in El Salvador, the guerrilla forces of the FMLN had demonstrated that they were capable of fighting a prolonged and perhaps endless struggle against the Salvadoran army and its U.S. backers. The U.S. embassy in San Salvador adjusted its own forecast for victory from two to eight years. At the continued refusal of the government and its U.S. mentors to negotiate a peaceful solution to the war, the FMLN launched a massive offensive at the national level in November 1989 which brought the fighting into the cities and left the Salvadoran and U.S. governments with their backs to the wall.

Guerrilla forces occupied all of the major towns and cities throughout the country, including San Salvador. In an act of desperation, the Armed Forces responded in the only way they knew, by bombing civilian communities – this time urban ones. And then they unleashed another massive wave of repression against civic leaders, academics, clergy and anyone else not clearly aligned with the government.

In the predawn hours of November 16, as fighting continued throughout the country, an army patrol from the nefarious Atlacatl Battalion entered the campus of the Central American University (UCA) and assassinated six Jesuit priests (Ignacio Ellacuria, the dean of the UCA; Segundo Montes; Martin Baró; Armando Lopez; Juan Ramón Moreno and Joaquin Lopez y Lopez), their housekeeper, Elba Ramos, and her 16-year-old daughter, Celina. The government immediately accused the FMLN of having perpetrated the crime, but a courageous university employee who had seen the soldiers on campus came forth with a detailed testimony that left little room for doubt about the true culprits.

It was clear that the decision to assassinate the priests – accused frequently by the military and the government of being the "intellectual authors of the revolution" – had been made at the highest levels within the military's Joint Chiefs of Staff. There were even some who insisted that then-president Alfredo Cristiani was involved, but there was no clear evidence to sustain this accusation. Logbooks recording arrivals and departures at the offices of the Joint Chiefs of Staff on the night before the murders were "lost" and no members of the military command were brought to justice until years later. The incident caused shock and horror around the world, however, and began to generate added pressure for a negotiated settlement to the war.

The offensive ended after several weeks of heavy fighting with hundreds of casualties and thousands more civilians displaced. It shocked the oligarchy, unaccustomed to gun battles in their own neighborhoods, and left the United States doubtful about the benefits of continuing a war that was now costing over a million dollars a day and showing no signs of being winnable.

I spent the first days of the offensive in coordination with FMLN cadres from the Felipe Peña Front, rendezvousing at points on the outskirts of the capital city where severely wounded combatants were receiving first aid and distributing those combatants among a chain of "safe houses" in San Salvador where collaborating physicians could provide more sophisticated medical attention. Several days after the fighting had stopped, as the smoke began to rise and as guerrilla units began to slip back to their camps in the rural countryside, I was deeply saddened by the news that my friend Lito from Morazán had lost his leg in combat and had been captured by the army.

He had told me once in confidence that he had never fired a shot in the war prior to 1989, but shortly after my departure from Perquín he was incorporated into the military structures of the ERP in preparation for the offensive. He was assigned the task of stashing ammunition and other military supplies in "safe houses" around the eastern city of San Miguel, the second largest city of El Salvador. Several nights into the fighting, as ammunition began to run low, Lito was chosen to cross enemy lines and recover part of the cache he had hidden. He was ambushed by government soldiers when he tried to return to the guerrilla-controlled sector,and his leg severed by fire from a 30-caliber machine gun. He had time to hide his weapons and remove his military garb before he was captured, and survived only because he was able to convince the soldiers that he was a civilian caught in the crossfire.

He was held for several months in a jail of the national police, during which time his leg was amputated just below the knee. I kept in touch with him through guerrilla channels during that time and was informed when he was finally released. I drove the next day to Morazán and picked up his pregnant wife, Jeaneth, whom I had met during my visit to Perquín months earlier and who was now living in the recently repopulated community of Segundo Montes just south of Perquín.

We drove together to the southern province of Usulutan, several hours away, where Lito had been living with an uncle since his release. He was suffering from obvious trauma at the loss of his leg and was drunk but coherent at the time of our arrival; so we loaded him into my jeep and set off for San Salvador. We passed through a number of military checkpoints en route and each time we were intensely interrogated by angry National Guard troops. It was due only to Jeaneth's pregnancy that we were not detained. We finally arrived at the safety of my home in San Salvador where Lito and Jeaneth remained for several months until we could arrange safe passage for them out of the country.

The geopolitical context which had served to justify the war was changing. The once threatening Soviet Union was gradually being dismantled. The "cold war" was evaporating, and El Salvador was losing its prime role as the "place to draw the line" against communism. A new urgency crept into U.S. policies, prioritizing a face-saving exit, and the message soon filtered down to the corrupt and recalcitrant political and military leadership of El Salvador that the days of juicy aid packages were rapidly coming to an end. War would no longer be a profitable business, so the Salvadoran government and its military began to take more seriously the growing clamor at the national and international levels for a negotiated end to the armed conflict.

A long and complex process of dialogue between the government and FMLN forces had been initiated back in October, 1984, in the northern city of La Palma in the province of Chalatenango, bordering Honduras. A second session occurred in November of that same year in the Catholic retreat center of Ayagualo in the province of La Libertad. The third session took place in Sesori in the province of San Miguel in September, 1986, and the fourth in October of 1987 in the offices of the papal nuncio in San Salvador. Years later, in 1990, a fifth session was held in Switzerland where an accord was signed defining the norms to be followed in a formal process of negotiations, demonstrating the political will on both sides of the conflict to seek a political solution to the war. In July of 1990, in Costa Rica, the San Jose Accord was signed, establishing the commitment of both parties to respect human rights and to end the practice of selective killings and forced disappearances. A complex series of meetings followed under the auspices of the UN in a stop-and-go process that culminated just before midnight on December 31st of the following year. Formal accords were signed in Chapultepec, Mexico on January 16th, 1992 and the country took to the streets to celebrate the end of 12 years of bloody civil war.

In tacit recognition of the underlying causes of the war, the Peace Accords included provisions for the demilitarization of Salvadoran society, for the building of political plurality and for economic reform. The spirit of the accords emphasized the need to eliminate the historical obstacles to democracy and to seek long-term solutions to the social, economic and political problems confronting the nation.

The sections of the accords dealing with socio-economic reform were unquestionably one of the weakest aspects of the peace initiative and did little to resolve the issues of poverty and landlessness that had sparked the massive incorporation of peasants into the struggle during the late 1970s. The accords that focused on demilitarization and the building of democracy were significant, however, and eventually produced an environment of political freedom unknown in the country's history.

The hated National Guard and Treasury Police were disbanded. The Armed Forces were reduced in size by half and their former mandate for internal security was rescinded. A new National Civil Police under civilian control was created with the participation of former FMLN combatants. The office of Ombudsman for the Defense of Human Rights was established, and agreements were reached for the reform of the electoral and judicial systems, which included the recognition of the FMLN guerrilla coalition as a legal political party.

In an effort to uncover the truth about decades of "dirty war," a Truth Commission was established with a mandate to investigate grave violations of human rights perpetrated by either of the parties to the conflict between 1980 and 1992. The Armed Forces insisted that violators not be mentioned by name in an effort to protect members of the high command implicated in some of the bloodiest acts of the war. Nevertheless, over 60 military officers were cited in the Commission's final report and close to 90% of the human rights violations perpetrated during the conflict were attributed to the army and other government security forces.

The United States tried to mask its own role as a party to the conflict, but it was clear to all that the war would never have survived its second year had it not been for the persistent aid and support of the U.S. government. It was later revealed that two thirds of the officers cited for grave violations of human rights during the war were trained by the United States at the infamous School of the Americas. Many of these same officers were later granted U.S. citizenship and were allowed to retire in luxury in the nation of their former mentors. As a final – and cynical – gesture of closure, the U.S. embassy in San Salvador built a monument within its walls to honor dozens of North Americans killed in the war, including the four churchwomen, raped and shot by a military that the United States had built and trained.

It was in this hopeful but still volatile context that I was blessed with the birth of my second son, José Andrés, on March 24, 1993, the 13th anniversary of the slaying of Monsignor Romero. He was a peace baby, this bright and pugnacious young soul who would never know or understand the heartbreak of the 1980s, but who would bring decades of magic and laughter to our lives.

Those who had fought the war, and those victimized by the violence were left to adapt emotionally as well as physically to the new reality of peace. Many had lost families and homes. Hundreds were left handicapped by the loss of limbs and much of their sanity. Adaptation and reconciliation would not be an easy task. Rural communities, some completely abandoned during the war, started rebuilding as people continued to come home, but the repopulations blended ex-combatants from both sides of the conflict, facing the impossible challenge of leaving the past behind.

A myriad of illnesses, ignored for years in the mystique of self-sacrifice that the struggle demanded, began to manifest itself. Combatants from both sides began to break down in both body and spirit. Back ailments from supporting heavy loads over endless marches, tooth decay, and more serious illnesses like chronic malaria and tuberculosis suddenly demanded attention. Post-traumatic stress and depression were common, and many once-disciplined combatants succumbed to the lure of alcohol and drugs.

I had not been a combatant in the war, nor had I lived it as intensely as many, but, at age 44, my aging body had also paid a price that I could not ignore. I had travelled to the most remote and dangerous corners of a region in constant turmoil in solidarity with the heroes and martyrs of my time. In the process, I had suffered from dengue, malaria, hepatitis, typhoid fever and every parasite known to man. During a trip deep into the Mosquitia jungles of northern Honduras, an area lacking in the most rudimentary forms of health care and without transportation, I came close to death from a burst appendix. In the small cave in the mountains of Morazán I came close to losing a leg to gangrene. And serving witness to the tragic bombing of civilian villages, frequent *guindas*, night ambushes and massacres would haunt even this hardened heart forever.

Following a motorcycle accident in 2003 that should have killed me or left me paralyzed, Ana Eugenia's mother teased me that I had lived more than the nine lives attributed to the proverbial cat. I don't know if this is true. But I treasure the memories and the lessons they brought, and am thankful for every God-given day and for the amazing human beings with whom I have shared this journey.

CHAPTER EIGHT

The Struggles of a
New Millennium

With the promise of peace, Teresa, Antonio and their children moved to the lowlands of Guazapa where new communities were being built for ex-combatants and civilian supporters of the guerrilla army as part of the Peace Accords. Antonio's sister Fidelia had already resettled there, along with her remaining children. It was a good distance from their home in Amayo, but it offered a view of China Mountain, and it was close enough to feel the spirits of loved ones who had been lost during the war.

The family settled in an isolated corner of an abandoned sugar plantation. When the plantation's new owners began to implement plans to reactivate production, Antonio was hired as a caretaker. He was lent a small parcel of land to plant his corn and soon had a menagerie of small farm animals, including chickens, pigs, ducks and dogs, wandering throughout his simple adobe house and yard.

Teresa busied herself again with the routine chores of peasant life. Within the first year in Guazapa, she gave birth to her final child, René. Like my youngest son, Andresito, he was a peace baby saved from the experience of war and the long years of struggle that had devoured the lives of so many of his ancestors. All of the older daughters married in the months that followed and moved to the capital city, leaving Teresa and Antonio with only their two youngest children to fill the enormous void.

With the first rainy season, Teresa planted a colorful flower garden to add some contrast to the dusty brown surroundings of their simple home. It was a demonstration of faith and offered the first promise of a future for this family in many a season.

Life was finally looking up for this resourceful couple, but El Salvador, like the Ireland of my ancestors, is not a place of happy endings. During the second year in her new home, Teresa was diagnosed with breast cancer. She received the news with her characteristic stoicism, as she had received so many other heartbreaking revelations during her lifetime, and she took on her new struggle with the same tenacity that had accompanied her through the war. She received chemotherapy to reduce the cancer, then underwent surgery to remove her left breast. Her recuperation was rapid, and a year passed without further complications, convincing us all that she had won her bout with this horrible illness. Into her second year, she began experiencing severe pain in her lower abdomen, however, and medical diagnoses confirmed that the cancer had spread to her liver.

We took her to the best physicians in the country, but the consensus remained that there was nothing to be done other than calm the horrendous pain that was wracking her body. She spent her last days in the capital city in the home of her daughter Isabel. And Antonio joined her once it became clear that she would not be returning to Guazapa again.

The doctors had given her six months to live, but she died within a week in the pre-dawn darkness surrounded by Antonio and his six surviving children. The family called me at four that morning and I went with the first light of day to pay my last regards to this woman who had brought such radiance and joy into all of our lives. At the sight of her corpse stretched out on the bed, I lost all control and burst into tears. Her daughters, Victoria and Isabel, forgetting their own sorrow, came quickly to my side, putting their arms around me, as if I were the one most in need of comforting, and I received again the selfless love of this devoted family in its worst moment of grief.

If you were to throw together all the days and hours that I had spent in the company of Maria Teresa Polanco de Rivas, it wouldn't add up to much in the space of a lifetime. I had lived on the periphery of her world and was always keenly aware of the privilege and wealth that distinguished my life from hers.

But I had shared the darkest hours of her life's journey, and had accompanied her impossible dreams in all of their intensity and drama. And for that, I had won her deepest trust and love.

I had also learned much from her example as well as from her words. Some of her lessons were too profound to assimilate at the moment they were offered, but they eventually changed my life. She showed me the infinite goodness and love that abounds in the human heart, a clear sign of divine presence. She taught me that simplicity was a virtue, and that dignity can reside in the humblest of surroundings. I learned that struggle brought meaning to life – that struggle was life – and that the depths of one's suffering frequently defined the capacity to experience true joy.

I have thought about Teresa often in the years since her death, but I could never find the words to adequately describe her until I came upon a verse by Kahlil Gibran in his beautiful book, *The Prophet,* that made me smile with delight and immediate recognition of the spirit to whom it referred:

> *And there are those who give and know not pain in giving,*
> *nor do they seek joy, nor give with mindfulness of virtue;*
>
> *They give as in yonder valley the myrtle*
> *breathes its fragrance into space.*
>
> *Through the hands of such as these God speaks,*
> *and from behind their eyes He smiles upon the earth.*

The signing of Peace Accords in El Salvador brought a dramatic shift in priorities, replacing the political goals of overthrowing dictatorship through military means with strengthening an incipient democracy, eradicating poverty and promoting sustainable development through non-violent struggle. As the repression and violence of earlier years began to diminish, new forms of social organization began to emerge reflecting this new agenda for change.

Postwar reconstruction, lasting from 1992 to 1995, focused initially on the formal implementation of specific provisions of the Peace Accords and rebuilding physical infrastructure destroyed in the war. The first phase of the process called for the demobilization, reinsertion and reintegration of ex-combatants; the implementation of a Land Transfer Program; credit and educational programs; a courageous effort to find and remove land mines throughout the war zones and other aspects deemed essential for a sustainable peace. It was hindered from early on, however, by continued resistance from ultra-conservative political and economic interests, by insufficient funding, by a lack of transparency, by inadequate coordination with non-governmental actors and by a continual debate between two fundamentally opposed conceptual frameworks.

The model for reconstruction promoted by the Salvadoran government, the World Bank, USAID and other large-scale donors prioritized rebuilding the country's infrastructure and instituting a misguided package of economic reforms to improve macroeconomic indicators and serve as the foundation for sustained economic recovery. The economic reforms were referred to as "Structural Adjustment" and were actually initiated in El Salvador in 1990, prior to the signing of peace. Its central precepts were contrary to all logic for a country trying to resolve the underlying structural roots of unrest and civil war, including the privatization of banks and public services, a reduction in government spending for social programs, the introduction of a value added tax (IVA), transferring the tax burden from the wealthy to the poor and other measures prioritizing the interests of wealthy elites over the underprivileged majorities.

Opponents of the official framework for reconstruction included the FMLN and its traditional supporters, most international NGOs and European governments. I represented a Norwegian development organization called Norwegian People's Aid at the time, and we, along with others, defended a different logic with a longer-term vision and with a focus on the economic, social and political empowerment of the poor. We pushed for a process that emphasized poverty eradication, the consolidation of democracy and sustainable development, viewing postwar reconstruction as an opportunity to resolve the worrisome gaps in the Peace Accords dealing with social and economic justice issues.

By 1996, reconstruction had come to a disappointing halt and I had accepted a job with the Washington Office on Latin America (WOLA), a small collective of committed U.S. citizens dedicated to human rights and best known during the 1980s for its opposition to U.S. military aid to El Salvador. In recognition of the enormous social, economic, political and cultural issues left unresolved in the Peace Accords, and the continued threat of political violence, WOLA had embarked on an initiative to strengthen citizen participation in El Salvador through training and accompaniment in public policy advocacy. I was asked to form part of a six-member team to develop and implement this program.

We developed an advocacy methodology based on the lobbying experience of WOLA in Washington and incorporating key lessons, strategies and tactics from the long years of political struggle in Central America. Our methodology reflected a conceptual framework of advocacy as an exercise in power, and prioritized the empowerment of civil society actors as the key to winning specific advocacy campaigns. Empowerment required strong organization and the building of alliances along with the development of advocacy skills in the areas of information and knowledge gathering, problem and policy analysis, the formulation of concrete proposals, the development of advocacy plans, effective lobbying, education and awareness-building, media work, and the mobilization of affected populations. The underlying proposition was that the struggles of the future would be won by intelligence, knowledge, creativity and persistence rather than through brute force.

Over the years that followed, we provided hundreds of workshops on public policy advocacy to civil society organizations throughout Central America and accompanied real campaigns on the most important issues of the day, including land reform, gender rights, labor rights, free trade, migration, corruption, indigenous rights, debt relief, fiscal reform, good governance and others. Our program became widely known, and we were soon travelling beyond Central America to work with organizations in South America, the United States and even my beloved Africa, providing workshops and advice on specific advocacy initiatives.

We were referred to at times as the "experts on advocacy," but I always saw myself more as a student, and felt enormously grateful for the opportunity to interact with knowledgeable and highly committed social activists and *compañeros* from around the world whose lives and courageous struggles brought lessons and insights of enormous significance.

In 2003, as my life continued to focus on training and accompaniment in public policy advocacy, I suffered a near-death motorcycle accident on a winding coastal highway in the province of La Libertad, breaking my back at the level of T-11 and taking me out of circulation for almost a year. I spent the next three months bedridden, followed by more than a year of physical therapy with gradually increasing physical exercise and a frustratingly slow recovery. It was during this time that I dusted off my diaries from the 1980s and began to write the first chapters of this book, driven by the determination to get well, get back on my feet and return to the world of social struggle that had become my life.

Among the long list of strategic issues not dealt with in the Peace Accords, yet key to assuring a viable future for El Salvador, were the urgent problems facing the nation related to the environment. By the year 2004, awareness was building among the citizens of El Salvador regarding the profound levels of deterioration of the country's natural resources, especially water, and people were beginning to perceive the need to organize and struggle around these issues.

El Salvador, with a population of over six million people in an area of slightly more than 8,000 square miles, is the most densely populated country in the western hemisphere and is considered by experts to suffer from the worst levels of environmental deterioration in the Americas, after Haiti. According to some analysts, the country possesses only 3% of its natural forests and its soils have been damaged by centuries of inappropriate agricultural practices reaching as far back as the colonial period.

Deforestation and the deterioration of soils make it difficult to filter the abundant seasonal rains that fall each year over El Salvador. Together with overexploitation, this problem is resulting in a worrisome drop in water levels around the country by almost a meter per year, according to the Ministry of Environment and Natural Resources (MARN). El Salvador's most important rivers are also slowly drying up; and MARN has reported that over 90% of El Salvador's surface water is polluted, leaving poor communities, both urban and rural, in a desperate search for adequate freshwater resources to meet their most basic domestic needs.

The crisis, according to experts, has several root causes. Global warming, of course, is among them. But it is generally agreed that the unregulated overexploitation of water by large-scale agriculture, industry and transnational corporate greed is the key environmental issue confronting El Salvador today. This problem, in turn, is the result of a lack of adequate government policies, programs and practices to ensure good governance in the water sector. All of these factors became key focal points in one of the most strategic battles El Salvador has fought in the new millennium.

In the midst of its environmental crisis, El Salvador, like many developing nations around the world at the turn of the century, began to attract the attention of transnational mining interests, primarily from Canada, interested in exploiting the country's numerous deposits of gold and silver. This had not been an economically viable proposition in earlier years due to the low grade of El Salvador's gold deposits requiring the extraction and processing of over 20 tons of rock and soil to produce a single ounce of gold. But, as commodity prices for precious metals began to rise dramatically on the international market, transnational mining companies began to aggressively assert their right of access to the country's minerals.

The majority of gold deposits in El Salvador are located in a mineral belt that runs across the northern regions of the country in the basin of the Lempa River, El Salvador's most strategic source of fresh water, providing electrical power, potable drinking water and irrigation for agriculture to over half of the country. The communities most threatened by mining were the same communities who had suffered most during the 12-year civil war, located in the northern province of Chalatenango (referred to during the war as the Apolinario Serrano Front), the department of Cabañas, including the municipality of Cinquera (known as Radiola in the war), northern Santa Ana province (the Feliciano Amas Front) and in the province of San Salvador, around El Paisnal (Piedra).

It was no surprise when these communities reacted quickly and strongly to the presence of foreigners prospecting for gold in the nearby hillsides. These territories had been bathed in the blood of family members and friends during the war, and were considered sacred ground.

Seventy percent of gold mining in the world today is done through open pit mining, destroying forests and topsoil, over-exploiting water and poisoning ecosystems with toxic waste. Mining is also an industry that requires enormous quantities of freshwater. In a sense, fresh water is the lifeblood of mining in the same way that it is the lifeblood of human existence. Mining companies compete with local communities, and with humanity at large, for this vital liquid.

The average gold mine in Central America uses more than a million liters of water per day. Some mines in the region use more than six million liters per day, and larger mines around the world use over 350 million liters of water per day, frequently leaving surrounding communities without adequate access to this life-giving resource.

Metallic mining, especially gold mining, also contaminates water. The separation of gold from ore requires enormous quantities of sodium cyanide, a toxic chemical that can kill a human being in quantities less than the size of a grain of rice. Cyanide solutions frequently seep into freshwater sources in and around mining sites or escape from poorly constructed tailings dams where toxic waste from the mining process is stored. Cyanide also evaporates at 36°C, contaminating the air in a radius of many miles around mining operations.

Apart from sodium cyanide, metallic mining utilizes explosives, fuel, antifreeze and other materials that leave toxic residues that seep into freshwater systems. The most problematic source of water pollution from metallic mining, however, is a process called acid mine drainage, a phenomenon which occurs when rock with high sulfide content (commonly found in Central America) is extracted from the earth, crushed and exposed to the oxygen from air and rainwater, converting the sulfides into sulfates and, finally, into sulfuric acid. The sulfuric acid, as well as other harmful metals that it leaches from the walls of the mine and from rocks in the surrounding area, flows into nearby streams, aquifers and other freshwater sources. Acid mine drainage is a process difficult to reverse and can be found today in gold mines in France and Spain that date back to the time of the Roman Empire.

Given all these factors, learned through the persistent study of scientific journals, talks with experts and visits to emblematic mining sites throughout Central America and the world at large, it was obvious that a country like El Salvador – already on the brink of water stress and suffering from water shortages and high levels of pollution – was not an appropriate location for largescale metallic mining. Supporting this position, a national poll, carried out by the Central American University (UCA) in 2007, found that over 62.5% of the population in El Salvador considered the country inappropriate for metallic mining. In a similar poll carried out by the UCA seven years later, the level of rejection had risen to 79.5%, and 77% of the population expressed the view that the government should move immediately to prohibit this industry.

The struggle against metallic mining in El Salvador lasted over 17 years, and can be divided into four distinct phases:

1. the period from the year 2000 to 2004, marked by the incursion of transnational mining companies and the growing resistance of local communities, especially those which continued to exhibit high levels of organization, citizen participation and a combative stance on community rights from the war years;

2. the period of 2005 to 2009, characterized principally by consolidation of the struggle at the national level led by the National Roundtable on Metallic Mining in El Salvador ("la MESA") and applying a rightsbased focus with a logic of nonviolent public policy advocacy to advance a clear policy agenda;

3. the period from 2009 to 2016, dominated principally by a prolonged legal struggle based on a suit brought against the Salvadoran State by Canadian mining company Pacific Rim and its new owner, OceanaGold and

4. the final phase of the struggle, from early 2016 to March of 2017, marked by the definitive battles for prohibition with the Archdiocese of San Salvador and the Jesuit-run Central American University (UCA) joining forces with the National Roundtable on Mining and assuming a central role in the struggle.

The first organizations working at the national level to respond to the threat of metallic mining were the community-based Association for the Development of El Salvador (CRIPDES) and the Association for the Economic and Social Development of Santa Marta (ADES). Both had been active in the accompaniment of thousands of families displaced during the war. CRIPDES, founded in 1984, continued to represent over 100,000 people residing in 400 communities around the country, many of whom were now being threatened by metallic mining. ADES, founded in 1993, also continued to accompany repopulated communities, many with ex-combatants from both sides of the civil war, engaged in a painful search to heal the wounds of a violent past and rebuild the social fabric of their communities.

With the aggressive incursion of transnational mining companies the communities represented by both of these organizations found themselves in another life-or-death struggle, this time in defense of their natural resources, especially water. With the formation of the National Roundtable on Metallic Mining in late 2005, these communities were joined by a broad variety of civil society organizations and institutions, including the Salvadoran Ecological Unity (UNES), an organization dedicated to the protection and conservation of the environment; the Center for Research on Investments and Commerce (CEICOM), a research institute which provided significant research and analysis on the impact of metallic mining in El Salvador and other related themes; the Environmental Committee of Cabañas (CAC) and the Association of Friends of San Isidro, Cabañas (ASIC), both mobilizing communities in the area where the Canadian mining company Pacific Rim wanted to build its first gold mine; the Foundation for Research for the Application of Law (FESPAD), a legal aid institution; Radio Victoria, a local community radio active on environmental and other social justice issues; the Unified Movement Francisco Sanchez-1932 (MUFRAS-32), a small community-based social movement in Cabañas; Communities for the Development of Chalatenango (CCR), a community-based organization coordinating closely with CRIPDES; the Foundation for Cooperation and Community Development of El Salvador (CORDES); the Justice and Peace office of the Franciscans (JPIC) and others.

In 2004, as my body continued to heal from my motorcycle accident and as I slowly adapted to life with incessant pain, I accepted a job with Oxfam America, a U.S. organization based in Boston dedicated to ending social injustice and poverty in the world and known best at the time for its global campaigns on fair trade. It had a strong and widely known international program on extractive industries, working in Latin America, Africa and the U.S., and I was hired as the Regional Program Coordinator for their work in Central America. I spent the next 13 years of my life consumed by the energy and fire of a struggle that occupied my every waking moment and provoked many a sleepless night as I obsessed over the plotting of the mining companies and searched for adequate strategies to stop them.

I was keenly aware at the time of the troubling similarities between the struggle against transnational mining interests and the devastating civil war that had shaken this country to its roots in the 1980s. We were again confronting a powerful transnational opponent allied with local economic elites with enormous resources at its disposition and the determination to advance its agenda at any cost. We also confronted, as we had in the 1980s, a devious attempt to win the hearts and minds of communities and policy decision-makers through aggressive multi-million-dollar propaganda campaigns built on lies and myths designed to derail serious and informed debate. The levels of greed and the blind determination of our opponents threatened the country with renewed polarization and violence, basic human rights were once more at the heart of our struggle and innocent lives were at stake.

The country was governed in 2004 by a right-wing pro-business political party prioritizing direct foreign investment and reluctant to prohibit an industry that promised a sizable increase in income for the State. Complicating things further, the communities most threatened by mining had little experience with this industry and, while their initial gut response provoked resistance, they had little knowledge of the social, economic and environmental costs of metallic mining, key to building a broad-based and sustainable struggle. Finally, mining companies were being highly effective in their communication techniques and unfounded promises of modern technologies more harmonious with the environment, of an economic boom for poor local communities, of increased revenue for health, education and other urgent needs and of greater respect for human rights.

According to the mining companies, it would be foolish for a poor country like El Salvador to forfeit the opportunities for economic growth provided by the exploitation of its mineral wealth. Nevertheless, the struggle for prohibition took root and gradually grew into a strong and persistent national campaign with the slogan "Yes to Life, No to Mining."

My job with Oxfam offered an opportunity to apply the accumulated lessons on public policy advocacy from my years with WOLA to a new and crucial issue that was quickly becoming a priority for communities and social movements throughout Central America and the world. As Oxfam America's Regional Program Coordinator on Extractive Industries, I travelled frequently to all of the countries in the region working with poor and mostly indigenous communities opposed to metallic mining. I also travelled to South America, the United States and Africa where I was able to observe the enormous costs of metallic mining, especially in terms of the environment. Everywhere I went, the story was the same. Metallic mining was overexploiting and contaminating scarce water resources and ecosystems, destroying traditional lifestyles, displacing villages, violating basic human rights, generating violence and destroying futures.

In an attempt to inform and educate the people and policy decision-makers of Central America on the issues related to metallic mining, Oxfam developed an abundance of materials that were shared with communities, civil society organizations, governments, researchers, think tanks, human rights activists, academics and other sectors in the early years of the struggle when few people knew much about this threatening industry. We participated, together with civil society organizations, in public forums and press conferences around the region. We met with governments and with mining companies to share our concerns; promoted unity and coordination among the broad variety of actors focused on metallic mining and embarked on an empowerment strategy with these actors, teaching the WOLA methodology for public policy advocacy, coordinating planning sessions to develop specific advocacy campaigns and training activists to improve the effectiveness of applied advocacy strategies.

The feature which most clearly characterized our struggle throughout its duration and which distinguished our methods from the war years was the profound commitment to non-violence. We were all keenly aware of the country's long and tragic history, beginning with the Spanish conquest and 300 years of brutal colonization, followed by a century of feudalism and oligarchic rule, 50 years of repressive military dictatorship, 12 years of bloody civil war and almost three decades of neoliberal capitalism. The country remained highly polarized and the threat of violence was always lurking nearby.

In the early years of the struggle, Pacific Rim, the point of the lance of metallic mining in El Salvador, mobilized its workers in confrontational street demonstrations against the Archbishop of San Salvador, Oxfam America, and the Office of the Human Rights Ombudsperson, all active supporters of prohibition. They gathered each Sunday in front of the National Cathedral while the Archbishop was celebrating Mass with signs and propaganda accusing him of lying and misleading the Salvadoran people. They demanded publicly that Oxfam be expelled from the country, accusing us of being the principal intellectual force behind the struggle, and held several concentrations in front of the Oxfam offices pasting signs on our walls that accused me directly of being an "enemy of the Salvadoran working class."

Then, in 2009, pro-mining interests in the country struck a more serious blow, assassinating four anti-mining activists from the province of Cabañas, where Pacific Rim was insisting on exploiting deposits of gold and silver. Marcelo Rivera, a quiet and mild-mannered school teacher, 37 years of age, who served as the director of the Cultural Center of San Isidro, Cabañas, was the first activist killed.

Local communities were being bombarded at the time with propaganda and lies about the benefits of mining. Tensions among pro-mining and antimining activists were building, feeding an environment that was becoming increasingly polarized and ripe for violence. Marcelo had become a leading figure in the resistance against mining in the province, founding the ardently anti-mining Association of Friends of San Isidro Cabañas (ASIC) and, for that, had become the target of pro-mining interests. He received threats for months; then, in June 2009, he was kidnapped and disappeared. His mutilated body was finally found a week later at the bottom of a well several towns away, missing eyes and fingernails and with other signs of torture.

In December of that same year, pro-mining interests struck again, this time in the municipality of Sensuntepeque, Cabañas province, killing Ramiro Rivera and Dora Soto. Both were shot to death by unknown gunmen for their opposition to metallic mining in the province, and for their frequent participation in the activities of ADES, ASIC, CAC and other community-based organizations working in Cabañas in defense of the environment.

The husband of Dora Soto, also an anti-mining activist, had escaped death several months earlier when gunmen shot at him near his home. Dora was eight months pregnant at the time of her assassination and held her youngest daughter in her arms as she returned from washing clothes in a nearby river. The hail of bullets that took her life struck her young daughter in the foot and penetrated Dora's womb, killing her and her unborn infant almost instantly.

My good friend, Francisco Pineda, the director of CAC, was in the community at the time. At the sound of gunfire he came running to Dora's aid, but there was little he could do other than hold her in his arms and assure her that her struggle would not be in vain. One tearful evening, years after the killing, I listened to Francisco relive that traumatic moment as he described putting his hands over Dora's midsection and feeling the last agonizing movements of her unborn child. When I speak today of the courageous anti-mining activists slain in Cabañas in 2009, I always include this brave young soul, a male I am told, robbed of his life on a rocky riverbank before he could take his first breath.

In June 2011, a fifth activist, Juan Francisco Duran, was disappeared and later found dead with two bullet wounds to the head. He was a fourth-year university student who, the day before his disappearance, had been placing anti-mining propaganda on storefronts and buildings in the city of Ilobasco, Cabañas province, where he lived with his parents and siblings.

The province of Cabañas continued to be highly polarized throughout the remaining years of the struggle. The brave and committed young journalists from the anti-mining Radio Victoria in Cabañas received frequent death threats by phone and by mail and were followed constantly by suspicious vehicles throughout the province. Local church figures were also threatened and frequently harassed. In 2016, the son of a prominent Salvadoran politician and legal representative of Pacific Rim at the time of the killings was caught and condemned to 11 years of prison for the assassination and mutilation of a person he had cut into pieces and left on the street in a plastic bag. In spite of this shocking development, there was no serious investigation by government authorities of any of the crimes committed in Cabañas, and the masterminds behind the killings were never identified.

The polarization and violence provoked by the mere presence of transnational mining corporations in the communities of El Salvador could have easily transformed our struggle into a bloody confrontation. There was certainly an abundance of activists who had known and, in some cases, participated in the violence of the 1980s and knew how to defend themselves, but our commitment to non-violence remained firm through the years, driven by the conviction that truth would eventually win out over the aggressive lies and propaganda of our opponents.

The anti-mining struggles of other countries around the region were also plagued by violence on the part of transnational corporations, pro-mining groups and local security forces protecting corporate interests. In Honduras and Guatemala, hundreds of environmental activists opposed to megaprojects violating the rights of indigenous peoples and endangering the environment were threatened and killed, and indigenous peoples in all of the countries of the region suffered from the violation of their right to free, prior and informed consent, established by Covenant 169 of the International Labor Organization of the UN.

The Mayan and Xinca peoples of Guatemala perhaps suffered the most from an industry that, by its very nature, is conducive to conflict and violence. In accordance with the cosmic vision of indigenous peoples in this country, the *Madre Tierra* (Mother Earth), or *"Pachamama"* as the Incas call her, is sacred. Mountains, especially, are sacred territory, regardless of the mineral wealth that might lie within their subsoil. Under these conditions, there is no "winwin" option, and there is nothing to be negotiated between affected communities and mining companies. The only non-violent option available to transnational mining corporations under these circumstances is to pack their bags and leave.

If mining projects are installed in indigenous territories, indigenous peoples lose. If the rights of indigenous peoples are respected, indigenous peoples will inevitably say "no" to mining, so mining companies lose. Within this highly volatile context, the organizers and key activists in anti-mining struggles around Central America promoted specific policy demands which differed in detail from one country to another. In El Salvador, we demanded the prohibition of metallic mining; Guatemalan organizations demanded the right of indigenous communities to free, prior and informed consent; in Honduras the demand was for the prohibition of open-pit mining. What all of these demands had in common were respect for the rights of threatened communities and a persistent commitment to non-violence.

The ultimate success of our prolonged struggle can only be explained by the determined and persistent action of thousands of Antonios and Teresas around the country and the strategic alliances built with key stakeholders at the national and international levels. Nevertheless, there are several actors that merit special mention for their persistent contribution to the struggle from its very first days and during its darkest and most trying moments.

Bernardo Belloso was an experienced social activist and highly respected leader of CRIPDES at the national level when the eyes of transnational mining corporations began to focus with eagerness on the rugged mineral rich terrain of northern El Salvador. He had been named to the board of directors of CRIPDES in 2001, and maintained a close supportive relationship to this organization's social base throughout its long years of struggle.

Like most of the base communities attended by CRIPDES since its founding in 1984, Bernardo himself had been displaced from his community of origin in Tecoluca, San Vicente along with his mother, 14 brothers and one sister. The war was just beginning at the time, but his father, Manuel, was already heavily involved with the guerrilla forces of the FMLN and, like Antonio Rivas in far off El Paisnal, served as the head of the local popular militia. As in the case of Antonio, the death squads and the army were in hot pursuit of this committed revolutionary.

The situation continued to worsen for Bernardo's family in Tecoluca, with continuous harassment and threats from the National Guard, and they were finally forced to flee, together with several hundred peasant families from the region, to the nearby slopes of the San Vicente Volcano where they would spend the next five years of their lives. Bernardo was eight years old at the time.

His childhood on the volcano quickly faded into an endless chain of military incursions, *guindas*, aerial bombings and all of the other permanent fixtures of life in the conflict zones of El Salvador. He lost three of his older brothers during that period and, like all youth in the war zones, began to dream of the day he would carry a weapon and join the local guerrilla column operating in the area. His father refused, however, so Bernardo served as a correo (messenger), carrying messages from one guerrilla camp to another.

At the age of 12, suffering from severe malnutrition, he was evacuated from the war zones and sent to a center for the displaced in San Salvador, and it was there that he had his first encounter with CRIPDES. It was many years later, however, after returning to his community in Tecoluca in 1991, that he was invited by CRIPDES to join their national team. As the head of CRIPDES's community organization efforts at the national level in 2002, he began representing this highly respected organization in broad-based social coalitions working on a variety of themes, and in 2005 was a key actor in the formation of the National Roundtable on Metallic Mining in El Salvador.

He travelled abroad frequently in the name of CRIPDES and the National Roundtable to build and consolidate international alliances for the struggle against mining and to receive the abundant recognition awarded to the National Roundtable for its anti-mining work. In 2014, three years before our victory against metallic mining in El Salvador, Bernardo was named president of the board of CRIPDES. He remained throughout the years a tireless and combative cadre and a force for unity in the difficult internal debates on strategies and tactics; and he continues to this day to work with CRIPDES with the same convictions, humility and perseverance learned in his childhood.

Antonio Pacheco was the director of ADES in Cabañas where the struggle against metallic mining had turned violent in 2009 and where it remained a source of heated conflict throughout the years. He is a quiet, unassuming but determined leader who had participated with the guerrilla forces in Cabañas in the 1980s and who had joined the anti-mining struggle in its early years.

Vidalina Morales also worked with ADES in Cabañas. She was born in the Honduran village of Los Hernandez, municipality of La Virtud in the province of Lempira, on May 5, 1968. She was the last of nine children in a family of humble peasant farmers with a Honduran mother and a Salvadoran father. Like Teresa in El Paisnal, her mother died at an early age and she was forced to take on the burdens of a grown woman before her time.

Also like Teresa, she lived her early years immersed in her studies and religious activities with the local church, but the war in El Salvador was right on her doorstep and soon smashed

The National Roundtable on Metallic Mining (with Vidalina Morales)
gives a press conference

Vidalina Morales

through the thin veil of tranquility that enveloped her life. Displaced families fleeing from the war in the Salvadoran provinces of Chalatenango and Cabañas began arriving in droves in the early part of the 1980s and eventually grew to a population of 7,000 women, children and elderly. A refugee camp was initially established in La Virtud under the auspices of the UN, but under pressure from the governments of El Salvador and Honduras, concerned about collaboration with FMLN guerrillas, the population was forcibly transferred to the camp of Mesa Grande in San Marcos, 15 miles from the border.

Vidalina's religious convictions led her into solidarity work with the refugees of La Virtud and later of Mesa Grande. As had occurred with me in Betania in 1982, her solidarity politicized her and eventually led to a direct relationship with FMLN forces just over the border. She transported food and medicines to guerrilla camps in northern Chalatenango; and it was in one of these camps that she met her husband-to-be, described by her in later years as "long-haired and bearded, with an elegant beret, like a photo of Che Guevara."

By age 19 Vidalina was pregnant with her first son and, with the massive return of refugees from Mesa Grande to El Salvador in 1987, she transferred with them to the province of Chalatenango in order to be close to her husband. She remained there for the next eight years, collaborating with the FMLN, learning from their revolution to "share the little one has" and to "live each day as if it were the last," as she would say today. She gave birth there to four more children and celebrated with the Salvadoran communities residing in the area when peace was finally signed in 1992.

After the war ended, she followed her husband to the town of Santa Marta in the province of Cabañas, repopulated also in 1987 by displaced families returning from Mesa Grande. There, she gave birth to her youngest child, built a small adobe house and, together with her family, began to farm the rugged and dry hillsides of Cabañas.

Vidalina joined ADES in 2000, and it was through this organization that she eventually became deeply involved in the struggle against metallic mining in El Salvador. By 2005, she was a member of the ADES board of directors and, with the formation of the National Roundtable on Metallic Mining, she began to represent ADES in this strategic coalition. She was close friends with Dora Soto and was deeply affected by her assassination in 2009. But her convictions remained firm as she travelled the country combating the lies and propaganda of Canadian mining corporations.

She visited mining sites throughout the region in coordination with Oxfam America and she shared the experiences and the lessons of our anti-mining struggle with communities, organizations, governments and churches throughout Central America, the U.S., Canada, Italy, Belgium, Spain, Switzerland and Australia.

Vidalina travelled to Washington, D.C. to represent the National Roundtable in a ceremony to receive the coveted Letelier-Moffitt award from the Institute for Policy Studies and, through it all, participated frequently in our press conferences, public forums, workshops and marches, speaking from the heart with a simple and moving message that won over audiences from all socioeconomic and cultural backgrounds.

She was the most effective speaker of us all, holding her listeners spellbound, and, for that, I often teased her about being our most strategic weapon – our "atomic bomb" – against the mining industry in El Salvador. She reminded me often of Teresa and the key role she had played in the struggles of a different decade, with quiet wisdom and an unas-summing manner , lighting our path like the North Star in the darkness of a midnight sky.

Another key actor in our struggle was Edgardo Mira of CEI-COM, a cantankerous old brawler and astute political thinker, former member of the Communist Party and ex-combatant in the civil war. Edgardo and I had many a disagreement over the years about strategies and tactics, but he was highly intelligent and persistent in his commitment to social justice, and I respected and admired him enormously. We had been together in 1983 when the Vanguard Units of the FPL in the Felipe Peña Front joined forces with a column of combatants from the Armed Liberation Forces (FAL) of the Communist Party for the attack on government troops stationed in Tenancingo. He was wounded by shrapnel in the attack and we must have crossed paths more than once during the horrible eight-day *guinda* that followed, but we never met until long after the war.

Saul Baños was a lawyer from FESPAD who also played an important role in the struggle, coordinating the National Roundtable on Metallic Mining, advising on legal matters, doing effective lobbying with policymakers, designing and coordinating public forums and media events and developing the proposal of the National Roundtable on Mining for prohibition presented to the National Assembly in 2013.

Luis Gonzalez, a young lawyer and environmental expert with UNES was an astute and committed leader of the National Roundtable on Metallic Mining and provided another strategic pillar to our struggle, and the list goes on.

Our struggle applied a wide variety of strategies and tactics in a persistent attempt to move our agenda of prohibition forward in

The author explains the threat of metallic mining
to ex-combatants in Cinquera

the National Assembly. This meant organizing, informing and mobilizing communities threatened by metallic mining; it meant developing clear and viable policy proposals and presenting them to the National Assembly; it meant lobbying policy decision-makers, conducting public opinion polls, doing effective and relevant research and holding public forums to inform and persuade citizens from all sectors of society, including those who tended to favor metallic mining. It meant developing and disseminating educational materials, conducting public opinion polls, working with the media to educate and inform public opinion, promoting popular consultations in municipalities threatened by mining, accompanying legislators on visits to former mining sights and, of course, taking to the streets when all else failed.

CRIPDES, ADES, CAC, CCR, JPIC AND ASIC, with their broad social base, held the key to organizing, educating and mobilizing affected communities. CEICOM and UNES conducted key research and developed educational materials. The lawyers of FESPAD developed specific legislative proposals for prohibition presented to the National Assembly in 2006 and 2013, designed public forums and did effective lobbying with government functionaries; and all joined for media work, public forums, lobbying policy decision-makers and for marches.

All of this required *compañeros* with a deep commitment and with the same mystique that had characterized the revolutionary struggles of the 1980s. Activists had to be audacious and willing to take risks; we had to be prepared to travel to distant communities in remote parts of the country to provide work-shops, sometimes to disappointingly small groups of people, to inform local leadership and to help organize. At the international level, we built strategic alliances with organizations from other Central American countries and from nations that were home to transnational mining companies, especially the U.S., Canada and Australia.

It was no surprise when the Catholic Church hierarchy of El Salvador allied itself with our struggle – grounded in the principles of Catholic Social Teaching – and assumed a definitive role in its final phase against metallic mining. Saint Oscar Romero, Rutilio Grande, the Jesuits of the Central American University (UCA) and others had shown the way years earlier in the midst of anoth-

International allies in solidarity with El Salvador.

er life-or-death struggle in El Salvador and, since the early 1970s, documents coming out of the Vatican had spoken out on the increasing threat to the environment from overexploitation and contamination of our natural resources. Most important among these was the powerful encyclical of Pope Francis, Laudato si', calling on the world's population to care for our common home by defending the environment and curtailing the abuse of natural resources, especially water.

As early as the year 2000, Bishop Eduardo Alas Alfaro of the northern province of Chalatenango had expressed his opposition to the incursion of transnational mining corporations into the communities of his diocese. In 2007, the Episcopal Conference of El Salvador formally positioned itself against metallic mining in their document entitled *Take Care of our Common Home (Cuidemos la Casa de Todos)* arguing that:

> *Our small country is the space in which God the Creator has called us to life. This is the portion of the world that He has entrusted to us to care for and to use according to His will. But this blessed land that we dearly love suffers from growing and unmerciful deterioration. We are all responsible for conserving and defending it because the environment is the home of us all: of this and of future generations.*

Following presidential elections in February, 2009, Archbishop José Luis Escobar Alas of San Salvador addressed a formal meeting of the three branches of government, including the outgoing president, the newly elected president and his cabinet. In that session, held in the Legislative Assembly, he gave the following message:

> *To the departing government as well as the incoming government, whatever party you are from, I call upon you to prohibit the mining of precious metals. I ask this due to the grave damage it would cause to the health of our people through the contamination of our water.*

In the years that followed, Archbishop Escobar Alas continued to speak out against metallic mining in press conferences, during Sunday Mass in the National Cathedral and in other public forums. And his auxiliary bishop, Cardinal Gregorio Rosa Chavez, did the same.

As the struggle continued to grow in El Salvador, the persistent messaging of Pope Francis in defense of the environment and his urging of the Church to take to the streets in solidarity with the poor motivated and strengthened the resolve of the Salvadoran Catholic bishops, priests, nuns and laity.

The commitment and role of the Salvadoran Church took a strategic leap in 2016 with the formulation of a new proposal for prohibition developed by legal experts and environmental specialists at the Jesuit-run Central American University (UCA). I had been invited to join the UCA team a year earlier, allowing me to contribute to this historical initiative.

I was assigned to the Office of the Assistant Dean for Social Action as an advisor on Public Policy Advocacy and Specialist on Water and Mining. Administrative support for my work was provided by a highly committed staff from the University Institute for Public Opinion (IUDOP). This institution, under the Assistant Dean for Social Action, had conducted highly strategic opinion polls on mining in 2007 and in 2015 demonstrating broad-based opposition to this industry, and its leadership and staff maintained a fervent interest in the anti-mining struggle over the years.

Ours was not the first bill on prohibition to be developed and presented to the National Assembly. The National Roundtable on Metallic Mining had presented their first bill back in 2006 and a revised version was presented in 2013. In spite of the persistent and valiant efforts of this highly representative coalition, however, rightwing parties serving the interests of big business and closely aligned with transnational corporate interests had refused to debate either bill. It was up to the Church to interrupt this long and irresponsible chain of resistance to good governance and open the debate on prohibition.

The UCA bill was shared with Archbishop Escobar Alas in the later part of 2016. He immediately gave it his support. It was then presented to the Commission on Environment and Climate Change of the Legislative Assembly on February 6, 2017. Several days later, the UCA requested and was granted a formal audience with the Commission to present our arguments in favor of prohibiting metallic mining in El Salvador.

It was during this presentation that I perceived the first small sign of change in the balance of forces around the mining issue among legislators. Right-wing party members of the Committee who previously would have boycotted the session listened intently and asked well-meaning questions as I dismantled the myths of "modern mining" promoted by the mining companies and used emblematic cases in the region to describe the enormous costs of metallic mining for a country like El Salvador.

Following our presentation, my hopes were boosted again by the encouraging feedback we received from the Secretary of the Commission and member of the right-wing ARENA party, Johnny Wright:

> *February 10, 2017*
>
> *My esteemed Professor McKinley,[2]*
>
> *It was a pleasure to receive you in the Commission and hear your presentation. It is always refreshing to have the opportunity in the National Assembly to learn from experts like yourself, especially when it is evident that the theme impassions you so greatly.*
>
> *I need no further convincing that metallic mining is not viable in our small country….for reasons related to the environment and for political reasons. Fundamentally, because it is wrong.*
>
> *I will make a personal effort to convince my parliamentary group that we should pronounce ourselves in favor of prohibition. I didn't have the opportunity to do this in our last meeting, but will try again next week.*
>
> *As you might imagine, there is resistance, but with the right arguments I hope that reason will prevail. You will be the first to know if I am able to attain a "breakthrough." My hope is that we are successful, and, as you say, "as soon as possible."*
>
> *We will be in touch, and next week I will propose a time to you for us to meet and talk.*
>
> *Best regards, Johnny*

---

2 Loose translation

In spite of the encouraging letter and continued verbal support from Johnny Wright, by early March of 2017, our bill had still not been debated and was far from being approved by the Commission, so the Catholic Church called for a massive demonstration to be held on March 9th. More than 6,000 priests, nuns and lay parishioners responded to the call, joined by the Protestant churches, the member organizations of the National Roundtable on Metallic Mining, environmentalists, development NGOs, human rights groups, directly affected communities and concerned individuals from around the country. Following a brief press conference in Bolivar Park in the center of the capital city, we marched to the National Assembly, led by Cardinal Gregorio Rosa Chavez, Archbishop Escobar Alas, bishops from the Protestant churches and authorities of the UCA.

Upon arrival, we were met by representatives from all of the political parties as well as national and international media. As the speeches began, marchers flowed out into the parking area of the National Assembly and into the downtown streets of San Salvador, holding their banners and posters on high and shouting in unison, "Yes to life, no to mining." Cardinal Rosa Chavez, Archbishop Escobar Alas and Andreu Oliva, dean of the UCA, spoke about the urgency of prohibiting metallic mining in El Salvador

and the growing frustration among the citizenry due to the lack of political will on the part of legislators. The heads of political parties insisted, one by one, that they were supportive. Then, the president of the Legislative Assembly took the microphone and promised the eager crowd that our bill for prohibition would be approved before Easter Sunday, several weeks away. I remember thinking at the moment that it was too much to wish for, but it was a third sign of hope that things were changing and that 17 difficult years of struggle might be approaching a victorious end.

In the days that followed, transnational mining corporations, like Pacific Rim and its new owner, OceanaGold of Australia, began to perceive a dangerous shift in public opinion and official thinking. They were aware before we were that, as a result of years of organizational and educational efforts, the tide was finally turning and that consensus was building in opposition to metallic mining in El Salvador. Recognizing the growing threat, mining companies returned to their earlier strategies of trying to win hearts and minds through aggressive and persistent propaganda and media campaigns. As they had been in the past, the campaigns were filled with promises of new technologies in a mining industry billed to have learned its lessons and now applying "modern" technology more harmonious with the environment. They referred to these developments as "responsible mining" and used as their model the OceanaGold gold and silver mine in the province of Nueva Vizcaya, Philippines.

In my job with the UCA, I tried to remain informed about metallic mining around the world, and was aware of the environmental destruction and human rights violations associated with gold mining in the Philippines, especially in Nueva Vizcaya. In order to confront the lies of Pacific Rim and OceanaGold, I coordinated with Mining Watch Canada, who had programs in the Philippines and knew the actors well. With their help, we established contact with the governor of Nueva Vizcaya, Carlos Padilla, and invited him to visit El Salvador.

Some said it was overkill, but I was taking no chances, and was pleased, and amazed, when the governor agreed to travel from the other side of the planet in solidarity with our struggle. With the administrative support of IUDOP in the UCA, especially from its young and committed administrator, Xiomara Mariona Zepeda, who had supported my work so fervently over the years, we planned a week of media work, public forums, meetings with communities threatened by mining, meetings with the President of El Salvador and his cabinet and, most importantly, a second audience with the Legislative Assembly's Commission on Environment and Climate Change.

The Commission, at the time, was being intensely lobbied by OceanaGold, but, in our meeting with its members on March 28th, the governor of Nueva Vizcaya presented visual evidence of the destruction caused by OceanaGold in his province and made convincing arguments against metallic mining. His 26 years as a congressman in his own country gave him credibility with Salvadoran legislators and, immediately following his prssentation, our bill for prohibition was approved and sent to the full Assembly.

On March 29th, I was planning to watch the final vote on closed-circuit TV, but I was called in the morning by Lina Pohl,

Johnny Wright (left) and other members of the Commission on Environment and Climate Change of the National Assembly vote in favor of prohibition.

the Minister of Environment and Natural Resources, and invited to accompany her in the VIP gallery of the National Assembly. When I arrived, the vote was in process, so I joined the Minister to watch the final results. Jeannette Aguilar, Laura Andrade and Xiomara Zepeda from IUDOP were also in the gallery and we hugged warmly upon my arrival. My heart was racing and bursting with pride as legislators gave recognition to the National Roundtable on Metallic Mining and to the UCA for our educational efforts over the years, and offered special thanks for the testimony of the governor of Nueva Vizcaya. With so many speeches from the legislators, the voting proceeded slowly, but finally concluded with the unanimous approval of our bill. At that moment, I found Vidalina Morales standing nearby in tears of joy and disbelief, and we embraced at the realization that our prolonged struggle, which had seemed impossible, was finally at an end.

There are times in life when things come together, forces galvanize, pieces fall into place and processes take on a magical quality that makes you wonder when the dream will end. That's what it felt like on this magical day for those of us in the struggle against metallic mining in El Salvador. There are simply no words to adequately describe it. It was a moment more precious than gold.

With the new law in place, El Salvador became the first country in the world to prohibit metallic mining in all of its forms at the national level, establishing an important precedent for other communities and nations confronting environmental destruction and the violation of basic human rights by transnational mining corporations. It generated an enormous sense of national pride in El Salvador, a country traditionally described with negative superlatives, and it gave hope to a people adly in need of successes in a long history of failed struggles for change. Perhaps most importantly, it vindicated the tragic death of anti-mining activists killed during the struggle and somehow brought honor and purpose to the deaths of Teresa, Eva, Santos and so many other heroes and martyrs from the struggle for social justice of the 1980s.

The new law surprised and angered transnational mining companies around the world and left them determined to overturn this historic win. Nevertheless, public opinion and the will

Celebrating our victory with the president of El Salvador
and the governor of Nueva Vizcaya, Phillipines

of lawmakers remain staunchly in favor of prohibition and the people of El Salvador remain ready to defend our victory.

With the effective blockage of metallic mining in El Salvador, environmental activists around the country began to focus on the broader challenges related to building good governance in the water sector, and CRIPDES, UNES, ADES and the other organizations of the National Roundtable on Metallic Mining continued to play a leading role. New broad-based coalitions like the National Alliance against the Privatization of Water were also formed with a new generation of activists joining the struggle. I continued to work with the UCA, assisting in the design and implementation of advocacy strategies and coordinating with these newly emerging social movements.

It is broadly recognized that current water shortages and pending water stress in El Salvador are due primarily to over-exploitation and contamination by large-scale agriculture and industry, and our struggle has led us frequently into confrontation with opponents from the past. In the 1990s, the investment consortium the Roble Group, owned by one of the famous 14 families of El Salvador's traditional oligarchy, built shopping malls and parking lots on a former coffee plantation, El Espino, located on the outskirts of San Salvador. The site had been declared a natural reserve following the war, given its importance as a filtering system for millions of gallons of rainwater each year to replenish the San Salvador aquifer, a key source of drinking water for almost half of the inhabitants of the capital city. As a result of the destruction of this key natural resource, poor urban barrios today suffer from chronic freshwater scarcity for domestic use in the midst of the coronavirus pandemic.

In more recent years, construction companies owned by wealthy Salvadoran families have been building luxury homes with swimming pools and golf courses in the southern municipality of Zaragoza, near the site of our former refugee camp, Betania, an area already suffering from water shortages. And around the country, large-scale producers of sugar cane extract enormous quantities of freshwater each year for irrigation, leaving surrounding rural communities dry.

In 2010, the battery recycling plant of Baterias Record was found by the Ministry of Environment and Natural Resources (MARN) to be contaminating the primary sources of freshwater for over 7,000 inhabitants from the village of Sitio del Niño and six surrounding communities near the town of San Juan Opico in the province of La Libertad. And, in the municipality of Nejapa, the transnational Coca-Cola bottling plant continues to extract water from a strategic aquifer at a rate that experts warn will leave it dry within the next 30 years. And the list goes on.

Large-scale agriculture is responsible for approximately 60% of water use in the country and for almost 70% of pollution from the uncontrolled utilization of toxic pesticides. And large-scale industry continues to contaminate surface water with its practice of dumping almost 90% of its toxic waste directly into rivers and lakes without processing. Both agriculture and industry are guilty of drying up strategic aquifers around the country and leaving poor communities in both the urban and rural sectors without access to clean water.

In the face of this threat, the UCA, in coordination with committed activists from around the country, continues to push legislation for a general water law to ensure the effective regulation of water in El Salvador and to develop the institutional structures in the public sector to ensure efficient, equitable and sustainable access to this key resource. At the same time, we continue a long-standing struggle for constitutional reform, recognizing water as a basic human right.

It has been a joy for me to find in this struggle a new generation of young social activists, many of them university students. They are too young to remember much about the war, but they remind me of the youth of that period, driven by conviction and ready to sacrifice all for the struggles of their time. At the age of 74, I am seen by them as the old *gringo*. They know little of my past or my joys and sorrows from a lifetime in their country, and I frequently give silent thanks when I am with them that

they were not born during those difficult years, since they surely would have joined the ranks of young revolutionaries fallen
victim to torture, disappearance or death, as did so many other
amazing human beings that I have known.

In September of 2018, a new and horrible challenge appeared in
my life and left me again walking the same desperate path as Teresa had walked more than two decades earlier. I was diagnosed
with an aggressive form of prostate cancer with metastasis to the
bones throughout my body. At this writing I have received several series of radiation and almost two years of hormone therapy
in El Salvador's public health system and am feeling strong and
hopeful. I have been given between three and five years of life,
but with the support of a loving God, strenuous daily exercise, a
good diet and much loving support from family and friends, I am
anticipating a more hopeful and victorious outcome in my last
life-anddeath struggle in this country.

CHAPTER NINE

Trading Places

Antonio and I have remained close and intimate friends throughout the years, and continue to enjoy the enduring bond of *compañeros* who have struggled together in a cause we both would have died for. He was keenly interested and supportive of our battles against metallic mining and the ongoing struggle in defense of water, recognizing both as key strategic issues for El Salvador, much like the issue of land had been in his earlier years.

He participated in workshops and public forums that we held in the nearby town of Suchitoto, and frequently travelled to the larger cities to participate in massive anti-mining demonstrations. I teased him incessantly about the fact that he had once been a miner himself for a short period of time prior to becoming a cane cutter, and he took me one hot afternoon to the tunnel near El Paisnal where he had labored shoveling ore in the sweltering heat for 75 cents a day. His life as a miner had lasted only seven months, but he saw enough during that time to understand the threat that mining posed to workers and to the environment. As we sat on the dusty hillside drinking cold beer from a cooler, Antonio shared the harsh memories of that period of his life.

Following the death of Teresa, Antonio bought a small plot of land in the lowlands of Guazapa not far from where he and Teresa had last lived. With his two sons, he built a simple adobe house close to a small river where his remaining family could bathe. His daughters were all married with children by then and living in the capital city or in the coastal city of Sonsonate. Aníbal, his oldest son, whom he had carried on his shoulders in *guinda* during a different life, remained in the countryside with his father, together with Rene, the youngest son, now married and with a young child of his own. They rent acreage a short walk from their home for planting corn and beans and for raising

Riding in Guazapa with Antonio and my son, Andrew

a few head of cattle, and it is pleasing to see this family gradually begin to think of their future again.

Soon after he moved, Antonio and I went together to the tiangue (auction for cattle and horses) in nearby Aguilares where we purchased several horses, complete with bridles and saddles, and, for many years afterwards, spent long hours in the saddle riding the same trails that I had walked with the *compañeros* during the war. My two sons loved horses and I taught them both to ride at an early age, so they frequently joined us, racing through the cane fields, jumping over barriers and pursuing imaginary enemies across the lowlands. When we rode alone, Antonio and I would often times return to his house late at night under a starlit sky, trusting the horses to find their way in the darkness while we shared the enduring memories and unresolved issues of a war that had taken over 75,000 lives and caused such immense suffering.

We travel together, on occasion, to Antonio's village of Amayo where another small adobe house once stood in the shadows of China Mountain, and where Teresa and her children spent long and terrifying days and nights in dark, muddy tunnels whenever government troops penetrated the subzone. During one of our visits, we searched in vain for a buried tin container in which Antonio had hidden the letters of his daughter, Eva, written while she was serving as the radio operator for the guerrilla command in the subzone of Radiola. We found pieces of the container, but the letters were missing, and Antonio agonized over the loss of this sacred treasure.

I also visit with Fidelia and her surviving children, who live in a small village of ex-combatants an hour's walk from Antonio. Patrocinia and Rosita have both married and have a growing brood of small children of their own,

My son, David Miguel

whose names are too many to remember. From their village, you can look out over the northern slopes of the Guazapa volcano and see Mirandilla where their father, Santos, still lies buried in an unmarked grave. And we have talked several times about searching for his remains and transferring them to a more accessible site.

Rosita and her husband, along with the husband of Patrocinia and several of their children, finally joined the ranks of "illegal" aliens in the U.S. making the horrendous journey by land through Mexico. Brothers and sisters and other family members who have remained behind are dirt poor, with little schooling, working small plots of corn and beans for their subsistence and hiring out as cane cutters during harvest time to boost their meager incomes. Life for these rural peasants has a troubling resemblance to the lives of their forefathers, and we often speak, when we are together, of the dashed hopes and aspirations for change that their generation once possessed.

With the signing of peace and the approach of a new century, El Salvador gradually slipped off the map. The issue of poverty was too complex, and the solutions too elusive, to attract the international audience that had once been so mindful of the war. The continuing social and economic polarization of a small Third World country failed to generate lasting concern.

There is a keen awareness, on the part of Salvadorans, of the important changes in the country at the political level as a result of 12 years of struggle and Peace Accords. Repression has been significantly curtailed. Headless bodies with bloody messages from the death squads carved into their chests are no longer turning up along the country's highways, and visitors to El Salvador today would have a hard time believing the horror stories of kidnapping and torture, massacres and the indiscriminate bombing of civilian villages that were so much a part of daily life during the 1980s. Nevertheless, the Peace Accords did little to eradicate the underlying social and economic causes of the civil war.

The FMLN, a legal political party since 1992, participated in its first national elections in 1994 and finally won the presidency in 2009, then again in 2014. In spite of its heroic history as the vanguard force in the liberation struggles of the 1980s, however, two terms in office brought little improvement to the lives of the poor in El Salvador. Those who placed their trust and risked their lives in the struggles for change of the 1980s observed in horror as FMLN leadership gradually distanced itself from the party's historical base of support. And they became increasingly embittered as the FMLN squandered its political capital trying to convince the world that it could play by the rules of bourgeois democracy and western capitalism while the revolutionary project, built on social justice, national sovereignty, equity and sustainable development, was left behind in the dust.

Neoliberal economic reforms, in place since 1990 and pushed by the U.S. Agency for International Development (USAID), the International Monetary Fund (IMF) and the World Bank in order for El Salvador to qualify for new international loans, did little to promote economic stability and exacerbated the existing levels of poverty in the country. As opportunities for sustainable development began to evaporate, so did opportunities for young people, and participation in youth gangs, especially in poor urban barrios, began to rise.

Fifty years of military dictatorship and 12 years of civil war, followed by almost three decades of neo-liberal reform, have left over 50% of El Salvador's population impoverished with 40% unemployment and many families surviving on less than a dollar a day. Health and basic education are constitutional rights, yet thousands die each year from curable diseases like pneumonia, dengue and intestinal infections, and the country struggles desperately to stay afloat in the oncoming storm of coronavirus. Violence and street crime have rendered El Salvador one of the most dangerous places in the western hemisphere and hopes for change are slowly waning on a distant and unreachable horizon.

The principal issues in the country today, besides the growing health and economic pandemic of coronavirus, continue to be poverty, unemployment, violent crime, corruption and a worrisome level of environmental deterioration, all of which leave El Salvador with a questionable future. The only viable solution, in the minds of many, is migration, generating a steady flow of desperate seekers north to Mexico, the United States or Canada or to a variety of other destinations that increasing numbers of Salvadorans now call home.

Migration is not new to El Salvador. Salvadorans have been moving around the world for much of modern history, much like the Irish from the time of my ancestors. And, like the Ireland of that day, El Salvador's long history of migration has been deeply rooted in political, social and economic injustice, foreign intervention and violent civil strife.

Approximately 25,000 unemployed Salvadorans migrated to Honduras in the 1930s, seeking work on the U.S.-owned banana plantations on the north coast. Pushed by the continuing concentration of agricultural lands and shrinking wages in El Salvador, this number grew to 350,000 by 1969. The Honduran government, that same year, initiated a policy of expulsion that eventually affected over 300,000 Salvadoran workers and provoked a five-day war between the two nations. The war was readily won by El Salvador, but the massive return of Salvadoran migrants swelled the ranks of landless peasants in their home country and drove unemployment rates to over 45%, exacerbating the existing social and economic inequities plaguing the country and contributing to the causal factors of the political and military violence in the decades that followed.

During these early years, Salvadorans also migrated in search of work to Panama where they found employment as laborers, carpenters and masons during the construction of the Panama Canal, and to U.S. shipyards during World War II, particularly in San Francisco. Back at home, workers migrated internally in search of seasonal employment on the large coffee plantations of the oligarchy. The constant absence of men from the home remolded the traditional Salvadoran family, forcing women to assume dual roles as breadwinner and caretaker, becoming more independent in the process.

The U.S.-supported war in El Salvador during the decade of the 1980s forced almost a million people, one fifth of the population at the time, to flee the country in search of refuge. Another 500,000 were displaced from villages of origin by indiscriminate bombing and military incursions, but remained within the country.

El Salvador today remains a militarized society with too many people unable to earn enough to meet their most basic needs, providing fertile terrain for the recruitment of youth by drug cartels, organized crime and street gangs. Deportations of gang leaders from U.S. prisons exacerbate this complex situation and contribute to growing insecurity for poor urban communities. Over 500,000 people have again been forcibly displaced from their communities, this time by violent crime, ranking El Salvador among the top 18 countries in the world suffering from this phenomenon.

Every poor family in El Salvador today holds tightly to the dream of getting at least one family member up north (al norte). During high points in migration from the region, international transport companies were carrying over 500 young men and women a day from towns and villages with names like Chirilagua, Olomega, Pasaquina, Intipuca and El Carmen out of the country en route to Guatemala and the northern border of Mexico. More recently, migrants have chosen to travel together in large caravans to protect themselves from the gangs, the drug lords and corrupt security forces in Guatemala and Mexico. Few of those risking the trip attain their goal of crossing into the United States. Most are halted at the border or caught by migration officials, la migra, either in Mexico or the United States, incarcerated and returned home.

The unlucky ones die of thirst in the arid wastes of the Sonora Desert, suffocate to death in the back of enclosed trucks or railroad freight cars or spend months in overcrowded camps along the Mexican border. Women and young girls run the risk of being raped or forced into prostitution in the brothels of northern Mexico to pay their way to the land of milk and honey.

Those who have miraculously reached their destination over the past several decades live in the poor barrios of large U.S. cities, crowding 10 to 15 people to a room in dilapidated buildings and working any job that comes their way. They stand on the corners of busy city streets offering their labor. They are the hacelotodos (jacks of all trades) who can fix your plumbing, rake your yard, paint your house or repair your roof for a few dollars a day. Those who find more permanent employment work as domestic help, construction workers, waiters, office cleaners or in other service industries. Those with access to capital set up their own restaurants and small markets selling traditional produce and foods from El Salvador, like the popular dish, *pupusas*.

Following the terrorist attacks on the United States in September 2001, the U.S. government gave top priority to halting the growing wave of "illegal" migration. The new Department for Homeland Security, with responsibility for border security through the Bureau of Customs and Border Protection, pushed forward a series of anti-migrant policies under the guise of national defense, classifying migrants, along with terrorists and drug smugglers, as a national security threat, while the U.S. Border Patrol began to implement an aggressive plan for migrant deterrence.

Under George W. Bush, Barack Obama and Donald Trump, the Border Patrol has been beefed up in staffing and equipment and has installed the latest devices of modern technology for the detection of a human presence along America's southwestern border. The government has also moved forward with Trump's ardent dream and campaign promise of building a 500-mile wall between Mexico and the United States at an estimated cost of $5 billion, which Trump insists will be paid for by Mexico.

The efforts to halt migration to the United States through its southern border have forced Mexicans and Central Americans to opt for increasingly dangerous routes, winding through inhospitable stretches of desert and claiming the lives of hundreds of the region's poor each year. Migrants facing growing hazards due to heightened security measures are increasingly driven into the hands of highly professional but often unscrupulous smugglers, referred to as coyotes. The smugglers charge enormous sums of money for this service, leaving those left at home faced with the task of paying off this debt, often requiring the mortgaging or sale of their small plots of farm land or shanty-town homes to do so.

Nearly 1.4 million immigrants from El Salvador, one fifth of the country's population, reside in the U.S. today, making Salvadorans the second largest Latin American migrant group in the country, after Mexicans. The remittances that they sent home every year prior to the coronavirus pandemic totaled over $5 billion, providing over 20% of the country's gross domestic product and helping to keep families and the economy afloat.

"Illegal aliens" in U.S. cities like Los Angeles, San Francisco, Houston, Washington D.C. and New York have become El Salvador's most important export, in spite of Donald Trump's description of them as "rapists" and "drug traffickers." Trump has warned of an "invasion of our country with drugs, with human traffickers, with all types of criminals and gangs" and refers to their countries of origin as "shithole countries," but this hateful rhetoric does little to identify the underlying root causes of a complicated issue. Solving the problem requires a more humble assessment of the priorities and practices of Central American governments and the decades of failed U.S. policy in the region.

When I talk with Salvadorans today about all of these issues, they frequently express curiosity about my decision to stay in this small and troubled country, plagued with so many problems and the ever-present threat of violence. They occasionally honor me by telling me that I have become a Salvadoran, and they tease me about trading places with the throngs of their countrymen and women seeking their future in the north. I can never find adequate words at such moments to explain my life's decision; but if I were to be more forthcoming, I would tell them the truth, that I was not here for the *pupusas* or merengue music, the warm weather or surfing, so popular with most foreigners. I am here for the struggles of the humble-spirited and combative people of a country I have come to love.

When I first arrived in Central America, my plan was to return to Africa at the first opportunity. More than four decades later, I have relinquished this dream and given in to my captive soul. I have returned to my beloved Africa on a number of occasions, and it still stirs my emotions as it did in my younger years. But too much shared history, with its joys and its sorrows, has rendered El Salvador a hard place to leave.

I have learned much during my years in Central America about the evils of empire, the corruption of power and the perils of greed. I have been frequently amazed at the arrogance and cruelty of U.S. policies toward the region, but I have also learned that they can seldom be explained by the hearts and minds of the American people. I have found a critical peace with the nation of my birth, if not with its leadership, and have fallen in love again with its unique history and myriad of peoples. I have rebuilt relationships with family and friends in the U.S. and am left with the single regret that my mother passed away before I was able to come to grips with my rage in the decade of the 1980s.

I have become an aspiring pacifist in my old age, a gift from the Quakers and the unpalatable violence of the civil war, and I treasure the amazing diversity of peoples and ideas on this earth as the source of all fascination with life. I reject the notion that the interests of one nation or people can ever take precedence over those of another and I join in solidarity with my American brothers and sisters who struggle to put these principles into practice both at home and abroad.

In 2020, I asked my sister Kathleen to contribute to my book by sharing her own perspective on my life's choices. She knows little about Central America and will not read a book on the subject, but she has her own beautiful and simple way of understanding things, and shares them on occasion as one would share a small but precious jewel. This is what she wrote:

> *There are times when I recognize a person's life in broader perspective.... I believe our lives are much bigger than the small role we play within a concrete reality....Having a broader perspective allows for greater love and compassion.*
>
> *Because we have been so close, I have struggled with feelings of abandonment by you. I have been extremely angry at different times, but I knew you were doing something so much bigger and making your own difficult decisions, and I begin to see you in a different light, with a different way of reconciling yourself to the issues related to your family of origin.*
>
> *Central America became your family, lots of chaos, three countries of people and personalities to be your brothers and sisters. Anger was justifiable, fighting was necessary. The military represented your father, controlling, hateful, and repressive. The older women, strong, capable and loving... your mother... Archbishop Romero your faith. You fell in love with people and you wanted to make things right. You were faithful to your life's choices!*
>
> *I am not certain that all of this is true. But if it is, then I have traded one highly traumatized dysfunctional family for another, and remain deeply in love with them both.*

I continue to visit Antonio frequently and we talk incessantly about the war and all that has come after, especially the worrisome trends of the country today and the persistent problems of poverty, corruption, violent crime and environmental deterioration, assuming new dimensions in the deadly context of the coronavirus.

We also talk about our shared concerns for the new presidency in El Salvador, its clear leanings towards authoritarian rule and its lack of respect for democratic institutions, won at great cost by the struggles of the 1980s. Militarization once again threatens democracy as the army is dispersed throughout the country under the guise of fighting violent crime, in flagrant violation of the Peace Accords of 1992 and of the Constitution of the Republic. And we worry at the ease with which the current administration excuses the increasingly systematic violation of basic human rights, threatening to return El Salvador to its violent past.

Compañeros

Some days Antonio and I drive to nearby Suchitoto in search of cold beer and *pupusas,* stopping briefly in the town of Aguacayo to visit the old roofless church that was bombed in the mid 1980s and to share stories of the war with niña Rubia, an aging woman who lost most of her family in the fighting. Then we continue on our route to Suchitoto, located on the shores of Lake Suchitlan.

We have our favorite places to eat and drink beer in the restaurants overlooking the lake, and as I gaze out over its mirror-smooth waters, my thoughts never fail to take me back to the war and the long dark nights paddling in small boats en route to a distant subzone or a place of temporary refuge.

My sons are grown now. They are Salvadorans by birth and by culture, still awakening to their mixed ethnicity, and I derive great pleasure from watching the Third World shine from their dark Latin eyes. David Miguel, the oldest, resides in Las Vegas, Nevada with his wife and two young children. People frequently say that he posseses the tranquil and wise soul of his mother and, for that, I am thankful.

He worked for several years for a small U.S. solidarity organization focused on human rights in El Salvador and we coordinated closely for a time in the struggles in defense of water in El Salvador. He accompanied numerous delegations from the U.S. to El Salvador as I once did long ago, and he participated in our marches in the capital city filling me with pride and gratitude at being able to share our struggle with this amazing spirit that I have the honor of calling my son.

My younger son, Josè Andrés, is named after my Irish grandfather and me, and takes after us both in many worrisome ways. The strength, the magic and determination of the Irish dominate his character. He recently married the love of his life and will be graduating from medical school in a few years, and leaves little doubt about the important role he is destined to play in the country of his birth.

Antonio continues to grieve deeply at not having had the opportunity to bury his oldest daughter, Eva, killed by helicopter gunships in the subzone of Radiola in 1985, and I regret to this day not having been able to locate the site where her remains were buried. He is also worried about losing a friend to the same illness that took his wife, and our times together have taken on new meaning for us both.

He is thankful for his life and for his children that remain and welcomes with joy all who visit him. He still loves to talk about Teresa, and the mere mention of her name evokes a warm and inviting smile. I am reminded at such moments of the key role this amazing woman played in his life, replacing the humiliation of his poverty with light, laughter and culture and easing the harshness and toil of his days.

When I visit Antonio today, I can feel the presence of Teresa everywhere. She is in Antonio, himself, and in all of Antonio's remaining children and grandchildren, who carry her unconquerable spirit, radiating light and endless hope in their still impoverished world. With the coming of rainy season each year, the countryside of El Salvador turns a radiant green and the blossoms and wild flowers that Teresa loved so much return. With the flowers come the butterflies dancing on the wind as they did in the gardens that Teresa once planted, full of grace and beauty and delighting in life, much as she had done in her short lifetime. It is a time of hope and of new beginnings for the poor rural farmers of El Salvador and it frequently brings to mind an anguished mother's words from a distant past, assuring me that this long dark night, where "time moves so slowly" would indeed one day meet the dawn. And I am gently lured to a place beyond rage, in this country of eternal struggle that I now call home.

Andrés (Drew) McKinley is a U.S. citizen raised in the picturesque New England town of Hingham, Massachusetts. After four years of teaching school in the jungles of northern Liberia, he spent over forty years in Central America working for a variety of international and local organizations on issues related to human rights, social justice and sustainable development. He has resided in El Salvador since 1980 and currently works as an advisor on public policy advocacy and environment at the Jesuit-run Central American University, José Simeón Cañas (UCA).